At the Confluence of Two Cultures:

William and George Bent Confront Manifest Destiny,

1829 - 1918

ᛒ

CAMILLA KATTELL

Light Horse Publishing
Santa Fe, New Mexico

At the Confluence of Two Cultures:
William and George Bent Confront
Manifest Destiny, 1829 - 1918
Camilla Kattell

Light Horse Publishing
Santa Fe, New Mexico
www.lighthorsepublishing.com

ISBN 978-0996675437

Library of Congress Control Number: 2016918168

Printed in the United States of America

First Edition

Dedicated to my family:
Chris, Trish, Doug, Sam, and Jake

ᘒ

CONTENTS

William Bent
Courtesy Palace of the Governors Photo Archives,
(NMHM/DCA), Negative 007029. The New Mexico
History Museum, Santa Fe, New Mexico.

George Bent and his wife Magpie
Courtesy of Stephen H. Hart Library, Denver Colorado.
BPF-Bent, George, #10025735, History Colorado.

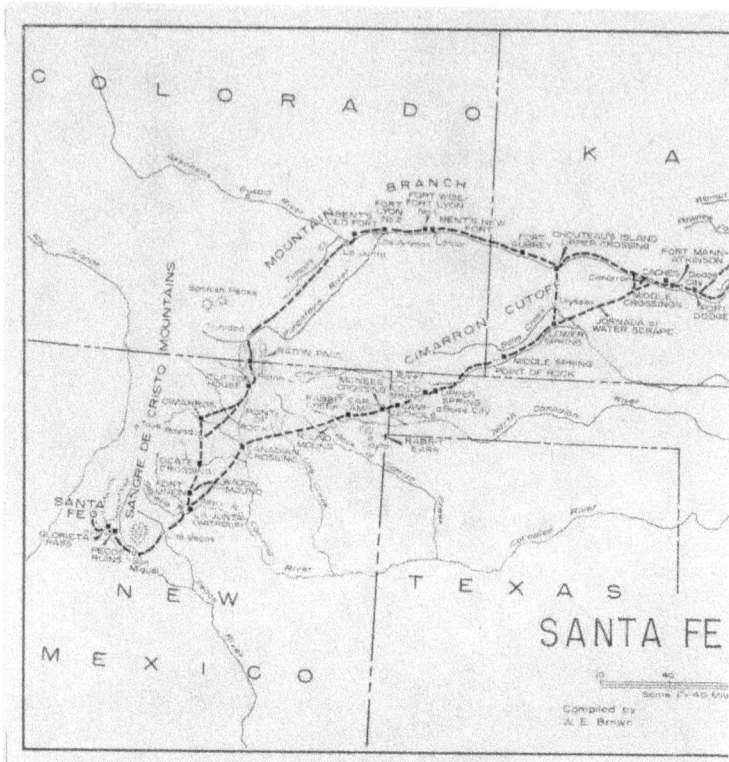

Map of the Santa Fe Trail

*Courtesy of the New Mexico History Museum, Fray
Angélico Chávez History Library, Santa Fe, New Mexico.*

PREFACE

WHILE RESEARCHING A BOOK about young people who traveled the Santa Fe Trail in the nineteenth century, I became fascinated with Bent's Fort and the story of the Bent family. Now a historical landmark, the fort represents the remarkable account of two brothers, Charles and William Bent, young men who went west in 1829 and built a successful trading business. The center point of my preoccupation was the incredible adobe fort that they built in what white men perceived as an empty wilderness—it was a trading post, a sanctuary, and a fortress that was never attacked either by Indians or armies, despite its vulnerable location in what is now southeastern Colorado.

Trade has been a motivator for exploration and conquest since man first made a swapping transaction. Charles, William, and their third partner, Ceran St. Vrain, were three young men with a lot of ambition and a shared vision of a future based on commerce. As they formed and developed Bent, St. Vrain, and Company, they divided their work according to their talents.

Ceran, having come from a St. Louis trading family that was already successful in the Missouri Territory, was an experienced retailer and knew Santa Fe and New

Mexico when it was still Spanish territory. He would run their operations in Santa Fe and Taos, New Mexico.

Charles was a gregarious and energetic young man with a good head for business. He liked doing the buying in St. Louis and was adept at marshalling the trade caravans across the prairie between Missouri and New Mexico to deliver quality goods in the West.

When the partners decided to build a trading post, William developed his part of the business, starting in 1833, around trade with the Indians, fur trappers, and other traders. It worked out that William was the perfect partner for building and running the only site of white civilization along the eight hundred miles of the Santa Fe Trail. Sometimes referred to as Fort William, mostly the fort became known as Bent's Fort. They hired adobe workers from Taos and constructed an amazing post with all the facilities and comforts that travelers and traders would want, including luxuries like ice for drinks and a pool table for fun.

But William's strong suit in the enterprise was his empathy with the Indians, especially the Cheyennes. He eventually married into the tribe, raised five mixed-blood children, and grew to love and respect the indigenous people. He brought a better quality of life to them with the trade goods he provided, and they recognized that they wanted the conveniences that he could offer. Since the beaver trade was dying, they traded mostly with buffalo robes that Bent & St. Vrain transported to the East for a profit. In some years this high-risk business paid off handsomely; in other years there were losses.

As the nineteenth century progressed, William's children grew up with freedom and tolerance among many ethnicities. They were raised as Cheyennes but also had the advantages of learning white ways from their exposure at the fort to all kinds of people who passed through or lived there. William also sent them to St. Louis for a more formal education.

The Mexican War (1846 – 1848), the 1849 California Gold Rush, the 1858 discovery of gold in Colorado, and the Civil War (1861 – 1865) brought many changes to the West, including to the life of young George Bent, William's second son. In his life, we see encapsulated these changes. George was the sibling who learned best how to straddle white and Indian cultures. He, like his siblings, was eventually forced to make a choice whether to live as white or as Indian. Especially after the 1850s, being of mixed race became more of a burden and less of a strength, even in areas that had been more than eighty percent mixed race. A great shift in racial relations loomed on the horizon for those who lived on the Plains.

Of course, this affected the Indians as well. As the number of white people traversing the plains increased, the Indians in the 1850s and 1860s became more and more concerned and fearful about their own survival in the face of the white destruction of their nomadic lifestyle. With their dependence on the buffalo, tribes began to fight back with a growing anger. At the heart of many ethnic conflicts was that Indians did not have a concept of private ownership of land. They were territorial, but none ever determined that they should own and take over all the land. Their resource needs were limited to the all-providing buffalo, water sources, and the freedom to follow the herds seasonally as nomads.

The white man's concept of individual ownership and dividing the land could not exist compatibly with the Indian's approach. As whites moved west, abrogating Indian claims to the land, developing railroads, mining, and farming, George's lifestyle, like that of the Native Americans, became more and more marginalized. And as government policy toward the Indians changed, becoming harsher year by year, George and his siblings paid a dear price for their mixed-race blood.

I researched the story of these two men, William and his son George. William left little in writing, and we know little of his thoughts and feelings. He was not a man who kept records or journals, and only a few books have been written specifically about him. Unlike Kit Carson, Jedediah Smith, and Buffalo Bill Cody—who won notoriety in their own time—William Bent earned reputation and respect but not lasting fame. Nevertheless, from the actions of his life we can piece together a great deal about the kind of man he was. He was certainly a survivor, and he dedicated much of his life to the fight for the welfare of the Cheyennes. He became as one of them. Yet William also maintained a residence at his trading post, and he traveled a great deal both to Indian camps and back to Missouri for business, making him a representative as well of the white migration and settlement.

George, on the other hand, recognized late in life that the story of his people, the Cheyennes, needed to be preserved. Though they had a rich oral history, Indians did not write their history. To guarantee that the story of his people was preserved after the elders were gone, George put his education to use and ensured that their story was recorded. He made contact with two men who helped record the Indian history.

George Hyde was a young, house-bound man in Nebraska. Between 1905 and 1918, he and George Bent developed a prolific correspondence, with Bent having written three hundred and forty letters. Based on these letters, Hyde wrote Bent's story as *Life of George Bent*, but his manuscript was not published until 1968, after it was found in an attic and a second manuscript was made available through the Denver Public Library. Editor Savoie Lottinville published George Hyde's book from these manuscripts. The reader learns not only about George Bent's memories of growing up as an Indian with many freedoms and as a young man fighting for a way of life, but also learns about the Cheyenne people.

George Bent also contributed significantly to George Bird Grinnell's ethnographic research among the Cheyennes. In *The Fighting Cheyennes*, Grinnell used much of the information that George Bent could provide about Indian life, especially in the 1860s when the Indians were fighting to sustain their traditional existence. Recognizing that as they died off, so would their way of life and the remembrance of their times, George helped record the memories of the elders of the tribe.

George Bent left us an incredible first-hand account of what daily life as an Indian was like, what the fear and outrage were like when the government sent armies to fight the Indians, and what the outcomes were. We owe him a debt of gratitude that he never knew would be recognized.

While indulging my passion for this subject, I also realized that writing for academics was not my goal. I'm not a member of an academic community, nor would I be accepted there. Rather, I wanted to write the story of these two men for an audience who, like myself, simply loves history and believes that we can't know ourselves until we know where we came from. Our educational system and public information sources adhere to a traditional view of our history as an especially admirable one, overlooking the nature of our government to conquer repeatedly throughout our history. Conquest does not take place without one people brutalizing another people.

In dealing with the indigenous people of North America, European immigrants used their superior technology to subjugate, destroy, and exploit. That is not by any means the totality of our history, and through the story of the Bents my intention is to show Americans of European descent who were energetic, productive, and in many cases, ethical.

There are definitely two sides to our story. I believe we need to recognize both and hope that in the future our civilization uses knowledge of itself to seek a more inclusive approach to all peoples.

These are two fascinating men who contributed so much to the development of the Southwest and to our knowledge of the Indian experience. Their stories reveal happiness, when times were peaceful and the family was growing and prospering. Other chapters describe terrible tragedy and heartache. But in all cases, this is the story of two outstanding men who did the best that they could in trying times.

Notes

As was conventional in the nineteenth century, William named his children after his siblings. His sons Robert, George, and Charles are easily confused with his brothers of the same names. Therefore, when referring to William's brothers I have indicated that I'm referring to a brother; e.g., "brother George." More often the names of his children are central to the story, so I simply refer to them by name, with the exception of his son Charles. This namesake of Williams' most famous brother, Charles, was referred to by the family as Charley (often also spelled Charlie), so I have followed that precedent.

Confusion also surrounds William's wives. William married Owl Woman in traditional Cheyenne manner, and together they had four children. At some point, he also took her sisters, Island and Yellow Woman, into his lodge. That was a common practice in the tribes for an affluent man to care for extended family. Whether or not William "married" either of these sisters is variously reported. However, Charley is the son of William and Yellow Woman. Where sources have disagreed on a fact, I have made note of the discrepancy

Use of the term *Indian* is controversial. One legend explaining its origins relates that Columbus thought he had reached the East Indies and, therefore, the people he encountered he called Indians. The name stuck for all indigenous people of the continent. Again, because much of my source material is from the nineteenth century, my use of the word *Indian* reflects this historical context.

Finally, some sources refer to William's father-in-law as White Thunder, others as Gray Thunder. I have used White Thunder throughout. It is a matter of interpretation of the Cheyenne language.

1 ∾ THE FRONTIER

THE FRONTIER OF THE United States was relentlessly pushed westward, from the inception of the country. Just twenty-seven years after the Declaration of Independence, when America consisted of thirteen colonies clinging to the East Coast, President Thomas Jefferson negotiated the Louisiana Purchase—creating a new frontier. The price of $15 million dollars bought 827,000 square miles west of the Mississippi River.

Euro-Americans considered this land empty and undeveloped, even though it was occupied by indigenous, mostly nomadic people. This wilderness had also been explored by the Spanish coming up from Mexico, the French explorers from Canada, and the English who also came from the northern climes. But to the people of the United States, it was an unmapped territory, ripe for the taking.

Government-sponsored expeditions, usually military, were sent out to determine just what the United States had purchased from France in 1803. Only a few years after the famous trek made by Lewis and Clark, white people from the East ventured forth to explore and settle that blank space on their maps. A growing influx of mountain men, traders, settlers, and other adventurers flowed westward and began transforming the frontier.

The indigenous people, who lived by and roamed with the hunt, believed the land belonged to God and was "no more susceptible of individual ownership than the air."[1] Beginning early in the nineteenth century, increasing numbers of whites crossed their land—people who lived by the plow and believed the West could be "put to a better use than merely as habitat for nomadic Indians and wildlife."[2] This clash of two cultures did not bode well for the future of the tribes. Thomas Jefferson struck the first death knell when he proposed a policy for avoiding warfare between the cultures that would remove and relocate the Indians farther to the west of the advancing frontiers.

By the 1820s settlers had already pushed across the Appalachian Mountains to build homes and the beginnings of towns as far west as the Mississippi River.

> The main business of the people of the United States from 1790 to 1890 was to advance the frontier from the Appalachians to the Pacific. No folk movement in history, except perhaps the barbarian invasions of Rome, compared in mass, density, or velocity with the sweep of Manifest Destiny.[3]

Manifest Destiny was the nineteenth-century doctrine and belief that the expansion of the U.S. throughout the American continent was both moral and inevitable. To justify breaches of the established Indian country, policy makers in Washington conceived this idea that lifted land greed to a noble plane.

As ambitious men kept advancing westward with their families, they moved the frontier boundaries of what they considered "civilization." Some were immigrants seeking land and settlement, while others were more opportunists. Many of both groups sold well-established homes and farms to move on and see what was "beyond." The country's character was shaped and stamped by a restless, seeking, inner drive.

The plains Indians were territorial to the extent that they required the use of enough space to support the buffalo and other wildlife that they depended on. They tolerated friends and allies in their territory as long as there was enough food. Beginning in the 1820s, as increasing numbers of Euro-Americans traveled the Santa Fe Trail and other trails west, the killing of precious game became alarming to these early native environmentalists who understood the harmony and balance of nature.

Indigenous people that occupied this "blank space" on the map of the plains were Pawnees, Arapahos, Cheyennes, Kiowas, Comanches, Crows, Sioux, Prairie Apaches, and others. Originally horseless, once these tribes acquired the horse, their lifestyle centered on increased mobility. In *Soldiers on the Santa Fe Trail*, author Leo E. Oliva addressed this effect on the Santa Fe Trail. "Horses were important to each of these groups, and the stealing of horses was considered an honorable deed. Consequently, they were a constant threat to travelers over the Trail."[4]

About the Cheyenne acquisition of horses, George Bent said:

> All these tribes near the hills had horses when the Cheyennes first came, and the Arapahos, Kiowas, and Crows, all have stories that their tribe was the first to give horses to the Cheyennes. The truth probably is that our people secured some horses from each of these tribes.[5]

Thus the indigenous people became aggressive fighters and expert, well-mounted horsemen with great skills for obtaining the animals on which they depended for their livelihood. Though most tribes were slow to anger, the ingredients were present for future clashes when their territory was threatened.

The movement of increasing numbers of interlopers continued throughout the nineteenth century, culminating in 1890. By that time the eastern white population had joined with the early settlements of the Spanish on the Pacific Coast, and the Census Bureau declared the frontier closed.

Throughout this century of migration, beliefs, attitudes, and government policies changed. In the West, an emerging philosophy based in racism and bolstered by the increased involvement of white government and society, led to policies of conquering the land and its original inhabitants. This story is personified in the lives of two men, spanning the 1820s through the end of the century. William Bent and his son George experienced significant generational differences in the challenges of their lives as "civilization" progressed and brought with it white racism.

Men of the West

Among these restless, westward-bound people, some became well known and successful, like Lewis and Clark, Jedediah Smith, and Kit Carson. They imprinted the American character with the values of curiosity, love of the wilderness, and toughness. Effort and endurance became the bedrock for building a better future. Any man who worked hard and built a farm or a business had opportunity to secure a better life for his family. Migrants less well known than these famous men formed the masses that ran the risks of disease, accident, hunger, Indian raids, and failure. Despite dangers, there developed, like a flow of lava, a steel rod of determination that would build a strong society inexorably moving west.

Young men were in the majority of the earliest trappers and traders who began to roam this great unknown. Most had learned frontier skills as their families eked out a living in the woods of the East. Among the thousands who took the early trails across the plains was a German-born American doctor, explorer, and botanist named Dr. Friedrich. A. Wislizenus. After setting up residence in St. Louis, he took the opportunity to accompany an expedition of the Rocky Mountain Fur Company to collect scientific data. In 1839, this was primitive and risky travel.

Dr. Wislizenus journeyed to the source of the Green River in the Wind River Mountains (current-day Wyoming), crossed the Rockies with bands of Flathead and Nez Perce Indians, and returned to Missouri via the Arkansas River and Santa Fe Trail. Seeming to divine the future, he wrote that the waves of civilization would move from east to west until reaching the Rocky Mountains. Then even the fiercest tribes would be overwhelmed by the swelling tide of immigrants, and the buffalo and antelope, too, would be buried with the Indians. He spoke of how this influx of a different people would bring vices along with civilization. He forecast that the rape of the mountains would bring to light the most precious of metals and that would result in strife and envy. The plow would turn the virgin soil that up till then was only touched by Indian and hoof. "Every decade will change the character of the country materially, and in a hundred years perhaps the present narratives of mountain life may sound like fairy tales."[6] His prophetic words are haunting.

The Bent Family

One family that had a tremendous influence on the development of the West, especially in the Southwest, had a long history of success, proliferation, and contribution to this young nation: the Bents. A mere eighteen years after the 1620 landing of the Mayflower, John Bent escaped the taxes imposed by Charles I in England and, with his wife and five children, ventured to the new colony of Massachusetts. The Bent name thrived and prospered. "By the time of the Revolution, Massachusetts teemed with Bents—farmers, yeomen, blacksmiths, mill operators, bakers, innkeepers, lawyers."[7]

The Bent brothers, Charles and William, brought innovation to the early Indian trade, carrying on a family practice of leading-edge involvement and adapting on the frontier, eventually developing a unique position in the Southwest. There is even family lore, though not verified, that Silas Bent, grandfather of brothers Charles and William, led one of the bands of "Indians" who dumped British tea into the Boston harbor, carrying on the family tradition of rebelling against unjust taxation.[8] It is also known that Silas fought in the Revolutionary War.

After the war, Silas Bent joined two hundred and eighty Revolutionary veterans to form the Ohio Company of Associates to buy shares in unsettled land under the Northwest Ordinance. They bought a million and a half acres of land on the northern side of the Ohio River in territory that would become Ohio.

The Congress of Confederation had passed on July 13, 1787, the Northwest Ordinance, a prototype for later territorial organizations, to regulate how states would be established in the unsettled land beyond the

Appalachian Mountains between British North America and the Great Lakes on the north and the Ohio River on the south (land that would become Ohio, Indiana, Illinois, Michigan, and Wisconsin). The intent was for a strong central government to regulate how the land would be governed and divided into new states rather than extending existing states. The prohibition of slavery established the Ohio River as the boundary between free and slave states. It also set aside land for churches, schools, and universities.

Silas's share gave him 1,173 acres, situated in what is now southeastern Ohio. He sent Silas Jr. ahead to scout the new land, while he sold his farm and prepared to travel west to make his claim. It must have provided quite a logistical undertaking to move his family of twelve children overland in 1789 by oxcart through the mountains and by scow down the Ohio River. Unfortunately he and his wife lost one of their children along the way. Such massive undertakings often took the highest toll.

In 1790, moving on from the location Silas Jr. had chosen for them, they resettled and helped establish the town of Belpré, sixteen miles from the territorial capital of Marietta. Thus the family continued their westward trek that began years before in England.

Silas Jr. was ambitious to succeed, but it took him a few years to establish himself. When he married, he settled in Pennsylvania, and his first son, Charles, was born in 1799. Six sons and four daughters followed. With that size brood to support, Silas Jr. tried the law, storekeeping, and served as postmaster, but none of these proved sufficient to his needs. He applied for a job with the Surveyor General of the United States and was appointed to a position in the Marietta surveyor's office. Eventually he was appointed associate judge of the Washington County Court of Common Pleas in Ohio. When Albert Gallatin, Secretary of the Treasury, appointed him to the position of Principle Deputy Surveyor in charge of the Louisiana Territory, he finally found the avenue to success that had evaded him.

Silas Jr. moved his family to St. Louis, arriving in September 1806, six days before the return of the Lewis and Clark expedition. This was a timely opportunity right on the cusp of understanding what the Louisiana Purchase could mean to the future of the United States. The resources of this vast unknown would call men to move into this seeming vacuum seeking to exploit its wealth, and St. Louis would be the center for trade and shipping.

Silas Jr. was very successful and was one of the few who were accepted by the old French establishment of St. Louis, including the descendants of Auguste Chouteau, a founder of the city. At some time between 1810 and 1813 President Madison appointed Silas Jr. Judge of the Supreme Court of the territory, a post he held until Missouri was admitted to the Union in 1821. It was said of him that he never had "his ability or his integrity questioned by the fierce partisans among whom he worked."[9] He passed along the same traits of ability and integrity to his sons Charles and William.

Silas Jr.'s ten surviving children grew up among the wealthiest families of St. Louis. Though they lived on the edge of the wilderness, they lived with all the graciousness that lucrative trade on the Mississippi River provided. Oldest son Charles welcomed the birth of his favorite brother William on May 23, 1809. These two brothers would be close all their lives and partner in the eventual building of a trade empire in the Southwest.

St. Louis of that time was a thriving trade center and must have been an exciting place for young boys growing up. There were long wharves with warehouses full of trade goods from New Orleans, Europe, and up-river. Tales of adventure, both on the river and in the wilderness, sparked imaginations resulting in dreams of wealth and opportunity for brothers like Charles and his shadow, William. This promise of adventure up and down the river and west into the fur country planted dreams in both older brother Charles's mind and in the desire of younger brother William to travel with Charles.

But before these young men could pursue their dreams, Silas Jr. sent teenager Charles east for an educa-tion at Jefferson College in Canonsburg, Pennsylvania. Though many wealthy boys from St. Louis were sent east to Catholic schools, Silas Jr. chose a Presbyterian institution in the area where his father still lived. It is not known how long Charles was there or what he stud-ied or precisely what schooling William received, except that "he stayed with his books long enough to be able to figure shrewdly, express himself with a rough-hewn directness, and spell after a phonetic fashion which, al-beit extraordinary, was no worse than his brother's or Governor William Clark's."[10]

During this period the fur trade was very lucrative, as both the French and English had already proven, and Anglo-Americans began to enter this high-risk busi-ness. The men who went to trap in the wilderness had to learn many new skills to survive. The weather in the mountains during winter was fierce and unpredictable, but the furs were the best quality when it was cold. Exploration was a necessary part of finding streams rich with beaver but could lead to being dangerously lost. If a man got sick out in the wilds, he could get little help, though the early trappers seemed to have better health than the later settlers who followed in wagon trains, by which diseases were more readily transported.

The early traders also noticed that Indians often arrived on horseback at the rivers to trade. They began to envision land travel to trade for furs with the Indians in the mountains. As early as October 1812, Robert Stuart, working for John Jacob Astor's Pacific Fur Company, heard from the Indians of an easy lowland gap in the Rocky Mountain range known as South Pass, in later Wyoming, eventually leading to the speculation that wagons could travel into and through the mountains. In 1824 famous explorer and trapper, Jedediah Smith rediscovered the long-forgotten pass when Crow Indians guided him through the pass going east to west. Eventually this route led to the development of the Oregon and California Trails.

As trade with the Indians up the Missouri River and its tributaries became established and lucrative, entrepreneurs were motivated to take the risks that the fur trapping business required. Success depended on hiring the help of strong, capable young men who had grown up on the frontier and had wilderness skills. Competition for controlling the fur trade became intense. May 3, 1824, seems to be the best-documented version of when young Charles Bent, under the management of Joshua Pilcher, joined in the cutthroat race for profitable trade (although he may have been with the Missouri Fur Company as early as 1819).[11] At age twenty-five, Charles already was developing a solid reputation as a hard-working, honest member of a team that depended on each man for mutual safety, success, and survival. Later, as mentor to younger brother William, Charles conveyed the skills of wilderness leadership.

Opportunity opened up when the Missouri Fur Company went into bankruptcy. On July 4, 1825, Charles and five partners applied to explorer and Missouri Territorial Governor William Clark, of Lewis and Clark Expedition fame, for a trapping and trading license. General William Henry Ashley's company of men had just returned from west of the mountains in the Green River region with a valuable load of furs, proving that packing horses overland could be a money-making venture, sparking the dreams of the Bent brothers and their peers.

As fur trading on the upper Missouri River became more and more competitive and smaller businesses failed, trappers began to hear of successful trading in the northern reaches of Mexico, in the towns of Santa Fe and Taos. In 1821 Mexico had won its independence from Spain. Previously, Spain had kept the borders closed to trade because they did not want competition from the United States, where superior-quality merchandise was produced at less cost. Citizens of the newly independent Mexico, however, wanted the better quality at better prices and were open to the idea of trade. Political changes in Mexico made the possibility of successes like General Ashley's even more intriguing.

William Bent, nine years younger than Charles, probably joined his brother about the time (believed to be in 1827) that Charles was looking for better opportunities. These two enterprising brothers brought similar attributes to their dreams of success. They were much alike. Both brothers had dark hair and a small stature. They both spoke fluent "river French" and Indian dialects, with William later showing a strong aptitude for learning Indian languages and Spanish. They each displayed courage from a young age and proved to have an instinctive entrepreneurial drive.

What motivated these young men to walk away from a life of ease and security in St. Louis, where they could probably have done anything, is not documented. They never left a record of their thoughts on the subject.

Adventure was certainly a draw for them, and maybe it was just in their blood to prove themselves as strong men. Danger did not seem to be a deterrent. They demonstrated themselves to be innovative businessmen—the Bent blood was running true.

In the winter of 1827 – 1828, in a cold camp on the Green River, fate played a role in the development of the Southwest. Charles and his four partners had set out late in the season, during September 1827, with a hundred pack horses loaded with trade goods and forty-five good men. Under the leadership of Joshua Pilcher, they were abandoning the cutthroat trapping on the Missouri River and following earlier experiments to travel overland to trade with the Indians. William probably rode with Charles.

As the party struggled through South Pass in a blizzard, with their goods cached back on the Sweetwater River, the Crow Indians stealthily stole all their horses in the night. They were forced to make their way in deep snows on foot. As they struggled through the pass, they understood that "much of their hope for the future [was] buried with their cached goods back on the Sweetwater."[12] They finally made it to the Green River and chose a campsite there for the winter.

At the same time, young Ceran St. Vrain was serving as clerk in a party of trappers led by Sylvestre Pratte. They hailed from Taos, the Southwestern center for fur trappers. When Pratte died, twenty-five-year-old Ceran was selected to lead the group in their efforts to stay alive through the winter and catch enough beaver to return to Taos and make a profit. Like the Bent's party, Ceran's was struggling through deep snows to reach the valley of the Green River.

Ceran came from a French family in St. Louis that had been very successful in the Indian trading business for some years. We don't know if the Bent brothers had known Ceran growing up in St. Louis, but their families very likely moved in the same circles. It is known that both parties met up and passed that winter in the valley of the Green River.

Trappers gathering in the valley and setting up winter camps would be able to socialize. As they sat around the fires at night to keep warm, these ambitious and skilled young men—Charles, William, and Ceran—likely talked about opportunities in trade and may have thought of joining forces in business. Charles and William were looking for a more promising business model than sitting in the freezing river valleys through the winter and competing for the decreasing number of beaver. Ceran may have spoken with excitement of his successes in New Mexico.

Charles and William now began to formulate a plan that would look to the Southwest for a future that would not require the hardships of trapping. Trapping was a dangerous undertaking and they would not make a fortune in that end of the business. Eventually they formed a company, Bent & St. Vrain Company, which would exert great influence on the development of the Southwest and the American expansion and dominance that followed trade across the plains.

ENDNOTES

1. William Y. Chalfant, *Cheyennes and Horse Soldiers, The 1857 Expedition and the Battle of Solomon's Fork* (Norman: University of Oklahoma Press,1989), xx.

2. Ibid.

3. George Catlin, Edited by Michael M. Mooney, *Letters and Notes on the North American Indians* (New York: Gramercy Books, 1975), 46.

4. Leo Oliva, *Soldiers on the Santa Fe Trail* (Norman: University of Oklahoma Press, 1967), 16.

5. George E. Hyde, *Life of George Bent , Written From His Letters* (Norman: University of Oklahoma Press, 1968), 20 - 21.

6. Friedrich A. Wislizenus MD, *A Journey to the Rocky Mountains in 1839* (St. Louis Missouri Historical Society, 1912), Kindle Edition, last sentence.

7. David Lavender, *Bent's Fort* (Lincoln: University of Nebraska Press, 1954), 16.

8. Ibid, 17.

9. Ibid, 20.

10. Ibid, 25.

11. Lavender, *Bent's Fort*, 397. Various dates from 1819 to 1824 may have been when Charles first went north up the Missouri River. The best documented is 1824, Footnote 7, p. 397 of Notes.

12. Ibid, 80.

2 ∾ THE CHEYENNES

A S EASTERN INDIANS WERE consistently pushed westward
by white settlement, they likewise put pressure on the
tribes in residence in territory they appropriated. For
example, in the 1770s, the Teton Sioux had overrun the
Arikara on the Missouri River and moved as far west
as the Black Hills, where they displaced the Kiowa and
Crow tribes. Over the next one hundred years, the Sioux
forced the Crows farther west and raided to the north
and south against the Assiniboine, Shoshone, Pawnee,
Gros Ventre, and Omaha. "These lands once belonged
to [other tribes]," the Oglala [Sioux] Black Hawk explained, "but we whipped those nations out of them
and in this we did what the white men do when they
want the lands of Indians."[13]

The Cheyennes were of the great Algonquian speaking people. They called themselves the *Tsistsistas* or "the
People." We don't know where they came from, but they
probably separated from the larger Algonquian people
living in the north and east, probably north of the Great
Lakes or from the upper drainages of the Mississippi
River. In 1673 they lived along the Wisconsin bank of
the Mississippi. By 1684 they had begun their gradual
migration westward toward the plains. They acquired

their first horses in the middle of the eighteenth century. This transformed them from people practicing agriculture, making pottery, and living in villages to nomadic buffalo hunters on the plains.

The Cheyennes lived in a manner we can only imagine. They had freedom, they lived close to the beauty and harshness of nature, and they had a spiritual belief system that kept them close to the land and the other creatures with whom they shared it. Among themselves, they adhered to a complex political and social structure. "The Cheyennes . . . were democratic and deeply religious. They were not ruled by hereditary chiefs vested with the powers of an absolute monarch. . . . [T]heir social structure was firmly grounded in a strong sense of freedom and family."[14]

Marriage was a serious institution. They had a strict code of morality, and their women were known for their virtue. Men, women, and elders all had their specific roles in contributing to survival of the group. Divorce was permitted if the relationship wasn't working, but extramarital relationships were not tolerated.[15]

Their political structure was led by the Council of Forty-four that was responsible for overall leadership of the whole tribe. In their division of responsibilities, warrior societies planned and conducted raids and were accountable for discipline and security. They had great power and influence. Survival required unity within the band and tribe on all crucial matters which resulted in control by the tribal council and the warrior societies. They had developed a hierarchy with communal priorities.[16]

There were ten bands within the tribe that were subject to this central control. These were organized in matrilineal clans, and a married couple lived with the bride's parents. The five warrior societies were fraternal, military, and semi-religious, each with special privileges, duties, and dress. Originally they were the Fox, Elk, Shield, Dog, and Bow-string groups; over time there was some evolution in these groups.

The Cheyennes had two powerful medicines for their protection, the sacred arrows and the buffalo hat. These were revered fetishes that were the center of the tribe's ceremonials. One person, known as the Keeper of the Sacred Arrows, had the sacrosanct duty of their care. The Sacred Arrows had been preserved since the prophet Sweet Medicine, in the beginning of time, presented the tribe with four sacred arrows. Two buffalo arrows with red shafts assured a food supply and two arrows with black shafts assured success in war. Their power was for the men. The buffalo hat was made from the skin off the head of a buffalo, including its two horns. As with the sacred arrows, a chief medicine man or other important man in the tribe was charged with the care of the buffalo hat. The buffalo hat represented food and pertained chiefly to women.

Their religious rituals were conducted seasonally as the tribe came together at certain times of the year and then dispersed into smaller bands for less environmental impact. They had to move camps regularly for grazing, water, and sanitation, so that during much of the year they roamed in smaller bands.

As they were pushed westward, the Cheyennes encountered the tribes in the northern plains, from whom they learned about the horse. This brought a revolution to the lifestyle of the tribe. Horses allowed for the accumulation of wealth among the Cheyennes for the first time. Speed and mobility provided more successful and far-flung capacity for raiding, and among the riches they appropriated, horses were the most valued plunder. Success in raiding brought glory and acclaim to individual warriors and a material improvement for the band. As the Cheyennes moved farther and farther south, where more horses could be found closer to Spanish settlements, they learned to capture, train, and raise fine herds. Horses became their measure of affluence.

In the 1820s the tribe split into a Northern Cheyenne element and a Southern Cheyenne faction. The Northern bands shared with the Sioux the Powder River and Bighorn country, in present Montana and Wyoming. The Southern Cheyennes began to settle below the Platt River living on the plains of what would become Colorado and Kansas. Their hunting grounds between the Republican River and the Smoky Hill River were rich in buffalo. Eventually the Southern Cheyennes settled as far south as the Arkansas River. The Cheyennes were still one tribe and often intermingled. They were closely allied with the Arapahos and the Lakota Sioux. The Sioux tribe is a confederation of several tribes that speak different dialects, the Lakota (also called Teton Sioux), the Dakota, and the Nakota. The Lakota, comprised of seven bands, were the largest and most westward of the groups.

A strict division of labor existed between the sexes. The women were gatherers of vegetable foods, while the men were hunters and warriors. With the horse culture, however, came a shift in lifestyle for Indian women. As the braves could travel further and further afield and bring home more and more plunder, the workload of the women grew. They did all the work in the camp, including the preparation of buffalo hides for trade. When a warrior became wealthy enough, he took more wives, who in turn provided more labor to cure hides and care for his household and children.

A Cheyenne warrior measured his own value against his successes raiding other tribes. They evolved a fighting ethic that would be very different from the fighting tactics of the white men they would encounter, as pointed out by David Levender, in *Bent's Fort*:

> The Indian fought for glory. . . . Just as he dreaded contempt above all else, so he craved admiration. . . . But he wanted to enjoy his glory personally. Though desire for revenge was a powerful motive . . . neither this nor any other cause was worth dying for when battle was actually joined, and there was nothing contemptible in his mind about running away to fight another day. The result was Indian raiding parties rather than Indian armies, with emphasis on guile, stealth, swiftness, and, above all, a careful playing of the odds.[17]

Thus, the Cheyennes became accomplished guerilla fighters. Despite their warlike attitudes toward other tribes, the Cheyennes generally sought peace with the white man. They did not initially meet the white man as hostiles.

> When they first met the white people, the Cheyennes were shy and timid, and endeavored to avoid the newcomers. Lewis and Clark speak of this, and old men among the Cheyennes say that they have always been told that in former times the chiefs advised that the white strangers be avoided.[18]

Trade, however, improved the quality of their lives and drew them into more frequent contact with whites. In these transactions, as George Bird Grinnell explained, the Indian was taught to value individual freedom and decision making. They could be headstrong and obstinate. Grinnell further described the character of these tribesmen as having a strong inclination to the "virtues of honesty, trustworthiness, and bravery in the men, and of courage, devotion, and chastity in the women."[19]

Until the mid-nineteenth century, many Indians were friendly to the white traders. French traders from Canada wandered the western wilderness for many years, often living among the Indians and marrying into a tribe. Some of those marriages were temporary, until the trader moved to the next camp, but many were enduring relationships producing half-white, half-Indian children. Grinnell commented, "A fighting and a fearless people [the Cheyennes], the tribe was almost constantly at war with its neighbors, but until 1856 was friendly to the whites."[20] Basically, their exposure to whites was transitory and non-threatening in the early years.

Even as late as the 1840s, the Cheyennes were known to be peaceful. Santa Fe trader James Josiah Webb tells of making camp along the Arkansas River at the Big Timbers. When one of the men went to the river to drink, he heard a dog bark. Much to his discomfort, he realized there was a camp of about twenty lodges across the river. The travelers slipped away undetected, "although we presumed they were Cheyennes and there would be little or no danger if we had camped there in the day time."[21]

Addressing the effects on the Indians of first receiving white trade goods, Pulitzer Prize-winning historian Bernard DeVoto in *Across the Wide Missouri* said:

> The first step in the white man's exploitation of the Indian, and it was the inevitably fatal step, was to raise his standard of living. From the moment when the Indians first encountered manufactured goods they became increasingly dependent on them. Everything in their way of life now pivoted on the acquisition of goods.[22]

It will be seen how strongly this fact especially affected the Southern Cheyennes.

As the frontier moved westward, it brought contrasting consequences for the Indians. Michael M. Mooney, editor of *George Catlin, Letters and Notes of the North American Indians*, wrote:

> It has always been assumed that the first contacts beyond the frontier were beneficial to the Indian. Europeans brought horses, guns, steel needles with which to sew. . . . Surely, the first contacts were beneficial. But the frontier itself—the advancing boundary between the cultures—was always the zone of disease, despair, and desperation, precisely because it was a tumultuous zone between two Medicines, two conceptions of time and earth and reason, two systems of imagination and faith.[23]

Before the flood of American immigration that transformed the West, before missionaries, the army, or real estate speculators, artist George Catlin, the first professional painter of the West, had been searching for years for a worthy subject for a lifetime of devotion and enthusiasm. He found it one day in Philadelphia, when he witnessed in the street a group of noble and dignified-looking Indians from the West. He had found his calling.

From 1832 to 1836, he traveled the West, visiting tribes and painting the people and the landscapes. George Catlin had made a commitment.

> Man, in the simplicity and loftiness of his nature, unrestrained and unfettered by the disguises of art, is surely the most beautiful model for the painter—and the country from which he hails is unquestionably the best study or school of the arts in the world. The history and customs of such a people are themes worthy the lifetime of one man, and nothing short of

the loss of my life shall prevent me from visiting their country, and of becoming their
historian.[24]

As two very disparate cultures pushed against
each other, their basic beliefs dictated that eventually
there would be strife. In his introduction to Catlin's
writing, Michael M. Mooney summed up these op-
posing views.

> The Indian believed that he was part of Nature,
> as were his brothers the deer, the bear, the wolf,
> and the turtle. He believed that Medicine—
> what the white man called God—was accom-
> plished by ceremonies in reverence of the sun,
> the rain, the animation of the land. He believed
> that The Great Spirit—Medicine—was imma-
> nent, in the inherency of things themselves.[25]

This Indian concept of being part of the whole was
very different from the white man's approach to the
gifts of the earth:

> The white man believed that God was tran-
> scendent, up there somewhere looking down,
> and that from God the Father he [man] had in-
> herited the earth. The deer, the bear, the wolf,
> and the turtle were for man's increase, for his
> use.[26]

George Catlin's empathy for the native people produced a prodigious body of art, including paintings,
drawings, watercolors, and a collection of Indian ar-
tifacts. Though some of Catlin's work was destroyed
by fires over the years, he did leave us with a wealth
of information about the Indians before the changes in
their culture as the result of white man's influence. He
foresaw the destruction of their culture and felt pain
for that.

Catlin recognized that many whites thought of the Indians as thieves and rogues, but he saw the reality of the world from the Indians' point of view.

> Thieving in their estimation is a high crime, and considered the most disgraceful act that a man can possibly do. They call this *capturing* [horse stealing], where they sometimes run off traders' horses, and make their boast of it, considering it a kind of retaliation or summary justice, which they think it right and honorable that they should administer. And why not? For unlicensed trespass is committed through their country from one end to the other, by mercenary white men who are destroying the game and taking all the beaver and other rich and valuable furs out of their country, without paying them an equivalent or, in fact, anything at all for it. And this too, when they [white men] have been warned time and again of the danger they would be in if they longer persisted in the practice.[27]

There was often empathy for the indigenous people by whites, like the Bents, who saw them as individuals, as fellow humans, as equals, and as family. However, many whites saw them as less than human, and within government, later in the century, there were even those who felt that they stood in the way of progress and, as savages, should be exterminated. But they weren't savages. We have seen from the observations of witnesses to the Cheyenne character that they were different from white men. Just as with white men, they were sometimes brutal when at war, but they had their own set of values that also represented a warm humanity. William Bent grew to understand them because he came to them without bias.

ENDNOTES

13. Nathaniel Philbrick, *The Last Stand, Custer, Sitting Bull, and the Battle of the Little Bighorn* (New York: Penguin Books, 2011), 29.

14. Chalfant, *Cheyennes and Horse Soldiers*, 309.

15. Ibid.

16. E. Adamson Hoebel, *The Cheyennes, Indians of the Great Plains* (New York: Holt, Rinehart and Winston,1960), 49.

17. Lavender, *Bent's Fort*, 126.

18. George Bird Grinnell, *The Fighting Cheyennes* (Norman: University of Oklahoma Press, 1956), 5.

19. Ibid, x.

20. Ibid, ix.

21. James Josiah Webb, *Adventures in the Santa Fe Trade 1844 - 1847* (Lincoln: University of Nebraska Press, 1995), 59.

22. Bernard DeVoto, *Across the Wide Missouri* (Boston: Houghton Mifflin Company, 1998), 12.

23. George Catlin, Michael M. Mooney, editor, *Letters and Notes of the North American Indians*, 45.

24. Ibid, 89.

25. Ibid, 46 - 47.

26. Ibid, 47.

27. Ibid, 121 - 122.

3 ⁊ TRANSITION TO A LIFETIME IN THE WEST

A S THE BENT BROTHERS struggled with how to make their fortune, their thoughts turned more and more to the trade with Mexico. The Santa Fe Trail had opened to commerce in 1822 after William Becknell had led a successful trading expedition to Santa Fe in 1821. Legend has it that when Becknell returned to Franklin, Missouri, with a bag of silver coin that he spilled in the street to demonstrate a profitable trip, the whole area caught the fever, and the Santa Fe Trail was in business. A loose association of small operators could band together for safety, leaving Missouri and arriving in the exotic city of Santa Fe with wagons loaded with trade goods. No one had yet established a trade monopoly, as had happened on the Missouri River.

Though many traders made very large profits, the returns in some years were, after costs, painfully insufficient. For example, in 1824, $35,000 worth of goods taken west by traders returned $190,000 in furs and specie brought back. Actual profit usually ran from ten to forty percent, but in some years traders took a loss. 1830 was a bad year, when sixty proprietors divided $25,000 in profits. Mexican tariffs could run as high as $50,000 to $80,000. Caravans returned east with silver, furs, mules, and wool. In 1839, $45,000 in specie that traders deposited helped avoid a run on the Bank of Missouri during difficult economic times.

In 1829, "with the opportunity given them by their father's recent death and a small inheritance, the Bent brothers went into business as Santa Fe traders,"[28] Anne Hyde tells us in *Empires, Nations, and Families*. We don't know how many wagons loaded with trade merchandise they were able to supply, but whatever they had, they were ready to undertake a great adventure. They joined with other wagons headed west and organized for the long prairie haul. The caravan had thirty-eight wagons and seventy-nine well-armed men, including French Canadians, Spaniards, backwoodsmen, hunters, and merchants. William had ample opportunity to continue honing his language skills.

Charles was chosen captain of the caravan, taking on many onerous duties and responsibilities that one might have expected going to a more mature man. He had to organize the train, divide the messes for cooking, regulate the march, select the campgrounds, make assignments for night guard duty, deal with Indians, and settle disputes. At the young age of 29, his experience trapping on the Missouri River gave him an aura of leadership that he lived up to.

> As captain, Charles intended to lead the [sic] his seventy-eight men to Santa Fe, where, if all went well, they would trade their goods for furs, buffalo hides, blankets, and Mexican silver, which they would carry back to St. Louis and sell at a handsome profit.[29]

It was leadership training with the finest possibilities, and William was at his older brother's side. Both young men embarked on an adventure that would decide the direction of their adult lives and their careers.

Indians had begun harassing traders on the Santa Fe Trail since its opening. By 1828 losses were heavy due to Indian attacks, and the federal government was pressured to provide military protection for the caravans. When the Congress adjourned without acting on the request, lead traders, in 1829, appealed to newly elected, Indian-fighter President Andrew Jackson to provide protection as far as the boundary with Mexico. The business was too lucrative to abandon. Orders were issued to Major Bennet Riley to escort the 1829 caravan with four companies of infantry (the army had no cavalry at that time).

Many traders were still hesitant, doubting the effectiveness of foot soldiers against mounted Indians. They also had to be concerned about safety after crossing the border—defined as the Arkansas River—into Mexico. Ultimately, only one fourth as many men made the 1829 journey as in the prior year.

As an economy the quartermaster had outfitted the military supply wagons with oxen rather than mules. The traders grumbled at the slow moving oxen and made complaints. Charles, with his amazing mind for commerce, was always on the lookout for ways to improve their trading business. Unlike others who scoffed at the use of oxen to pull the wagons, he knew that oxen were heartier than mules and less expensive to buy and maintain. They were also no temptation for the Indians, who much preferred mules or horses and had no use for oxen. He asked Major Riley if he could borrow a yoke of oxen to see how they performed, and the Major agreed. After this trip, Charles planned to make the transition to using oxen, since they consistently proved to hold up better than the mules. His decision would have a lasting impact about the value of oxen on the trail for future caravans.

With Charles as captain and Major Bennet Riley as military escort, things were uneventful until they approached the Arkansas River, where they had a choice of two crossings. Charles wanted to lead the wagon train along a shorter route, crossing the Arkansas at the Caches and following a dry trail to the Cimarron River, a sixty-mile trek without water. Major Riley was not authorized to cross the Arkansas River into Mexican territory, and the traders were afraid to be without the military escort. They wanted to travel along the river for another laborious thirty miles to the upper crossing at Chouteau's Island, delaying the loss of the military escort. Charles agreed to follow the longer route that would add a couple of days to their travel. When they eventually reached Mexican territory, Major Riley was to camp by the river and wait for the traders return trip in the fall.

River crossings were always dangerous undertakings, with uneven riverbeds, quicksand, and unpredictable currents. But on July 10 they worked all day, doubling and tripling teams so they could maintain forward progress through the shallow but treacherous shifting channels of the river.

When it was time for the wagons to separate from the escort, Major Riley gave Charles some advice. He said to keep the wagons together and to keep guards both fore and aft of the wagon train. Both he and Charles had come to realize that controlling the independent traders was much less than perfect. The traders were disinclined to follow orders, especially the necessity to keep the wagons together and in a desired formation for defense. They argued with each other, and they thought more in terms of how to make a profit than in how to keep everyone safe. They tended to be an unruly bunch. Charles told Major Riley he would do "what he could," probably somewhat tongue-in-cheek.[30]

The next day the caravan set out without the military escort. William rode either as a scout or hunter, at some distance from the caravan and out of sight of it. Suddenly Indians dashed at him from out of a gully where they must have been watching and waiting for such an opportunity. William fired off a quick shot and raced toward the wagons. He didn't know if the Indians might be Kiowas, Comanches, or Gros Ventres, but any of them could lift his scalp as well as the other. Though inexperienced in Indian fighting, he had the best possible instinctive reaction to this alarming sight.

He rode a black mule with split ears—the mark of a Comanche mule. As William approached the wagons, Charles and two other men were also in danger and under attack from their position as an advance party. Samuel Lamme was shot and killed by the Indians. When the Indians stopped to scalp him, Charles and the other man had time to make their escape.

Charles saw that the Indians were going to charge through gaps in the wagon train, a typical tactic, and he recalled some advice that seasoned mountain man Milton Sublette had given him. He changed strategy from defense to offence and turned back to attack the Indians, with William riding to join him. This strategy scattered the Indians enough to allow time for the teamsters to circle the wagons into a defensive position. The Indians surrounded the wagons and the battle became a standoff. These young Bents had strong survival instincts that led to good decisions. This strategy, probably originating with the army, was one also noted by

Lieutenant James William Abert, an army topographical engineer. He wrote that in selecting campsites they tried to pick terrain that would "render abortive any attempt to charge through the camp, which is the most usual mode of attack."[31]

When the traders recovered from their panic, they fired their cannon. Though the shots were ineffective, they did scare the Indians off for a time. Nevertheless, a stalemate ensued. Charles asked for nine volunteers to run the gauntlet of the Indians and ride back to the river and get Major Riley to come to the rescue. William may have been among the volunteers.

When the troops arrived the next morning, the Indians withdrew. Samuel Lamme, the man killed the day before, was quickly buried. The usual trail burial was to dig a hole, wrap the victim in a blanket, and drive over the sight to prevent Indians and animals from desecrating the grave. There was little ceremony.

The traders were not fighters, and they didn't have much of a taste for combat with Indians. They pressed Major Riley to stay and escort them, which he did for two days, but he had violated his authorization by entering Mexican territory. After two days he returned to the Arkansas River to await their autumn return.

Fortunately the caravan soon encountered more than a hundred *ciboleros*, Mexican buffalo hunters, who were also very frightened and pleaded to join up for safety in numbers. They thought there were two thousand Indians on the warpath. The traders were relieved at the idea of joining forces for they had slept little, constantly on the alert for attack.

When word of their plight reached Taos, New Mexico, a rescue party of forty men, led by frontiersman Ewing Young, rode out to meet the caravan. When these forty men were driven back by the Indians, Young sent for more help. It took an additional fifty-five men to finally run the Indians off.

According to both David Lavender, in *Bent's Fort*, and David Fridtjof Halaas and Andrew E. Masich, in *Halfbreed*, among the rescuers was young Kit Carson. Kit was seven months younger than William, and they soon found they had a lot in common. A strong bond grew between them, and their friendship lasted throughout their lives. Kit named two of his sons after Charles and William Bent.[32]

When Charles and William finally relaxed their day and night vigilance, thanks to the reinforcements, they knew that "ninety-five Rocky Mountain trappers were a far better shield than five times that many traveling merchants or Mexican buffalo hunters."[33] The traders and buffalo hunters just didn't measure up to the fighting skills of the experienced mountain men. Charles no doubt felt that leading caravans of traders was like herding cats, but he developed into a renowned and respected leader of the trade caravans.

After going through Taos, the Bent brothers moved on to Santa Fe. They were on an exploring mission to determine how this trading business would work and if it held a future for them. Both were now seasoned leaders and would find their niche in the building of the Southwest.

When their caravan arrived in Santa Fe, about August 4, the quick sale of all his merchandise convinced Charles that he needed to return to Missouri to pay off loans, load up more merchandise, and return to make a profit. In less than a month he headed east again to make a speedy turnaround and be back in Santa Fe by December. In the span of about nine months he would travel more than twenty-three hundred miles. His energy and enthusiasm for this new business was impressive. He had found his role in the buying, selling, and transporting phase of the business, even though the work would become more challenging. In 1830 the government refused to escort the trading caravan as they had the year before. The traders were left to their own protection in the future. Without military escort, Charles would have to use all the skills he had developed to get the caravans across the prairie without incident.

Newly acquired partner Ceran St. Vrain, who already knew the Mexicans, would market the merchandise. Ceran ultimately acquired Mexican citizenship to have more favorable business dealings with the tax collectors in Santa Fe. His strength in the partnership was to operate their wholesale/retail sales in the city. He was a reliable partner, and as things developed, each of the three partners would be able to play to their individual strengths contributing to the growing business.

However, William had other ideas than returning east to travel with another caravan. At age twenty, he decided to stay in the West. Following a caravan did not particularly appeal to him. He decided to look into what other opportunities might be available. "This turned out to be a momentous decision for the history of the region."[34]

William's role would be determined as the business expanded. As a very young man, he had arrived in the West to seek his fortune. Now his task was to determine how he was going to do that. Of his preparation we know he traveled west with Charles in a caravan of traders with a military escort to the border. We know that he was initiated into Indian fighting on the trip. We know that he had the opportunity to learn what it means to escort traders across eight hundred miles of grueling trail and to have a financial interest in the outcome. And we know he was learning about the business of trading.

Did he want to be a trapper? Did he want to escort trade caravans and sell their merchandise? What other options might he discover? Being a true Bent, his inclination would be to find his own innovative course. Charles was a born pioneering businessman, while William, though dedicated to the business, had a different talent to offer. William's strong suit proved to be his competence with the people who would be a major constituency and his primary market, the Indians. Running the financial aspects of the business was best left to Charles and Ceran.

The Dream Fulfilled

After the caravan arrived in Santa Fe in 1829, William was restless. It was decision-making time. He had decided not to return with Charles to Missouri and instead stayed in Taos. Eventually he joined a party of independent trappers headed north. The fact that they were carrying trade goods indicates their intention to do more than just trap. They set up a winter camp on the Arkansas River.

One day a war party of Cheyennes, on foot to raid the Utes for horses, came across their camp. The Indians were curious about what these white men were doing and approached the camp making signs of peace. Both they and William spoke Sioux and knew sign language so they could parlay. The Indians were attracted to some of the trade goods these young men offered. Here William experienced Indians that he wasn't fighting, which provided a turning point in his future. This meeting between the Cheyennes and William would lead to a life-long relationship having an influence on the lives of both parties.

When the Cheyennes left the camp, two warriors lingered. They were repaid for their curiosity by getting the scare of their lives when the camp received a surprise visit from a band of Comanches under Bull Hump, who aggressively rode into the camp. The Comanches struck terror into the hearts of everyone. These fierce warriors were unchallenged from Texas to the Platte River. New Mexicans lived in constant fear of their brutal raids, and in Mexico, they also captured women and children in addition to horses. Due to the number of female Mexican captives that they took, the tribe had become infused with Mexican blood.[35]

Comanche horse herds numbered in the tens of thousands. Though they usually got their horses in Mexico, this time Bull Hump was after Cheyenne horses. William quickly hid the two Cheyenne visitors among the pelts and trade goods. Fortunately the Comanches had not come to shop, but they noticed the many Cheyenne moccasin tracks and demanded to know the whereabouts of the Cheyennes. William had to make a quick choice between betraying the two Cheyennes and winning the favor of a powerful tribe or saving the two frightened Cheyennes. William chose to tell Bull Hump that the Cheyennes had ridden on their way. Bull Hump departed in pursuit of the Cheyenne band. If instead he had discovered the lie, he would have killed the whites and the two Cheyennes. There was apparently nothing in the camp to motivate Bull Hump to aggression against these white men. He was focused on Cheyenne destruction that day.

At age twenty, William had just made a quick-thinking decision that had a huge impact on the rest of his life. He won the gratitude of the Cheyenne people, though he didn't know it yet. "No one had any idea that a seed had been planted that would help influence the growth of America."[36]

When it was safe, the two Cheyennes went their way. At the end of the season, William, with his fellows, gathered their skins and returned to Taos. In these early years, William was developing into an honest man who would carry that trait into his future business dealings. He realized he preferred working with the Indians to fighting them, and he was honing many skills that would make him a leading ally to the Indians. His vision of the future was one of peace and doing business that was advantageous to all parties.

On August 25, 1830, William joined three other Missourians for a trapping trip into the Gila wilderness farther south of Santa Fe in Mexico. They took nine pack mules, twenty-four traps, and a Mexican roustabout. Ceran, knowing of several other trapping disasters in that area, probably advised against the danger of Apache attacks, but these adventurous young men did not heed any warnings.

After a long search for beaver, they found some on the Gila River. However, the Apaches also found them. When William's party camped, they picketed six of their horses and let seven loose to graze. After a very quiet night, they found the loose horses were gone and seventeen of their traps were missing. This says a lot about the stealth of the Indians.

The next morning Robert Issac counted about a hundred and eighty-three warriors camped across the river. When the warriors strung their bows and swarmed across the Gila, the whites sheltered behind their baggage and exchanged threats back and forth with the Indians. In an attempt to placate the Indians, the whites promised the Indians that they planned to trap upstream the next day and they could trade then. They wanted to seem vulnerable and unprepared, to mislead the Indians about their intentions. They spent a worrisome night and in the morning made the appearance of moving upstream. The Indians characteristically had an ambush planned, but the whites veered off course and made a stand at the top of a bluff. While the Indians let loose a hail of arrows, the riflemen picked targets and successfully found their marks with eleven of twelve shots. When the Indians saw how effective their firepower was, they lost interest and left.

William and his cohorts hastily returned to the settlements, but William's reputation as an Indian fighter and leader in a tough situation was firmly established. He was now known as far east as St. Louis. Though he didn't make any money, William had learned a lot and gained widespread respect.

No record tells us what William did next, though he likely gathered a small party and returned to the Arkansas River, in present-day Colorado, intending to trade with friendly Indians. He did not choose to wander with pack mules, and he had more goods than a nomadic trader could carry. He must have planned for the Indians to come to him. This was the embryo of his course for the future.

Demonstrating the natural Bent talent for business, probably in the winter of 1830 he built a small picket stockade where the Indians could come to him to trade — a model that allowed him to be more settled. He also wanted to import from Missouri merchandise that was superior to what he was getting in Santa Fe. He wanted wagons loaded with top-quality goods that could be bought in St. Louis and customized to the Indian trade.

For the next twelve to eighteen months we can only surmise what William's life was like from what he did in the trading business. He probably pursued a hybrid trading model: sometimes traveling from Indian camp to Indian camp, trading calico, knives, beads, mirrors, salt and pepper, dried onions, beans, and pumpkins for pelts; and sometimes conducting trade at his stockade. Clearly, though, William continued to think of a central location for trading, as that was the direction he moved in over the next months.

Additional motivation for William to do something other than work as a trapper was his recognition that the beaver in the Southwest were giving out. The life-style of trading with the Indians seemed preferable to him than the life of wading freezing streams in the winter to trap the ever more elusive beavers and losing everything to Apaches. He wanted to find a better way of making a living in the West that he loved. Trial and error were helping him decide what direction to go with his career.

Probably in the summer of 1832, Charles left a load of merchandise in Santa Fe and made the arduous trip over Raton Pass to the north and then found a route to go seventy miles east to William's stockade. Charles was getting help now in his transporting of goods from younger brothers George, who was eighteen, and Robert, who was sixteen. William probably rode to meet them to show them the route.[37] The Bent family effort now included four brothers.

By the mid-1840s this route over the pass would begin to be a much-used branch of the Santa Fe Trail, and it became known as the Bent's Fort route during and after the Mexican War. However, in 1832 it was still an arduous trip to cross Raton Pass. It isn't known when the first traders' wagons were able to travel this branch, but in 1845 Army Lieutenant James W. Abert reported that it was only recently put into use. The Bent's, with

the location of their fort, were among the earliest to influence travel by this newer route, as opposed to the dry
Cimarron route. The mountain route had better water
and would grow in importance for Bent's Fort.[38]

When Charles saw the stockade, his entrepreneurial, creative energy met a new challenge head on.
Seeing the potential for business there, he envisioned a
monopoly of the trade business on the Arkansas River
with the Indians and trappers. The lessons of his experiences on the Missouri stuck with him. He couldn't
ignore the growing competition from other independent traders and wanted to avoid the trade wars that
had ruined the fur business on the Missouri River.
Together the brothers visualized a permanent, durable
fort in place of the stockade, a place where merchandise could be stored, trappers supplied, Indians traded
with, and one that would be strong enough to be safe
from attack. These brothers were born businessmen
who could look at an open plain and see a future of
thriving commerce where most people would have
seen only a hostile wilderness. They decided on a different way of doing business.

As the Bent brothers continued down the Arkansas
River that summer of 1832, heading back to Missouri
for trade goods, they made camp in a lush grassy area
where the livestock could rest, near the confluence of
the Purgatoire River (also called Purgatory River). This
spot would repeatedly play a role in their future. A
large group of Cheyennes of the Hairy Rope band came
along with a large herd of horses they had raided from
the Comanches. Led by Wolf, Wolf Chief, and Yellow
Wolf, the Cheyenne war party approached the brothers' camp. William recognized two of them and greeted
them in Cheyenne. Because they had just completed a
successful raid against Comanches and were in a good

mood, they were eager to trade. They were impressive men—big, healthy, well mounted, and well-armed.

Charles and William invited them in and treated them to coffee with sugar. Coffee with lots of sugar was a great favorite with the Indians and the gesture was one of amity. They also smoked the pipe, a sign of hospitality and friendship. The Cheyennes were very family oriented and meeting these four brothers made an impression. They gave each of the brothers an Indian name. When Charles and William told the Cheyennes, through William's knowledge of Cheyenne and Charles's knowledge of Sioux, that they were planning to build a trading fort, the Indians showed their surprise by putting their hands over their mouths in awe. This was big medicine!

Obtaining superior merchandise to improve their quality of life appealed to the Indians. Chief Yellow Wolf suggested a better site nearer to the movements of the buffalo at Big Timbers, farther down the Arkansas River. This site was in a traditional camping location for their tribe. He said he would bring his whole clan to trade. Then the Cheyennes accepted more tobacco and went on their way. "The careful observation of manners, the acceptance of good advice, and ritual naming made this a successful beginning to the Bent family business enterprise."[39]

The Cheyennes became a unique force in William's life.

> Native people on the plains saw trade items as part of creating relationships that set in motion cycles of mutual obligations. Anglo-Americans, in contrast, engaged in trade as part of simply earning a living, a scheme that was impersonal and individual. . . . William Bent understood the difference very clearly.[40]

William accepted his relationship with the Cheyennes as one of mutual obligation that eventually became a major responsibility for him.

The Bent brothers were conducting marketing research, though they wouldn't have called it that. The Bents were astute enough to know that the Cheyennes could provide a strong nucleus market. That the Indians had contributed their own ideas and offered the use of their own camping grounds was auspicious. Likewise, William and Charles respected these people by sharing their own dreams. They were beginning a partnership with the Indians that indicated a regard that the Indians rarely got from white men. This was a momentous occasion, when white men and Indians shared the plan for a beneficial future for both.

When William began to move into the Indian trade as his goal, he must have recognized that this trade would depend on peace among the Indians and with the white men. We see the future William and his deep concerns and values beginning to emerge. This was an opportunity untainted by racism, prejudice, or exploitation. William proved to be the epitome of a man whose true interest was to get along and respect rather than to think in terms of pushing people out of his way, as that philosophy later developed in the West. He brought a refreshing attitude to dealing with the people who occupied the land he already loved and where he wanted to build his life. After all, he was the interloper.

Eventually the Bents chose a site for the fort that was farther upriver on the Arkansas, in a border area between tribes. Arapaho, Prairie Apache, Utes from the mountains, Comanches and Kiowas from the plains, bands of Crows, Gros Ventres, and even some Wyoming Shoshoni roamed this transitional territory. It would also be a convenient location for trappers from

the mountains. They selected a spot a dozen miles upstream from the Purgatoire on the north side of the
Arkansas River in United States territory. In years to
come, caravans to Santa Fe would also pass through
when the Santa Fe Trail developed a mountain branch
over Raton Pass. They were in the trading epicenter of
the Southwest.

William recognized that the key to success in the
business was developing a more reliable trade with
the central Plains nations. He envisioned a neutral
location where Indians and traders could rely on
safety during their transactions, placing the emphasis
on business over strife. Thus various experiences co-
alesced into a vision.

After consulting with Ceran, the Southwest mode of
design was adopted and a permanent structure of adobe
was planned. An establishment of this nature would
give them a great advantage over the growing competition from nomadic traders. The Bent brothers took the
idea of trading with the Indians to another level in the
Southwest, where trade would also eventually bring
traffic from St. Louis through Westport, along the Santa
Fe Trail, and into Santa Fe by the 1840s. Two strong
sources for business, Indians and the international trade
route, would come to this unique point in the middle of
the wilderness where the Bents would offer welcome,
respite, and hospitality along with trading.

Marc Simmons, author of *Kit Carson and His Three
Wives*, summarizes in a concise manner this growth and
the final development of direction for William:

> St. Louis brothers Charles and William Bent
> made their first entry into the overland com-
> merce of the region in 1829, joining a wagon
> caravan with their goods for the Santa Fe mar-
> ket. . . . But a rise in the firm's fortunes led in

1833 to the opening of a store in Taos and the beginning of construction on the fortresslike [sic] trading post situated adjacent to the Southern Plains. William Bent, Charles's junior by nine years, was handed the job of building and then, upon completion, managing the fort.[41]

William had found his place in Bent, St. Vrain & Company. The partnership had been formalized in September 1830 and was now well on its way to succeeding.

Bent's Fort Realized

For nearly two thousand miles from the Mississippi River to the Pacific Coast, no other building like Bent's Fort existed. Unlike later government forts built along travel routes to protect travelers of all kinds, Bent's Fort was the result of private enterprise for the purpose of trade. It was a unique edifice that was the dream of the Bent brothers and Ceran St. Vrain.

The Bent brothers' experience of the fur trading wars on the Missouri River motivated them to get ahead of the competition and initiate a different, more enterprising approach for succeeding in this lucrative opportunity. Their timing was perfect. Between the fall of 1832 and the fall of 1833, due to the growing popularity of the silk hat, beaver pelt prices plummeted. The beaver trade was dying. From now on the driving trade in the West would be buffalo hides, and the Bent's were positioned to dominate.

Edwin L. Sabin, in *Kit Carson Days 1809 - 1868*, has provided a detailed description of the fort. Its location—near present-day La Junta in southeast Colorado—was ideal as a crossroads of the Southwest. There were outbound trails going up the Arkansas, a trail going north leading to the Platte River trading posts and to Laramie, a trail over Raton Pass south to Taos and Santa Fe, and from the east it was on the main route to the Missouri River and Westport.[42] Additionally, the site on the Arkansas River was chosen where there was good grazing land and a good water source at the river. This grass and water supply could support hundreds of travelers and their livestock who would come.

A substantial increase in traffic on the trail would begin in the 1840s with the Santa Fe trade, increase during the Mexican War with military usage, and with the 1849 California Gold Rush the traffic became so heavy that it was destructive to the trail across the fragile land.

The fort itself, however, was an enduring landmark along the trail. In his book on Kit Carson, *Blood and Thunder*, Hampton Sides describes it as "resembling an ancient Algerian citadel, with adobe walls three feet thick."[43] Charles and William had learned the virtues of adobe as a building material in the Southwest, where timber was in short supply. Adobe was durable, low cost, resistant to fire, and the thick adobe walls remained cool in the summer and warm in the winter. No doubt Ceran was instrumental in knowing the merits of Southwestern design and was involved in the planning.

Comforts almost forgotten while on the trail could be found at this sanctuary:

> Thus at the crossroads of the plains wilderness was stationed old Bent's Fort—its dun ramparts a stronghold and a hospice in one. . . . But within there were food, shade when needed, warmth when needed. And always tobacco and conversation.[44]

William hired laborers in Taos and they probably began to build in 1832. The plan was for a rectangular structure with fourteen-foot-high walls and about twenty-five rooms surrounding an interior courtyard or *placita*. Shortly after starting work on the fort there was an outbreak of smallpox, brought by the laborers. William contracted a mild case and bore the scars on his face for the rest of his life, as did many people of his time. William had seen how devastating this disease was to the Indians when he was on the Missouri. He nursed those who were too ill to travel and sent everyone else back to Taos, including Ceran, in an attempt to isolate the disease. When the disease had run its course, they continued building. By the fall of 1833, the fort/trading post was sufficiently completed to begin doing business.

In late 1833, after the small pox scare had subsided, William and Ceran rode north toward the Black Hills to find the Cheyennes and let them know it was safe to travel to the fort to trade. As a result, three hundred and fifty Cheyenne lodges and more than 2,500 people gradually made the move back to the Arkansas to camp in the vicinity of the fort. This relocation strengthened a split in the Cheyenne tribe that had been under way. Though the Southern Cheyennes and the Northern Cheyennes would remain one tribe, the fort and its promised trade were major factors in this permanent division.[45]

When the fort was ready to do business, Charles obtained a United States government trading license on December 18, 1833—something that had not been a part of their more nomadic business on the plains. The license authorized trading with the Cheyennes, Arapaho, Snakes (Shoshoni's cousins) Comanches, Kiowas, Sioux, and Arikaras.

In 1839 writer Thomas Farnham was hired by Horace Greeley and other Eastern entrepreneurs to travel west and write about the experience. In his journal Farnham likened the fort to an image of times long past: "A solitary abode of men, seeking wealth in the teeth of danger and hardship . . . like an old baronial castle that has withstood the wars and desolations of centuries."[46]

There were rooms for trading and storage, dwelling rooms with fireplaces, a blacksmith shop, a food storage area, a dining area, a kitchen, a tailoring shop, carpentry shops, and a wagon-repair space. It was about one hundred-thirty-seven feet by one hundred-seventy-eight feet. Watchtowers at two corners were equipped with small canons. The corral for enclosing animals at night had six-foot to eight-foot walls, with cactus planted on top to prevent Indians from climbing over. There was a well in the center of the yard, in case of siege, and a pelt press for packing furs. The fort was self-sustaining and well protected from Indian attack.

Eye-witness accounts from people who traveled to the fort reveal many interesting insights into what the fort was like and what it meant to the hardship-worn visitor. These irresistible accounts add so much color to the story, and their telling in the vernacular helps us to experience those times. With his writing skills Farnham provided wonderful detail. When he arrived at Bent's Fort, two of the Bent brothers were there, though he doesn't say which two. It is interesting to see the Bent brothers through the eyes of Farnham:

> Two of them [the Bent Brothers] were at the post when we arrived. They seemed to be thoroughly initiated into Indian life; dressed like chiefs—in moccasins thoroughly garnished with beads and porcupine quills; in trowsers [sic] of deer skin, with long fringes of the same extending along the outer seam from the ancle [sic] to the hip; in the splendid hunting-shirt of the same material, with sleeves fringed on the

elbow seam from the wrist to the shoulder, and ornamented with figures of porcupine quills of various colors, and leathern fringe around the lower edge of the body. And chiefs they were in the authority exercised in their wild and lonely fortress.[47]

Farnham believed that, while in St. Louis, these men dressed very differently. He speculated that the Bent brothers probably wore beaver hats, high stocks, and broadcloth coats when they represented the firm as merchants in St. Louis. But on the frontier, respectability called for different attire.

Even with the central trading location, William continued sending traders to Indian camps to trade, and he continued personally making some of these trips. His strength was in dealing with the Indians, whom he respected and treated fairly. He earned a reputation among the Indians as a good white man that they could trust. William was an early ambassador for developing wholesome relationships before the Indians learned hatred for the white men.

The duties of the partners now became well established. Ceran tended the stores in Taos and Santa Fe, Charles kept the caravans rolling with trade goods, and William ran the fort and managed the traders. "In time, William became the major driving force in the day-to-day management of activities at Bent's Fort, and he guided the company through its successful trading operations among the Indian tribes of the southern Great Plains."[48] These three men had just the right complement of talents to balance the needs of their enterprise.

However, William still had some hard lessons to learn before reaching his full potential. In the summer of 1834 a band of Shoshoni from Wyoming had fallen on Charles near Taos and had stolen a herd of mules and horses. On July 29, when a band of eight lodges of Shoshoni approached a stockade on the Arkansas where William was trading, he recognized some of them as having taken part in the attack on Charles. He and the other men with him attacked the Indians, even though they were coming in peace. The Shoshoni band fled in terror, leaving thirty-seven horses and all their possessions. Three Shoshoni were killed and one was wounded. An Arapaho bystander was also wounded. This event highlights how, in a land without formal law enforcement, a man's ethics—and his power—were judge and jury.

In time, an outraged witness of this incident filed a report with the Indian Office regarding the behavior of the whites. Charles was probably able to smooth things over, and there was no reprimand.[49] Part of William's heated reaction may have been due to the importance to a businessman of protecting his property and, of course, anger at his brother having been violated. The bond between these brothers was very strong. They had been as inseparable as two brothers, with nine years in their age difference, could be. Their commitment to each other was life-long.

This was the blackest mark on William's long history with the Indians. His instinctive response had exhibited the mountain man's philosophy that Indians must be kept in line or that force should be avenged with force. It was out of character with his later behavior. The guilt and a reprimand from Charles affected young William. From that time he worked diligently to discourage violence on the plains. He was learning to be the man he aspired to be.

Managing a Fort

A great variety of skills were required to keep the fort functioning. As many as sixty to a hundred people normally worked there. "Beyond the company men and hired clerks, there were blacksmiths and wheelwrights, stock tenders, cooks and their assistants, common day laborers, butchers, and assorted hunters, bringing in fresh supplies of buffalo, elk and antelope meat."[50] Additionally there were company clerks and men to perform other functions to keep up with the comings and goings. Many of the men living there had families with them, and the number of people in the area was increased by the Indians who lived outside the fort but close by in Indian lodges.

Many visitors to the fort commented on the diversity of the people working, trading, and traveling through this bastion. The crowd of people was eclectic, including Americans, English, French of St. Louis and Canada, Germans, Mexicans, Indians, and mixed-race individuals, mostly women and children.

©Camilla Kattell

Bent's Old Fort today, exterior view

Robert L. Duffus, in *The Santa Fe Trail*, provides some insight into who one might see at the fort. By this time the fort had been an outstanding landmark for nearly a decade:

> Here, too, or close by, pass the great seasonal migrations of the principal Indian tribes of the western plains. So, though the fort lies in the midst of a seeming desolation, it is actually at a veritable wilderness cross-roads. Stay here long enough and every famous trapper, hunter, and trader, and most of the famous chiefs of the day will come and knock at the gate.[51]

The fort also attracted the attention of the government and the army. Lieutenant James Abert was ordered in 1845 to explore the Canadian River region of the plains. He recorded how important to his troops the resupply at Bent's Fort was to their survival:

©Camilla Kattell

Bent's Fort main entrance from the inside looking out.
This could be well secured.

The interior courtyard of Bent's Fort with the fur press
for packing furs for shipment east (above)
and corrals (below)

©Camilla Kattell

Sutler's shop (above)
and partial view of plaza architecture (below)

©Camilla Kattell

Now, through the agency of Messrs. Bent and St. Vrain, we had procured eight *fanegas* [a unit of dry measure in Spanish-speaking countries] of unbolted Mexican flour, also plenty of coffee, and as much sugar as . . . would last us for two months; three or four boxes of macaroni and a small quantity of rice were added as luxuries; . . . with eight prairie-fed beeves . . . we considered ourselves pretty well supplied.[52]

The fact that the fort was American cannot be overlooked, and we have stories of July Fourth celebrations remembering national loyalty. On a typical Independence Day, the Bents greeted the day with booming cannons and a giant American flag. The soldiers, trappers, travelers, and traders danced and sang and enjoyed William's "hail storm" mixed drink, while the children sucked on ice—courtesy of William's ice cellar, stocked with ice harvested in the winter and preserved for summer use. This was just one of the luxuries that William made an effort to provide to guests.

Alone and distant from the states, situated on the Mexican border and in the heart of Indian country, the fort evoked feelings of patriotism. "Frederick Ruxton, who visited in 1845, remarked that the 'solitary stranger passing this lone fort, feels proudly secure when he comes within sight of the 'stars and stripes' which float above the walls.'"[53]

In 1846 young Lewis Garrard, traveling the Santa Fe Trail at age seventeen in the company of Ceran St. Vrain and one of the Bent-St. Vrain caravans, arrived at the fort after a weary day of travel in the rain. In his book *Wah-to-yah*, he left wonderful details of his travels and adventures.

[W]e arrived in sight of the fort, where our animals were soon unsaddled, and turned out at the gate, to wander in quest of grass. . . . We found Mr. St. Vrain, who introduced us to William Bent, a partner. . . . We sat down to a table, for the first time in fifty days, and ate with knives, forks, and plates.[54]

The Bents offered an amazing level of Eastern civility in this wilderness. They even imported a pool table for entertainment. The next morning Lewis marveled at the views of the Rocky Mountains from the parapets and observed the diversity of the people. What an amazing learning experience for such a young boy. He was quite adventuresome and got involved with many of the activities at the fort and beyond. There had to be some commitment on William's part to have this boy around the fort and let him follow along on some of the undertakings outside the fort.

Much later, in 1847, Lewis was close enough with William to help build an irrigation system on William's new ranch in the Purgatoire valley. Their construction party included William and three other men besides Lewis.

They had plows, and the *acequia* [irrigation ditch], by which the land would be irrigated, was nearly finished. . . . For two days we labored as though the embryo crop depended upon our finishing within a specified time. When the water flowed in the *acequia*, we watched the bits of wood and scum floating with the first tide with intense interest and satisfaction.[55]

Lewis reported much satisfaction from working with these men, and William, whether it was planned or not, was no doubt offering this boy a chance to work with the men and build his confidence and skills. A similar mentorship occurred in 1856 when James Larkin arrived at the fort with a caravan led by William. Larkin described how the fort entrance was to the east with a pair of antlers over the entry and commented on how the trade worked:

> It is used by Mr Wm Bent as a trading post with the Indians—the Cheyennes, Kioways [sic], Arrapahoes [sic] & Comanches ranging in the neighborhood—they bring their Buffalo Robes, Tongues & Dried Buffalo Meat, Antelope & Deer skins to him & take in exchange Coffee, Sugar, Powder, Flour & Balls—on which a large profit is made.[56]

Larkin also mentioned in his diary that he felt no fear of the Cheyennes and Kiowas living around Bent's Fort "as they are friendly with Mr Bent"[57]—this despite recent killings of white men by Cheyennes around Fort Kearny. William inspired a lot of faith and assurance in Larkin. This was an important effect of William's leadership in this only stronghold of security between the frontier and Santa Fe.

William was contented at Bent's Fort. He liked living at the fort and doing his trading from there, and within two years he established it as the center of a trading empire. During the summer the warring bands from various Indian tribes would come through looking to trade for ammunition and powder as they conducted their annual raids on other tribes. William had to be able to perceive the mood of these bands and their intent. He had to understand the Indians well enough to know when to overlook insults and when to give gifts to a chief without offending another.

He also learned when to allow some sale of liquor under pressure from his demanding customers.[58] Liquor was used by William's white competitors to gain business with the Indians. Contemporary reports of how the

Bent's handled the sale of liquor indicate that they dealt with the Indians honorably; they no doubt sold liquor when circumstances were appropriate. "Their virtue, if it is a virtue, lies in their having tried to hold the evil to a minimum."[59] One method William used to minimize the problems was to credit the sale of liquor and then deliver it to the Indians once or twice a year for the chiefs to distribute.

William had a delicate balance to maintain between peaceful business and outbreaks of violence. Easily all could have been destroyed in this isolated refuge if he had indulged offensive behaviors toward any of his clients. There was no law to protect him. But William was just the manager needed for this job.

He also became an unofficial spokesperson in the delicate dealings between the army and the Natives. As early as 1835, Colonel Henry Dodge led a peace-seeking expedition into the Southwest. Eventually all the participants ended up a Bent's Fort. Though it was an ineffective council with little accomplished, the fort played a central part in hosting the military and the Indians. After gifts were distributed, the chiefs professed friendship with the Americans. The meeting served to clarify "the role Bent's Fort would play. . . . [William] Bent's choice of location, his personality, and diplomatic arrangements allowed for the fort to be a free trade zone in this remarkably dynamic region,"[60] relates Anne F. Hyde. The Fort had quickly become a center for activities of trade and diplomacy.

Of course, he had to protect the fort while keeping good relations with volatile customers and at the same time produce a profit. He managed all those responsibilities in an exemplary manner. He saw to it that the gates were closed at night and all the Indians were sent back to their own camps. By 1835, just two years after the fort opened for trade, William had gained the trust and respect of the Cheyennes, Arapaho, Comanche, Kiowa, and Prairie Apache tribes. His knowledge of their languages and communication by sign language made dealing with them smooth and accurate and sent a message of respect.

William tried to treat all the tribes the same, though he was closest to the Cheyennes. He enjoyed a special relationship with the Cheyenne tribe and especially with White Thunder, a respected leader. In turn, the Cheyennes respected William as a man who had become successful in the manner that he had chosen.

Endnotes

28. Anne F. Hyde, *Empires, Nations, and Families, A History of the North American West, 1800 - 1860* (New York: Ecco, an Imprint of Harper Collins Publishers, 2012), 154.

29. Ibid.

30. Lavender, *Bent's Fort*, 100.

31. Lieutenant James William Abert, *Expedition to the Southwest, An 1845 Reconnaissance of Colorado, New Mexico, Texas, and Oklahoma* (Lincoln: University of Nebraska Press, 1999), 53.

32. Lavender, *Bent's Fort*, 105. Halaas & Masich, *The Remarkable True Story of George Bent — Caught Between the Worlds of the Indian and the White Man* (Cambridge: Da Capo Press, 2005), 8.

33. Lavender, *Bent's Fort*, 106.

34. A. Hyde, *Empires, Nations, and Families*, 154.

35. Lavender, *Bent's Fort*, 129.

36. Ibid.

37. Ibid, 140.

38. Oliva, *Soldiers on the Santa Fe Trail*, 18.

39. A. Hyde, *Empires, Nations, and Families*, 147. Lavender, *Bent's Fort*, 141.

40. A. Hyde, *Empires, Nations, and Families*, 164.

41. Marc Simmons, *Kit Carson and His Three Wives* (Albuquerque: University of New Mexico Press, 2003), 31.

42. Edwin L. Sabin, *Kit Carson Days 1809 - 1868* (Lincoln: University of Nebraska Press, Vol. I, 1995), 287.

43. Hampton Sides, *Blood and Thunder, The Epic Story of Kit Carson and the Conquest of the American West* (New York: Anchor Books, a Division of Random House, Inc., ©2006 by Hampton Sides), 43.

44. Sabin, *Kit Carson Days 1809 - 1868*, 287 - 288.

45. Lavender, *Bent's Fort*, 149.

46. Thomas J. Farnham, *An 1839 Wagon Train Journal, Travels in the Great Western Prairies, The Anahuac and Rocky Mountains and in the Oregon Territory* (New York: Greeley & McElrath, 1843, ©1983 by Northwest Interpretive Association), 35.

47. Ibid.

48. James A. Crutchfield, *Revolt at Taos, The New Mexican and Indian Insurrection of 1847* (Yardley: Westholme Publisning, 2015), 33.

49. Lavender, *Bent's Fort*, 161 - 162.

50. Simmons, *Kit Carson & His Three Wives*, 33.

51. Robert L. Duffus *The Santa Fe Trail*, (Albuquerque: University of New Mexico Press, 1972), 147

52. Lieutenant James Abert, *Expedition to the Southwest*, 19.

53. Halaas and Masich, *Halfbreed*, 46.

54. Lewis H. Garrard, *Wah-to-yah, and the Taos Trail* (Norman: University of Oklahoma Press, 1955), 42.

55. Ibid, 242.

56. James Ross Larkin, *Reluctant Frontiersman*, edited and annotated by Barton H. Barbour (Albuquerque: University of New Mexico Press, 1990), 81.

57. Ibid, 82.

58. Lavender, *Bent's Fort*, 181.

59. Ibid, 160 - 161.

60. A. Hyde, *Empires, Nations, and Families*, 160.

4 ⁖ ALLIANCE &
ALLEGIANCE

WILLIAM RODE TO THE Cheyenne camp in the spring of 1835, stopping at White Thunder's lodge, intent on finding a wife.[61] White Thunder was keeper of the tribe's sacred medicine arrows that protected the people, indicating he was a revered man—as close to a chief as the Cheyennes had. And his daughter, Owl Woman, came as close to being a princess as Cheyenne social structure recognized.

At twenty-eight (or thirty, according to some sources), William wanted to marry and have a family, while at the same time form a strong relationship with the Cheyennes that would provide a valuable alliance. Cross-cultural alliances were not uncommon. In David Fridtjof Halaas and Andrew Masich's *Halfbreed*, it is found that Cheyenne women were highly thought of as wives among the white men on the frontier. "Cheyenne women had an unmatched reputation for intelligence, beauty, and grace."[62] White men, however, were not similarly prized: "[T]heir hairy faces offended Cheyenne sensibilities . . . and their lousy clothing and dirty appearance made them less than perfect companions. Yet, for many Indian women the promise of wealth and an easier life for their families made marriage to such men acceptable."[63] On the other hand, "the Cheyennes bathed every morning, winter or summer, in running water."[64]

William had never been married. He had been in the mountains and plains for some years, and he loved the West. He probably foresaw the fort as his home for many years to come, given the investment and its success. His lifestyle at the fort was more compatible with the Indian cultures than the white. High society in St. Louis seemed to hold no appeal for him or to tempt him in any manner. Though William did not put his thoughts about a racially mixed marriage to paper, given all the considerations, Owl Woman made a good match. And politically, he could not have made a better choice.

Whether William went through the complex wooing rituals of the Cheyennes is not known. Courtship rituals of a young man involved first getting the attention of his chosen maiden. He then hung around, hoping for a sign of friendship on her part. He might then, from outside the circle of lodges, play plaintive tunes on his flute at night. If his maiden could, she would slip out so they could whisper together for a short time. If the girl was not responsive, the medicine man might be asked to put a spell on her. If the girl's consent was won, the suitor gathered as many horses as he could and tied them in front of her lodge. Of course, her parents were aware of what was going on by this time. The acceptance of the horses indicated approval and was followed by gift exchanges. During the period of engagement the maiden presented herself and her homemaking skills to her intended to show what a good wife she would be. Rarely did things progress to a point where the suitor was humiliated by a refusal, and elopement was all but unheard of.

At his age, William most likely made marital arrangements with White Thunder and shortened the rituals that teenagers would have followed. With suitable gifts, he sought the hand of White Thunder's oldest daughter, Owl Woman, and was accepted. This union of two important families would be a momentous occasion. She would be a Bent and he a Cheyenne, son of the Arrow Keeper. They would be family, something that was very important both to William and to the Cheyennes.

Both William and White Thunder understood the benefits of their alliance. Both had power and prestige in their own world. White Thunder would have direct access to goods, and William was seen as a man of consequence in both the white and Indian worlds.

Charles probably urged William to think about the strategic advantages of marriage. He and Ceran both had married high-born Mexican women, a critical step in the success of trade negotiations in Santa Fe and Taos. Nevertheless, indications are that William saw this as an affair of the heart, one of mutual respect and satisfaction.

The precise location of the wedding is not known but likely was near Bent's Fort. In a typical Cheyenne marriage, William would have moved into her village. However, this was not a common marriage. The newlyweds moved between the two worlds and two cultures. The fort seemed more a place of business than a home, and Owl Woman preferred her lodge in the nearby village. It was airy and roomy, with welcome light filtering in. The sounds of the village rarely intruded. Children played under the watchful eye of elders and older children. William kept a portable writing desk in Owl Woman's lodge. Yet Owl Woman also was attracted to the multicultural excitement when visiting the fort, which offered exposure to the exhilaration of foreign languages and customs. She and William rearranged the apartment in the fort, putting soft hides on the floor and hanging blankets on the walls.

William and Owl Woman made a working accommodation that embraced both of their cultures and gave their children a more extensive and worldly background than most frontier children received. Together, they had four children and gave them both Bent family and Cheyenne names. In 1838 William and Owl Woman's first child, Mary (after William's sister), was born.

> This relationship grounded life at Bent's Fort and made it successful and stable in a world that was anything but. The Bent children grew up understanding the significance of family, tribal, and imperial alliances as they participated in daily life at the fort. George Bent [William's son] . . . remembered hundreds of employees, many of whom had families of various ethnic mixes, all guided by the rhythms of the seasons and the trade caravans.[65]

These were the years when William must have been happiest. He was a business success, had a happy marriage, and his children were safe and near him. David Remley in *Kit Carson* summarizes these years as an ideal life:

> The story of their life together is an idyllic picture of the ideal suburban arrangement of the time. The family could stay at home during the day. Owl Woman did the domestic chores and visited with the other women while the children played in the river's sand under the cottonwoods. Meanwhile, their father, William Bent, walked or jogged along horseback to the office at Bent's Fort each morning.[66]

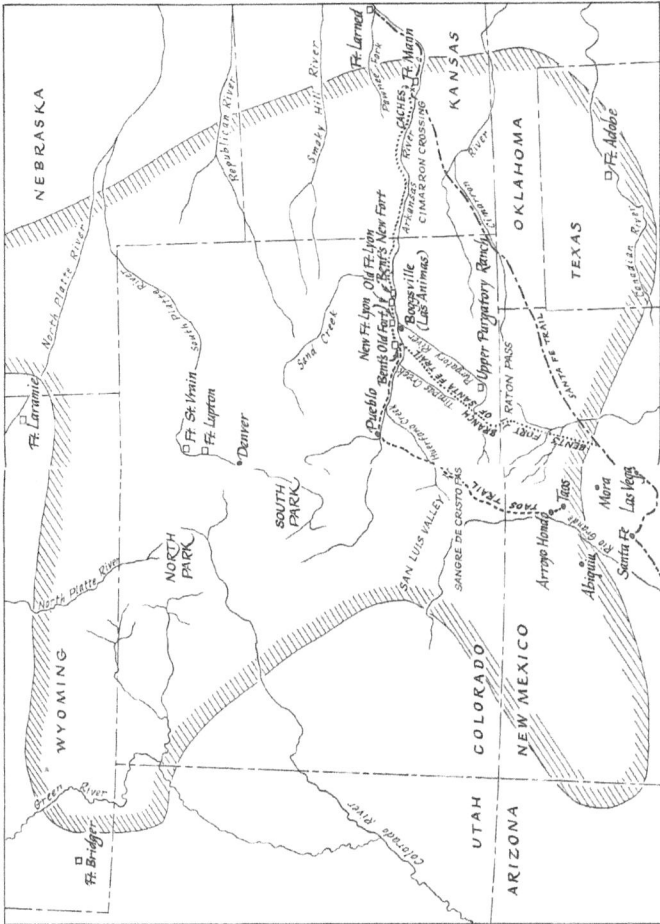

The Wilderness Domain of Bent, St. Vrain & Co.
Map originally published in Life of George Bent:
Written from his Letters, *by George E. Hyde, edited by*
Savoie Lottinville. Copyright ©1968 by the University
of Oklahoma Press. Reprinted by permission of the
publisher. All rights reserved.

William and Owl Woman were devoted to their family. William loved his children and never felt that the mix of races made them any less than if they had been only white. His acceptance and love of the people of the West had grown to a point where he simply saw people as people. He would later, however, send his children to St. Louis for a more formal education to better prepare them for life in two worlds.

Referring to far-flung communities in the Louisiana Purchase, like Santa Fe, Anne F. Hyde explains how strong family connections related to family success in the early settlement of the West:

> Bent's Fort acted as successful trading center because William Bent had made familial relationships with the Cheyennes, American, and Mexican elites....By 1838 Bent and his wife Owl Woman .... were the central business and social leaders of the region. Their four children, all educated in St. Louis and with their mother's people, moved easily among the New Mexican elite, St. Louis traders, and Indian diplomats.[67]

Competition among and between the Cultures

By 1837 Bent & St. Vrain had realized substantial returns on their investment, even after the expense of building and stocking the fort. Competition was still keen, though, and the company always thought in terms of advantage in business. William continued working for domination in the fierce competition for market share in the West. It was a cut-throat time for doing business, without any government regulation—except that whiskey was not to be sold to the Indians. That was the only government intervention. In 1802 an amendment had been added to the Trade and Intercourse Acts outlawing the use of liquor in the Indian fur trade. However, there was little capacity for enforcement over the vast expanses of the plains, and the rule was openly violated.

When the American Fur Company, from their post at Fort Jackson in Colorado, offered competition and a trading war, the Bents' solution was to buy Fort Jackson. That seemed the best way to control the market on the South Platte. In July 1838 Ceran went to St. Louis and pulled off this coup, aided in part because the American Fur Company had suffered a loss in trade the year before when smallpox decimated the northern tribes.

During the sale negotiations the American Fur Company (AFC) suggested that they and Bent & St. Vrain should divide the lucrative market on the plains: Bent & St. Vrain would not trade north of the North Platte River, and AFC would not compete on the South Platte River. Thus in 1838, big business agreed on what territories they would exploit without interference from each other.

The arrangement guaranteed the Bents the growth of their Southwestern trading empire. Though they faced uncontrolled competition from free-wheeling individuals, the Bents were very successful in gaining the business of tribes both north and south, especially at the fort. And by the 1840s Bent, St. Vrain & Co. dominated business on the Santa Fe Trail.

William worked to build and maintain business while violence was always present among passionate men who had no reason to fear legal retribution. The firm's Indian customers provided the greatest potential for danger, particularly in the summer when war parties were traveling the plains and stopping off at the fort.

Farnham commented on the location of the fort in the midst of so many Indians, many of whom were not friendly with whites or with other Indians. The buffalo brought the Utes and the Cheyennes from the mountains and the Pawnees from the Platte River to the upper Arkansas to intercept the great herds on their migrations north. The Comanches came from the south for the same reason. In June, August, and September there were "from fifteen to twenty thousand savages ready and panting for plunder and blood. . . . The Messrs. Bents feel comparatively safe in their solitary fortress . . . [though] every hour of the day and night is pregnant with danger."[68] Farnham's description of the "savages" certainly expresses a racial bias that is heard repeatedly in accounts of the period. Unquestionably the Indians were present in numbers that would have allowed them to overwhelm the newcomers—as the whites were well aware.

When rowdy crowds gathered, William dispatched armed patrols to the battlements. At sunset all Indians were sent out of the fort and the gates were locked for the night. With constant vigilance, William managed to keep the peace most of the time. In the middle of this vast isolation, William maintained this balance of peace against all odds, as no one else had ever accomplished. He assumed many leadership roles. He was by now a peacemaker, negotiator, benefactor, and counselor. He became a powerful advocate for peace, protecting both the health of his trade business and the lives of loved ones.

Inevitably, though, he could not always be successful.

The Battle of Wolf Creek

Not long after William's wedding, some hotheaded young Cheyenne warriors of the Bowstring society wanted to make a horse raid against the Kiowas and Comanches. They pressed White Thunder to perform the traditional Sacred Arrow renewal ceremony, which was required to assure their success. When he refused to be rushed through the ceremony, they beat the seventy-year-old medicine man and forced him to perform the ceremony in the time they had chosen. He warned them that it would be bad medicine, but they remained determined. Had William been at the fort, he would have protected White Thunder, but he was away. The raid did go poorly, and none of the forty-two in the party of the Bowstring society returned. White Thunder had anticipated that they were doomed.

That winter, White Thunder and Porcupine Bear, his son-in-law, agreed that the Sacred Arrows should be moved against the Kiowas to avenge the forty-two lost Bowstring warriors. White Thunder felt the proper procedures would be followed this time, and Porcupine Bear, Chief of the Dog Soldier Warrior Society, was sent as emissary to the scattered Cheyenne and Arapaho camps to recruit fighters.

Unfortunately, while Porcupine Bear was in a large camp on the Platte River, traders from the American Fur Company brought whiskey into that camp, and despite William's warnings against this poison, the Indians could not resist it. In the drunken chaos that followed, the unforgiveable crime of a Cheyenne killing a fellow tribesman resulted when Porcupine Bear reacted to a call for help from a cousin, and he killed Little Creek. For this deplorable deed, Porcupine Bear and his relatives were banned from the tribe and became outlaws. The Dog Soldiers were disgraced but were able to continue camping near the rest of the tribe.

The Dog Soldiers, though outlawed, fought valiantly through years of warfare, and they eventually won much respect from the rest of the tribe for their bravery and fighting skills. Their independence would have a long-term effect on the tribe, as they developed into the most adamant of white haters.

As the politics of the situation unfolded, younger men remained determined to carry a war of revenge to the Kiowas. White Thunder no longer had control. Leadership devolved to younger, less experienced men, causing a rift in the Southern Cheyenne tribe. In the spring of 1838 their war of revenge against the Kiowas and Comanches was planned by the allied Cheyennes and a small party of Lakota Sioux who gathered on the Arkansas.

The Cheyennes claimed victory at the resulting battle of Wolf Creek, but losses on both sides were devastating. The greatest loss for the Cheyennes was White Thunder, William's father-in-law and the only Arrow Keeper in Cheyenne history to be killed in battle. This spiraling cycle of revenge raids conducted during the summer raiding season each year was characteristic of the plains Indians' way of life.

By the winter of 1839 - 40, with pressures from a smallpox epidemic among the Kiowas and the traders pressing the Indians for peace, the Cheyennes and Arapahos and the allied Comanches and Kiowas decided to cease fighting each other. They recognized that the cost of their incessant warring was simply too high. Bent's Fort was chosen as the site for the peace negotiations.

As the tribes arrived at the fort and set up their camps, great festivities were held. Dancing, drumming, gambling, racing, storytelling, feasting, and general merrymaking took place. Trade flourished at the fort as the tribes participated in elaborate gift giving. William knew this could be an explosive situation, and he tried to suppress any use of liquor. He had learned that liquor and Indians didn't mix, and it was a bad combination for trade.

The conclusion of the peace talks left William in a considerably stronger position on the frontier. When the Comanches left the peace celebration, they begged William to again send wagons to them for trade. The partnership he helped broker between the Cheyennes and Comanches translated into a new era of trade and prosperity.

Forces of Change

A new challenge arose after the Indians made peace in 1840. Up to this point, the few fur men who crossed the northern plains had left little imprint on the Indian way of life, but the floodgates of emigration were about to open. In 1841 the first emigrant train moving up the Platte River unobtrusively changed the future of the plains tribes. Many of these travelers had seen their livelihoods destroyed during the depression of 1837. Their answer was to start over by moving west of the Mississippi and acquiring new land to rebuild on or to start a business where others were now creating new demand. Though they had few material goods to transport, they unwittingly carried with them white diseases.

The Santa Fe Trail and, therefore the fort, provided an avenue for infections that threatened the people who traveled west, as well as the native populations that had no immunity. Smallpox and cholera ravaged the tribes and threatened their future. Smallpox devastated the Comanche villages in both 1816 and again in 1839 - 40. The Mexican adobe makers, who worked for William while building the fort, had brought both skills and disease in 1832. But the cholera epidemic that was first carried up the Arkansas River by the forty-niners and spread throughout the Southwest by Comanche traders caused wholesale ruin to human life. These diseases made western travel and living very dangerous.

Arguably equally devastating would be the rise of bias and prejudice against Natives. As the swarm of emigrants grew through the 1840s, tensions were bound to develop, though the Indians were amazingly forbearing. Propaganda was used to justify what eventually became a mass need to free the western lands for white occupation and ownership. The insidious growth in the change of attitudes would be triggered by this first influx of travelers emigrating to California, Oregon, and points between.

Buck Rinker, in the story of his modern travel on the Oregon Trail by covered wagon, *Oregon Trail, A New American Journey*, reminds us of how the Indian has often been portrayed in myth for a purpose.

> Historian Richard Slotkin has shown how the myth of Indian savagery was required to justify the subjugation of the tribes so that their prairie kingdoms could be seized by the Americans crossing the frontier after 1843. But that image, faithfully passed down by purple-sage novels and Hollywood westerns, is wildly inaccurate. The initial encounters between the first covered wagon trains and the tribes were extraordinarily friendly, and the pioneers would never have made it past Kansas without their Pawnee and Shoshone guides.[69]

A comic episode that happened in 1841 shows how tolerant the Indians were in the early stages of this growing invasion. During the first missionary caravan west, on the occasion of their first Indian encounter, young Nicholas Dawson ran into camp without his mule, gun, pistol, and most of his clothes. He reported he had been robbed and maltreated by a horde of Indians. Panic ensued, but soon some fifty Indians peacefully rode into sight and pitched their tents. It turned out they were friendly Cheyennes. LeRoy Hafen tells this story in *Broken Hand*: "[T]hey had no intention of hurting the young man, but had been compelled to disarm him because in his terror at meeting Indians he seemed likely to fire at them. They readily surrendered his mule, gun, and pistol, and the incident was amicably closed."[70] These were not brutal savages but men with a sense of humor.

George Bent, William's Son

In the third year of peace, the third child of William and Owl Woman, George, was born on July 7, 1843, in his mother's lodge near Bent's Fort. He looked like any Cheyenne boy, with long, black hair, dark eyes, prominent cheekbones, and a long, straight nose. In dress and behavior, he was Cheyenne. The family now consisted of Mary, Robert, and George. Their half-brother, Charley, would be born in 1845, and a sister, Julia, in 1847.

In the mid-1840s, William took Owl Woman's sisters, Yellow Woman and Island, into his lodge—this was a common practice among affluent Cheyenne men. Yellow Woman was Charley's mother. After Owl Woman died in 1847, from complications at the time of Julia's birth, Yellow Woman and Island shared responsibility for raising the children. Island seemed to be the true mother figure for the children and took a strong interest in how they were raised.

Though the early years of William's union with Owl Woman seem to have been peaceful and happy, great changes were coming to the plains and to the Bent family. "Forces no one could have predicted would test the strength of these familial connections and the intercultural networks they had devised to make trade and family life possible. Global economic, diplomatic, and ideological shifts would prove seismic."[71]

William's five children would each have to deal with the fact that their father was white and their mother Indian. When William came west, he refused to live in a world of racial prejudice. Intermarriage between white men and Indian women was common, and William did not judge such relationships racially. He never signaled to his family that he was superior for being white, though he probably accepted male domination within the family. When he took his mixed-blood family back to Westport and St. Louis, he made no apologies.

The cultural and social environment would be different for his children. When they were little and living on the frontier, they had no reason to feel out of place or inferior. In fact, both their father and their mother were highly respected people. However, things would change for them starting when they were sent east to school. For each of the children a different path lay ahead, depending on the choices they made.

George would prove to be the archetypical example of dealing with both worlds, with both successes and failures. David Fridtjof Halaass and Andrew E. Masich provide a wonderful description of the youthful freedom and learning that George enjoyed. The children had plenty to keep them busy and they were well looked after by their Cheyenne mothers. For the Indians, "it takes a village" to raise a child was the kind of responsibility they embraced. As a young Cheyenne, he was never punished, though his grandmother taught him to respect his elders. He loved attention and got along with charm and a quick wit. Their play, both boys and girls, mimicked adult behavior as they learned future roles. George demonstrated uncommon intelligence and, like his father, had a facility for languages. He learned Cheyenne and English at home and later picked up Spanish, Comanche, Kiowa, and Arapaho.

George spent his childhood learning about horses, hunting, and battle. Living near the fort he also learned white man's ways of handling horses using force, but he preferred the Indian technique of gentling a horse. Similarly, seeing how white men often disciplined their children with harsh methods, he was probably glad his father deferred to his stepmothers in matters of discipline and education. George and his siblings had the run of the fort, which provided a lot of excitement and variation to their days. There was always something going on and much to learn in the multicultural atmosphere. George's own words, from George Hyde's *Life of George Bent*, recall a full and exciting childhood.

> When I was a boy there were a hundred men employed at the fort, and many of the men had families. There were Indian women of a dozen different tribes . . . and a large number of children. . . . [W]e children had no lack of amusements. In fall and winter there was always a large camp of Indians just outside the fort—Cheyennes and Arapahos, and sometimes Sioux, Kiowas, Comanches, and Prairie Apaches. The trade room was full of Indian men and women all day long. . . . [T]here was often a circle of chiefs sitting with my father or his partners, smoking and talking. Wagons came in from New Mexico loaded with gaudy striped Mexican blankets, silver dollars, silver in bars, and other strange things. . . . In summer the wagon train and many of the men were away . . . but there was still plenty of stir about

the post. Sometimes a war party going against the Utes, Apaches, or Pawnees stopped at the fort and gave a dance, and there were usually some white visitors staying with us.[72]

Growing up with compatibility between the races, George observed both Indian and white choices and values. It seems safe to say that, as with all children, George absorbed the behaviors and attitudes of the adults in his world. Fortunately, William Bent modeled tolerance as his mixed race lifestyle indicated. Living with an Indian mother and white father who were satisfied with their lives, there was no reason for George to learn about hate.

Endnotes

61. David Lavender, *Bent's Fort*, 186. Some historians place the date of this encounter as late as 1837.

62. Halaas & Masich, *Halfbreed*, 24.

63. Ibid.

64. Lavender, *Bent's Fort*, 188.

65. A. Hyde, *Empires, Nations, and Families*, 165.

66. David Remley, *Kit Carson, The Life of an American Border Man* (Norman: University of Oklahoma Press, 2011), 91.

67. A. Hyde, *Empires, Nations, and Families*, 162.

68. Farnham, *An 1839 Wagon Train Journal*, 33.

69. Buck Rinker, *The Oregon Trail, a New America Journey* (New York: Simon & Schuster Paperbacks, 2015). 16.

70. LeRoy R. Hafen, *Broken Hand, The Life of Thomas Fitzpatrick Mountain Man, Guide and Indian Agent* (Lincoln: University of Nebraska Press, 1973), 177.

71. A. Hyde, *Empires, Nations, and Families*, 225.

72. G. Hyde, *Life of George Bent*, 84.

5 ~ THE MEXICAN WAR

SINCE THOMAS JEFFERSON AND the Louisiana Purchase, men in the United States had dreamed of a nation that reached from the Atlantic to the Pacific. A significant step in that direction occurred in 1836, when Texas requested to join the union after winning its independence from Mexico. In 1844 President Tyler secured a treaty of annexation with Texas. That same year, James K. Polk was elected president as an expansionist candidate. On December 29, 1845, the new President Polk signed the bill that accepted Texas into the Union. He also settled the issue of the northwestern border of the Oregon Territory with Britain by a compromise solution. Now if only he could add the northern territories of Mexico to the nation—including New Mexico and California—the dream of a sea-to-sea nation would crown his presidency.

The rumblings of Manifest Destiny that had been gaining force would, in April 1846, lead to the outbreak of the Mexican-American War, the first United States war on foreign soil. Located on the border of these two countries, Bent's Fort would soon be a beehive of activity.

Colonel (later General) Stephen Watts Kearny led the first troops from Fort Leavenworth, in what is now

Kansas, toward the Southwest. They were known as the Army of the West. The orders he got on May 26 were to cross the Arkansas River into Mexican Territory, take Santa Fe, and then proceed to California to conquer it for the United States. Kearny led an army of raw recruits, mostly Missouri Volunteers, for eight hundred miles across miles of empty prairie, without adequate supplies. So hasty were the preparations that the inexperienced troops had loaded wagons improperly, making handling the wagons dangerous. And poor logistical planning led to provision wagons being ahead of or behind the marching troops that departed from Leavenworth in staggered waves between May 28 and July 6, 1846. As a result the men were short of rations through most of the trip.

The Army Arrives at the Fort

Kearny had designated Bent's Fort as the rendezvous point for the troops going to Santa Fe and to serve as a provision depot. Huge military supply trains would move across the "great American desert," using the Santa Fe Trail, through the summer and the rest of the war. There wasn't much for the Bents to do but agree to the arrangement. They were the only suitable site between Fort Leavenworth and Santa Fe. It was reported in the *New Orleans Picayune*, by Mathew Field, in 1839, that the fort could accommodate two hundred men and three to four hundred animals. With no other major facilities in between, it was a natural place for the army to stop and recruit its livestock and replenish its men. This burden fell on Bent & St. Vrain Company.

"[O]n July 31, the Army of the West was concentrated into a single force for the first time."[73] An interesting note on the travel of the poorly prepared, underfed troops was that the infantry passed the mounted forces and arrived first near Bent's Fort:

> This amazing phenomenon was possible because the infantry did not have to groom any horses, did not have to stop and graze, did not have to wait for runaway mounts to be caught before proceeding, and could make and break camp more quickly than soldiers who had the additional duty of caring for their horses.[74]

When Kearny's Army of the West reached the fort, imposing its invasive presence, Kearny took stock of supplies and found them woefully inadequate. The army made repairs to equipment, replenished supplies the best they could from what was available, and acquired replacement horses and mules from William and the nearby Arapaho camp. One has to wonder how an Indian pony, which had never been harnessed, was put to work on military tasks like pulling wagons.

Frank S. Edwards was discharged from Colonel Doniphan's troops after their campaign in the Mexican War. He published *A Campaign in New Mexico with Colonel Doniphan*, where he gave us an idea of how important Bent's Fort was to resupplying the war effort:

> At Bent's Fort we obtained a supply of draught mules to fill the places of the many horses we had killed by fatigue on the march—out of the hundred fine cannon horses with which we had started, not more than forty were left, and of these, not more than ten ever got to Santa Fe.[75]

This destruction of stock was typical of much of the travel across the plains. A *caballada*, or herd of horses, mules, and oxen, always accompanied the wagon trains to resupply the animals that faltered or were lost.

Through the next months, William tried to maintain business as usual, but his quiet fiefdom would never be the same. He would need to anticipate and balance the outcomes the war could bring and what effect each outcome would have on the various cultures—Indian, Mexican, and white. Conquest would have a price for many of the individuals caught up in the government's actions.

> The Bent family had always operated on the edges of many worlds. The ever volatile situation in the Arkansas and New Mexico borderlands required the kinds of diplomatic skills and economic clout that the Bents had amassed. It also required straddling many lines and political situations, a position made much more difficult during the U.S. War with Mexico. . . . As stakeholders in the largest trading enterprise directly on the major road to New Mexico, William Bent . . . watched the politics of territorial and economic expansion carefully.[76]

William worried about his tenuous situation as an American depending on trade with Mexico and the Native nations. He tried to trade with the Indians as usual, but it became impossible with the army's demand for supplies that were soon depleted. Twenty thousand head of livestock ruined the grazing around the fort. William's repair shops were soon overwhelmed, and his Native allies scattered. He received no compensation for his losses.[77]

William was kept busy with adjunct duties. There were officers to entertain, huge grazing herds to direct, storage and repair space to allocate, and sick people to house. The sutler's shop was wiped out of supplies. Mobs of Indians stood around gaping and looking for handouts. Hundreds of traders whose activities were interrupted by the advance of the troops called on the Bents for favors to help them in these circumstances as they worried about getting to markets—if there were any markets.

For traders headed west from Missouri to Santa Fe and beyond, there was much uncertainty about how they were going to be able to recoup their investments and make a profit in this unsettled situation. Their commitment to a business that depended on peace and good trade conditions was deeply at risk. Historian Bernard DeVoto, in *The Year of Decision 1846,* spoke of the magnitude of this war for the traders:

> This year [1846], ahead of the armies, beside them, and behind them, a good deal more than a million dollars' worth of goods, St. Louis wholesale, would move down the trail. The trade had already riveted New Mexico to the American economy and it paid a rich profit (from fifty per cent upward) in spite of risk, redskins, graft, and competition.[78]

Amid the turmoil, there were some benefits for William. Through the years, he came to know many officers—General Stephen Kearny, Major John C. Fremont, Colonel Henry Dodge, Colonel Alexander Doniphan, Lieutenant Colonel Philip St. George Cooke, Colonel Sterling Price, and Colonel Edwin Vose Sumner—and forged important connections with influential men. Later he was proud of his service as a scout for Kearny in the passes ahead of the army on the approach to Santa Fe. William was gratified with the honorific title of Colonel that remained with him for the rest of his life.

Unfortunately these benefits did not balance the losses of this chaotic invasion. LeRoy R. Hafen provides a visual for changes in the fort during this hectic time:

And now this old fortified trading post, built
in 1833 and for so many years an isolated fortress on the plains, took on the liveliest aspect
of its long history. Traders and freighters, officers and men of the army, mounted or afoot,
surged through its gates and crowded its inte-
riors, and its wonted calm was broken by clang
and clatter and uproar.[79]

Among the many pressures on William were his continued efforts to provide some comforts for guests of the
fort. Susan Magoffin was the eighteen-year-old bride of
successful Santa Fe trader Samuel Magoffin. She came
from a wealthy Kentucky family and was well educated. Her caravan trip to Santa Fe and further south
into Mexico inspired her to keep a diary published as
Down the Santa Fe Trail and into Mexico. She left us with
wonderful observations and vivid visuals of a busy year
on the Santa Fe Trail. Susan Magoffin's feminine and en-
thusiastic observations included many details of things
we might not ordinarily see in our imaginations from
this distance.

She described how, as they finally approached
Bent's Fort after an arduous trip, they passed an encampment of soldiers. There was a circular formation of about fifty tents with wagons scattered about.
Soldiers were seen loafing under the trees, watering
staked horses, or drying laundry in the sun. Magoffin
gave us a minute insight to what the camp was like
and how an unsophisticated young man of the frontier
executed his new duties:

At the outer edge of the encampment stood a
sentinel, who with all the dignity and pomp . . .
of his office shouldered his musket marched up,
and stoped [*sic*] us with the words "where go
you"? We gave him our directions, he reported

us to the sergeant at arms, and without farther
[*sic*] ceremony we were permitted to pass on.
In a little time we were in sight of the Fort.[80]

At the fort, she commented on the cacophony of
the ringing hammers shoeing horses, the braying of
mules, the laughter and crying of children while mothers chattered, the sound of men scolding or fighting.
The place was crowded to overflowing with no respite.
Nevertheless, the romance of this honeymoon adventure
for Susan comes through in many of her descriptions,
including her initial impression of Bent's Fort. "Well the
outside exactly fills my idea of an ancient castle."[81]

Susan, pregnant and very sick, had been badly bat-
tered on the rough ride, including a dangerous carriage accident. William ordered an upper-story room
set aside for her. On the day after her nineteenth birthday, July 31, she had a miscarriage. William had the
sad task of showing Samuel a decent place to bury the
dead child.

This story gives us another glimpse of the humanity
William was called on to express from a position of re-
sponsibility that was probably overwhelming at times.
He tended to the needs of traders, military, and a young
lady traveling under the most difficult of circumstances.
He had to be a man of many facets.

Another account comes to us from George Bent,
William's son, who recalled how this extraordinary activity was startling to the observing Indians: "The army
was very small—about 1700 men, mostly cavalry—but
the Indians had never supposed there were as many
men as this in the whole 'white tribe,' and they watched
the passing of the troops in amazement."[82] In the early
years most Indians had no idea of the relatively huge
population of white people in the east. Many were beginning to get a better idea.

Francis Parkman Jr., a young historian, traveled the Santa Fe Trail in 1846 on his return to Missouri after an extended stay studying the Sioux Indians. He too published an exemplary chronicle of his travels in *The Oregon Trail*. He and his party had traveled west on the northern route but rode south to join the Santa Fe Trail for the return trip. He spoke of the growing resentment that the Indians felt to all this traffic across their hunting grounds:

> There was some uncertainty as to our future course. The trail between Bent's Fort and the settlements, a distance computed at six hundred miles, was at this time in a dangerous state; for since the passage of General Kearney's army, great numbers of hostile Indians, chiefly Pawnees and Camanches [sic], had gathered about some parts of it. A little after this time they became so numerous and audacious, that scarcely a single party, however large, passed between the fort and the frontier without some token of their hostility. . . . Many men were killed, and great numbers of horses and mules carried off.[83]

While the Indians stole a few horses and mules from the Army of the West and other reinforcing units, they made no real attempt to attack the military's compact troops. They knew the price they would pay for attacking such well-armed, though semi-disciplined forces. They waited and watched, reserving attacks for more likely targets.

Parkman's description of the conditions at the fort, after Kearny had left, tells a lot about the cost to William of having accommodated the army:

> Bent's Fort stands on the river. . . . At noon of the third day we arrived within three or four miles of it, pitched our tent under a tree, hung

our looking-glasses against its trunk, and having made our primitive toilet, rode toward the fort. We soon came in sight of it, for it is visible from a considerable distance, standing with its high clay walls in the midst of the scorching plains. It seemed as if a swarm of locusts had invaded the country. The grass for miles around was cropped close by the horses of General Kearney's soldiery. . . . [W]e found that not only had the horses eaten up the grass, but their owners had made way with the stores of the little trading post. . . . The army was gone, the life and bustle passed away. . . . The proprietors were absent, and we were received by Mr. Holt, who had been left in charge. . . . He invited us to dinner, where, to our admiration, we found a table laid with a white cloth.[84]

The next morning before they departed for Missouri, they returned to the fort "to smoke with some Shienne [sic] Indians whom we found there."[85]

Wartime Policies

All of these changes at the fort were only part of what was in store for William. The army was about to disrupt the whole foundation of the lives of the Indians, the Mexicans, and the whites, like the Bents, who had established themselves in a no-man's land that was transitioning to US territory.

Colonel Kearny issued a proclamation at Bent's Fort on July 31, 1846, in which he told the citizens of New Mexico [sic] the objects of his mission. He declared that he was entering New Mexico" [sic] seeking union and to ameliorate the condition of its inhabitants."[86]

He would repeat his message as his troops passed through villages like Tecolote and San Miguel del Vado, and it didn't seem to matter whether or not he received the acceptance or allegiance of the people.

On July 31, 1846, Kearny summoned William to his headquarters. He told William that his invasion of New Mexico would begin on August the second, but he had no way of knowing what threats lay ahead in terms of resistance, especially in the mountain passes he had to cross. There were rumors that Governor Manuel Armijo of the northern province of Mexico may have been reinforced with troops from the capital, but rumors were the only means of intelligence.

Kearny asked William to form a spy company—or scouts, as we would call them today—to reconnoiter the passes and learn any advance information that he could. After the devastation to the business of the fort that had already taken place, when Kearny suggested hiring him, William lost his temper and "snapped that if Kearny wanted still more help he could damn well pay what it was worth. And out he went."[87] William was also concerned about creating a perception that he was taking sides against the native Mexican population.

Kearny, realizing there was no one else to call on for the help he needed, sent a peacemaker to William and worked out a compromise. William organized about a half dozen skilled men to ride in advance of the army to scout for them.

> On August 1 the Army of the West, with [Thomas] Fitzpatrick as guide [famous mountain man and Indian agent], and with William Bent added as an additional pilot, left the vicinity of the fort. . . . Three days later Bent and six men were sent ahead to reconnoiter the mountain passes. They met and captured a Mexican

squad of five men, who had been sent out to gain knowledge of the American approach. . . . A wretched looking lot were these captives, and when brought to the American camp were the objects of a great deal of derisive mirth.[88]

The Army of the West had a hard time taking the burro-mounted Mexican citizens seriously as a dangerous enemy, though they did still wonder what kind of army might await them near Santa Fe. William and his scouts were able to report that Raton Pass was free of the enemy, but it was not free of obstacles. The march over the pass would be hard on men, wagons, and animals.

On August 15, 1846, at Las Vegas, New Mexico, Major Thomas Swords caught up with Colonel Kearny after following him from Fort Leavenworth. Major Swords, chief quartermaster of the Army of the West, was carrying mail, orders, and Colonel Kearny's commission as a brigadier general, dated June 30, 1846.

Constant rumors of Mexican resistance kept everyone on the alert. Rumors that Armijo would defend Santa Fe at Apache Pass persisted, but William said he was "darned if he could find any sign of gathering opposition."[89] He was proved right. On August 18, 1846, Kearny's Army of the West entered Santa Fe without a shot being fired. At the last minute, Armijo gathered as much of his wealth as he could and ran south, abandoning his post in Santa Fe. He had never received the support of troops from Mexico City and would not stand alone.

The lack of resistance was misinterpreted by the Americans as welcome. In truth poverty was at the root of the New Mexicans' passivity. Residents of Spanish and Indian descent living at Pecos, Las Vegas, and other villages along the trail existed at a subsistence level and were hardly in a position to express any opposition.

> And such settlements they are—Here is a little
> hovel, a fit match for some of the genteel pig
> stys [*sic*] in the States—it is made of mud, and
> surrounded by a kind of fence made of sticks;
> this is the *casa grande* [big house]. It's neighbors
> are smaller.... They are inhabited by *rancheros*,
> as they are called, who attend ... *vacas* [cattle].
> Their food consists of a little cheese made of
> thin milk, a little *pan de mais* [corn bread]—and
> such little fruits & nuts as they can collect.[90]

Though the government in Mexico City was not popular with many New Mexicans, the inhabitants still resented the invasion of their land. Many feared that the Americans would ban their Catholic religion. That was not the case, but the suspicion caused an undercurrent of fear.

After Kearny took Santa Fe on August 18, 1846, he set up a local government naming William's brother, Charles Bent, Territorial Governor on September 22. This appointment of one of the Bent brothers to this position recognized their success and reputation in the territory. This civil government in Santa Fe seemed, due to the locals' acquiescence, acceptable to the local citizens. Kearny was anxious to depart for California, where he wanted to conquer a much more prosperous country for the United States than anything New Mexico offered.

Frank S. Edwards was impressed, as many were, with the quaintness and primitiveness of the capital of this northern province of Mexico.

> [T]here is no burying ground, and the dead are
> interred by the side of the road, just out of the
> city, with simply a pile of stones, and a small
> wooden cross on the top of it.... [Our] troops
> had brought the measles with them, and it
> was soon communicated to the children of

the inhabitants, and carried off many of them; therefore, funerals among the young were common.[91]

He seems to have had a somewhat limited view of the city, but one that surely impressed him and showed a side of the city not commonly heard about. One has to surmise that so many children dying of disease contributed to the fear and apprehension of the local people.

When Doniphan arrived in Santa Fe, the troops ahead had so decimated the grazing grounds around the city that Doniphan's men had to send their animals miles away for grazing. Edwards stated that when Josiah Gregg, an early trader, arrived in Santa Fe in 1831, he mentioned that the valley was rich in grazing grounds. Caravan traffic over the years had been seriously destructive to the local pastures.

On the night of September 24, a ball was held at the governor's palace in Santa Fe for Kearny and his army, soon to depart for California. Charles was a more political and gregarious personality than his brother William, who did not attend the gala.

> William Bent was not at the ball, though he was an honorary "colonel" now by virtue of his having scouted the way to Santa Fe. The embellishments of society made him uncomfortable. Even before his brother's inauguration he turned back toward the Arkansas, worried about the fort and about the new ranches.[92]

William and others were developing ranches in Colorado and New Mexico. He preferred to head back to the fort to tend to business; as always, he focused on the work to be done. William was a man more comfortable in the wilderness, tending to his duties among people like himself and living without the grandeur and pomp of society, even in backward Santa Fe. He had been on the frontier, living with Indians and mountain men, so long that whatever high society he had known as a young man held no attraction for him now. He was a changed man, or at least a man who had adapted to wilderness life and preferred it. It is easier to picture William sitting around with the chiefs smoking and talking than at a ball in Santa Fe.

The Taos Revolt

On September 25, 1846, Kearny departed Santa Fe, leaving Charles in charge of the capital and the territory. Over the next few months, as troops moved on to Mexico and California, Charles heard rumors of unrest and possible rebellion. Conspirators were encouraged by the reduction in military strength in New Mexico.

At the time of the Mexican War, the area of New Mexico was a melting pot of several very different cultures. Several Pueblo tribes had inhabited the area for hundreds of years. The more recently arrived Navajos and Apaches added another intricately interwoven layer to the culture. The appearance of the Spanish in the sixteenth century set in motion the development of the country of Mexico. Finally, the American presence of trappers, traders, and soldiers added to the complex cultural mix of distinct religions, mores, and lifestyles. Within this crucible, it is not surprising that political dissatisfaction with the American occupation might lead to a violent response.

Initially Diego Archuleta, Augustin Duran, and Tomas Ortiz led the plotters against the new government with amateurish night riding, whispered conferences, and assessment of arms available for a revolt. When Charles was informed of the plot he immediately initiated actions to determine who the conspirators were, but they all dispersed and got away. By January 2, 1847, it was believed that the rebellion had been suppressed.

Despite warnings that it was dangerous, Charles was determined to take a trip from Santa Fe to Taos to see his family and to show his confidence as his party traveled without a military escort. After four days of cold, wearying travel in deep snow, his party reached Taos.

There a delegation of Indians from the nearby Taos Pueblo greeted Bent, requesting the release of two of their jailed neighbors charged with theft. Bent responded by saying that he could not interfere with the process of the law.

Finally he reached his humble adobe home; it was good to be welcomed by the family and by a warm fire. But through the night a mob, further incited with liquor and accusations that the Americans had an intent to seize their lands, became murderous. When this mob gathered around Charles's home and threatened him, Charles could not believe that his friends and associates of many years would harm him. Yet in the early morning hours of January 19, 1847, the mob succeeded in breaking into Charles's home, and they brutally murdered and mutilated him.

It was a ghastly attack, with his wife, his children, and other relatives, including Kit Carson's wife, Josefa, witnessing the carnage. The anger and resentment careened out of hand, and the rampage continued through the night in Taos, where five more were killed—all were Americans or American loyalists. Over the next couple days the rebels murdered other Americans in nearby Arroyo Hondo, at Rio Colorado, and the village of Mora.

News of the death of his beloved brother did not reach William until days later when a messenger, Louis

Simonds, reached him at the Big Timbers, where he was camped with the Cheyennes. Charles was like a father to William, and this news of his brother being scalped and mutilated hit him hard. The Cheyennes wanted to attack New Mexico, but William restrained them, telling them this was a white man's problem.

Lewis Garrard, during his adventurous travel, had gotten to know many of the mountain men and had a great respect for the Bents. In *Wah-to-yah*, Lewis recorded that the next day he rode with William to the fort traveling without baggage and only robes strapped to their saddles. William had little to say and his pain was visible. Garrard pitied William whose older brother was his lifelong comrade. Garrard recounted that:

> [W]e saw . . . a Mexican, mounted on a strong iron-gray horse. . . . He was passing at a gallop, when Bent, with his cocked rifle, shouted in Spanish to stop. The man stated that he belonged to William Tharpe's company; but the skulk's restless eye and his every motion seemed to indicate more than he told. After a searching cross-examination, Bent told him to "vamos, prento!" (go quick), or he would send a ball through him. . . . I expected to see the Mexican pitch from his horse through the aid of a bullet. Bent turned to follow him, expressing a regret at not having taken a shot.[93]

When they arrived back at Bent's Fort from Big Timbers, confusion ensued. The only way to obtain valuable news was by word of mouth. News of the states, intelligence about supplies of wood, water, and grass, activities of war parties and buffalo herds, and the spread of dreaded sickness were the topics shared by passing travelers. But in times when events developed so rapidly, there was no reliable information about what was going on. All William knew was that there had been a revolt and Charles was dead. In the absence of up-dated reports, a small group of men had ridden out to Taos, knowing they were too few to take on the Mexican Army but thinking they could scout out the situation and maybe help in the fight against the rebels. No one yet knew the extent of the fighting. Though Governor Armijo's requests of the Mexican government in Mexico City for additional troop support in Taos were ignored, the Americans had no communications to let them know this. To them, all hell was about to break loose.

Captain (first name unknown) Jackson, in charge of US military presence at the fort, similarly would not provide William with the support of his troops, especially when Frank De Lisle arrived, having fol-lowed Lewis Simonds from the Purgatoire ranch with wagons. De Lisle believed Mexican troops were at his heels.

William was responsible for as many as sixty to a hun-dred fort employees and their families who depended on the fort business as their livelihood. Plains Indians—Arapahos, Kiowas, Comanches, Prairie Apaches—re-lied on William for guidance and trade. The Southern Cheyennes were the most dependent. They had moved near the fort, and it was the center of their seasonal movements. Even more, William was their friend and protector. He was married into the tribe and had be-come inseparable from them.

Fearing that the Mexican Army was approaching, the priority for William was protection of the fort and the nearby ranches. He decided that his responsibilities should prevail over the luxury of revenge. He would re-main at the fort, as the company representative.

Under William's organizing leadership, twenty-three men—the company's seventeen roustabouts and several "free traders," four of whom had families in Taos and were very worried—volunteered to go fight whatever rebels they could find. Young Lewis Garrard also joined the group for the excitement. He was a young man with a talent for being in the right place at the right time. Not knowing what they might encounter, it was thought that at least some volunteers could retrieve the cattle that had been driven off by rebels and burn out a few Mexicans on their way toward Taos.

When William's men had departed, he heard that John Albert was at Pueblo, about seventy miles away. Thinking Albert might have more information about what had happened, William rode to Pueblo but was disappointed, because Albert had not been in Taos. However, when he arrived fifteen Mexican men were being held captive. Had William signaled it, the mountain men would have gladly killed the Mexicans. Though he was filled with rage, vengeance, and grief, William refrained from allowing these Mexicans to be killed on the spot. He knew they had been on the Purgatoire and could not have been involved with what happened in Taos, so he said to turn them loose. The force of his leadership saved these men from unjust death. It was not his nature to take revenge on innocents, as he had seen so often on the frontier and would see more of in the future. This is the kind of incident that helps paint for us a picture of the kind of man William had become. Since Albert couldn't provide details about Charles, William rode back to the fort through the freezing weather.

Once Colonel Sterling Price, left in charge in Santa Fe by Kearny, had arranged for the security of the capital, he made plans to march to Taos. On January 23 Price, with an effective force of three hundred and fifty-three men, departed. All his troops were on foot except for a company of mounted Santa Fe volunteers commanded by Captain Ceran St. Vrain. En route they encountered rebels prepared to fight in easily defended canyon areas in the villages of Embudo and La Canada.

> After eleven days of travel over the cold, snowy, rugged countryside of northern New Mexico and following two pitched battles in which several of his men were killed and wounded, Colonel Price and his army finally arrived in Taos on February 3.[94]

The rebels' main force had established their defense at the Taos Pueblo, three miles north of Taos. Two large buildings protected by three-foot high adobe walls provided an impenetrable fortress. Price placed his troops around the compound and began bombarding the buildings with his cannon. It wasn't until the next afternoon, after the rebels withdrew and took refuge in the parish church, that they were able to breach the church wall and fire three rounds of grapeshot point blank into the interior. The few who escaped the building were picked up as they ran.

> The American losses at the battle of Taos Pueblo were seven killed and forty-five wounded, many of whom died later. Out of the estimated six hundred or seven hundred of the enemy who participated in the fighting, 154 were killed. . . . An unknown number of Indians and Mexicans were wounded. The following day, the Indian residents of the Taos Pueblo sued for peace.[95]

Through April there were hasty trials of the participants in the gruesome murder of Charles and the others. Charles's wife, Ignacia, and her sister Josefa (Kit Carson's wife), were key witnesses, as they had been present during the butchery. After fifteen days of trials, fifteen men were sentenced to death and were hung. William did not attend but secluded himself on his

©Camilla Kattell

Taos Pueblo. Site of the final fight of the Taos Revolt.
Continuously inhabited for over 1,000 years (above)

Remains of the church where Colonel Price's men killed
the rebels. Taos Pueblo (below)

©Camilla Kattell

ranch and grieved, away from the chaos of the trials. "In the blunt directness of his nature there was no room for the secondhand satisfaction of watching society exact its retributions."[96]

Many years later William's son George, an older man now, recalled the anger and confusion of the men at the fort when Charlie Autobeas brought the news of the killings and the response from Colonel Price in Santa Fe. George said many guilty Pueblo Indians were killed in the fight at Taos. He recalled that, "The Mexicans who had instigated the murders of course escaped punishment."[97] He reflected a prejudice against the Mexican leaders and probably felt the Indians were unjustly punished. However, some of the rebels who were tried were identified as Mexican and hung. They were buried by Padre Antonio José Martinez in the cemetery of the local parish church. Five Indians that were hung were taken back to the Pueblo for burial. George was correct that the instigators were never caught.

Charles, at forty-six, a man with great promise for the future, was buried headless in Santa Fe. The youngest Bent brother, Robert, at twenty-five had been killed in 1841 by Comanches while escorting a Bent train. He was buried at the fort. By 1847 only William and his brother George remained of the four Bent brothers who had set out with big dreams and ambitions.

When brother George got sick with what William called consumption, William did everything he could to save him. He "pottered fruitlessly with the medicine chest which each year was filled for him by a Westport apothecary. Calomel, rhubarb, camphor, Seidlitz powder, assorted pills—nothing helped."[98] On October 23, 1847, George died at thirty-three of a lingering illness, probably consumption, as William had guessed. George was buried outside the fort walls, near his brother

Robert, and later their remains were returned to St. Louis for final burial. Son George further recalled, "My father was now the only one of the Bent brothers left in the mountains, and he ran the business alone."[99]

In 1847 William also lost his beloved Owl Woman. She died after bearing their fourth child, a daughter, Julia. Owl Woman was, according to Cheyenne custom, dressed in her favorite finery, wrapped in a blanket, and placed with some of her possessions on a scaffolding high in the branches of a cottonwood tree. In this traditional manner of burial it was believed she could return to the earth, and much like in other religions, it was believed her spirit would travel to join the Great Spirit. She was left with the things she would need for her journey.

It was a devastating time for William and the children. One can only imagine how they dealt with all the tragedy in the family. We do know that young George helped tend the graves outside the fort by planting cactus over them, to keep scavengers away, and that the children were now cared for by Yellow Woman and Island, the younger sisters of Owl Woman who had joined William's lodge a few years before. Unlike many white men who lived with Indian women, William did not walk away from family responsibilities. William and his family continued living according to Cheyenne beliefs and customs.

Endnotes

73. Oliva, *Soldiers on the Santa Fe Trail*, 70.

74. Ibid, 69.

75. Frank S. Edwards, *A Campaign in New Mexico with*

Colonel Doniphan (Albuquerque: University of New Mexico Press, 1996), 18.

76. A. Hyde. *Empires, Nations, and Families*, 378 - 379.

77. Lavender, *Bent's Fort*, 275 - 276.

78. Bernard DeVoto, *The Year of Decision, 1846* (New York: Truman Talley Books, St. Martin's Griffin, 2000), 119.

79. Hafen, *Broken Hand*, 233.

80. Magoffin, *Down the Santa Fe Trail and into Mexico, The Diary of Susan Shelby Magoffin, 1846 - 1847*, edited by Stella M. Drumm (Lincoln: University of Nebraska Press, 1962), 59.

81. Ibid, 60.

82. G. Hyde, *Life of George Bent*, 85.

83. Francis Parkman, Jr., *The Oregon Trail* (New York: Penguin Classics, 1985), 380.

84. Ibid, 380 - 381.

85. Ibid, 384.

86. William A. Keleher, *Turmoil in New Mexico, 1846 - 1868* (Albuquerque: University of New Mexico Press, 1952). 7.

87. Lavender, *Bent's Fort*, 278.

88. Hafen, *Broken Hand*, 233 - 234.

89. Lavender, *Bent's Fort*, 280.

90. Susan Magoffin, *Down the Santa Fe Trail and into Mexico*, 90 - 91.

91. Edwards, *A Campaign in New Mexico with Colonel Doniphan*, 25.

92. Lavender. *Bent's Fort*, 287.

93. Garrard, *Wah-to-yah and the Taos Trail*, 119 - 120.

94. Crutchfield, *Revolt at Taos*, 92.

95. Ibid, 96.

96. Lavender, *Bent's Fort*, 316.

97. G. Hyde, *Life of George Bent*, 88.

98. Lavender, *Bent's Fort*, 325.

99. G. Hyde, *Life of George Bent*, 88.

6 ∞ THE CLASH OF CULTURES

DURING THE MEXICAN WAR, the Indians understood that the military forces of the West were being diverted to fight the Mexicans, leaving them with an opportunity to raid military supply trains and trading caravans with impunity. They had real grievances: more and more wagon trains crossing the plains were killing the buffalo, their main source of livelihood; other game was being driven from their usual grazing areas; and caravans also cut down the few trees available on the plains, depleting another major source of fuel, shelter, shade, and winter forage.

With the Indians striking back against this invasion of their way of life, more whites reverted to the practice of killing Indians on sight—something that had been occurring since the first influx of Europeans on the East Coast. For example, in 1641, Dutchman Willem Kieft sent soldiers to Staten Island to punish the Raritans for offenses that had been committed against white men. When the Raritans resisted, the soldiers killed four of them. The Raritans struck back by killing four Dutchmen. For that, Kieft, ordered two villages massacred while the Indians slept. The Dutch soldiers bayoneted men, women, and children, hacked their bodies in pieces, and burned the village.[100] This set a precedent for many years to come as the frontier moved west.

In 1847, such an incident occurred in the vicinity of Bent's Fort, but the Indians resisted the desire for revenge. An elder Cheyenne chief, Cinemo, approached a government wagon train of supplies, begging for some tobacco. One of the teamsters shot him. Though the furious tribe wanted to seek revenge for his life, with his dying breath Cinemo urged them to maintain the peace. William convinced them to turn the other cheek, and peace was maintained.[101] The Southern Cheyennes had never yet broken the peace with the white men, but that peace was to become more and more of a challenge for William and the Cheyennes.

Clashes between the Indians and the whites threatened everything William had built, including the Bent trading empire and his family life. Both had thrived on peace among the whites, Cheyennes, Arapahos, Comanches, Kiowas, Prairie Apaches, and Utes—and the futures of both depended on enduring peace.

LeRoy R. Hafen describes the Bent relationship with the tribes:

> Bent's Fort . . . was the main trading rendezvous of both the Cheyennes and the Arapahoes, and here they traded their furs and buffalo robes for scarlet cloth, beads, looking glasses, guns, and ammunition. William Bent was the resident owner. . . . His relations with the tribesmen were close and intimate, and no white man exercised more influence among them.[102]

William Chalfant, in *Cheyennes and Horse Soldiers*, also gave credit to William for his "considerable influence over the Indians of the region and [how he] did much to maintain a tenuous peace between the natives and the European intruders."[103]

Bernard DeVoto saw the Cheyenne tribe in 1846 as thoroughly under the influence of William and well pacified. "The southern Cheyenne were also here, a powerful and valorous people, but in our period they were not troublesome, having been pacified by the Bent brothers, with whom they kept their word."[104]

William had preached peace to the plains Indians for fifteen years, and his influence had kept them out of the fighting, but the Mexican War brought a shift in a vast power struggle that left the Southern Cheyennes and other plains tribes wanting to fight back and defend their way of life—even though many understood they already were in a losing battle. The future looked discouraging in terms of co-existence between the whites and the Indians.

In the summer of 1847 some Indians took advantage of the fact that troops were occupied against Mexico and there was a great opportunity for raiding and plundering. Comanches, Kiowas, and Pawnees killed forty-seven Americans, destroyed three hundred and thirty wagons, stole sixty-five hundred animals—and this doesn't include the work of the Navajo, Apaches, or Utes.[105] The Arapahos and Cheyennes were very close to joining all this destruction, motivated by revenge for the damage to their homeland. William continued to encourage his Cheyenne allies to forebear and keep the peace. He assured them that a new Indian Agent was due to arrive with supplies to reward their discipline.

Indian Agents

Government-appointed Indian Agents had a great influence on the balance of peace. As early as 1775, the

Second Continental Congress set up three Indian agencies to deal with Indian affairs and to negotiate treaties. Agents were the government's representatives to the tribes, and in 1789 agencies reported to the newly formed War Department. How successful the system was fluctuated through the years.

Land acquisition lay at the heart of the matter. Since early colonial days, it was believed that the Indians had a right to the soil they lived on, and thus the land must be acquired by purchase through treaties and agreements. Indian reservations were a consequence of these deals, and creating reservations became an entrenched part of the system. Of course, the US government also used conquest and military force to obtain indigenous lands, and it used Indian Agents to implement government policy on the Indian reservations. A core component of the job was to distribute subsidies, or annuities—allotments of supplies and food that were agreed to in treaties between the government and the Indians. Annuities were meant to help the transition from a hunting culture to a settled farming culture. Often the subsidies were mismanaged or inadequate.

Indian agencies moved west with the frontier. When the beaver trade collapsed, many out-of-work traders were appointed to these positions in the West, with little guidance or oversight. Not surprisingly, they managed their posts according to their personalities, and the agencies were rife with problems. Often the agents were corrupt and did more harm than good for the Natives.

Thomas Fitzpatrick, however, was a well-intentioned agent who understood the need for a gradual transition for the tribes to assimilate to a settled life of farming instead of nomadic hunting. He had been put in charge of the agencies on the Upper Platte and the Arkansas, and the government blithely designated Bent's Fort as his headquarters.

William received this news gloomily. The government had never cared about the Cheyennes or Arapahos. Now he didn't know what would happen, but he knew that once again things were changing. His life, like the Indians', was being curtailed by the US government—and there would be little restitution. Not only would he be uncompensated for quartering Fitzpatrick, but government teamsters had been encroaching on his ranchland, grazing their livestock on William's and others' properties.

William also saw wisdom in helping the Indians become farmers, especially given the clash of the foreseeable influx of settled, land owning whites in opposition to the nomadic needs of the Indians. The growing restlessness among the Indians intensified this belief. When in late August the Cheyenne government subsidies did not arrive because they had been distributed to New Mexican Indians, the peaceful Cheyennes mocked Fitzpatrick and protested that raiding tribes were rewarded by receiving their government gifts, but the peaceful Indians were punished. Bitterness was growing with a lack of patience.[106]

William was still depressed by the loss of his brothers George, his work-mate, and Charles, his hero, but as usual he turned to his work as he grieved and he focused on his continuing responsibilities. To be the sole surviving brother of four, who had come west to make a life, must have been haunting and lonely. Discouraged throughout that winter, William feared a general uprising of the Indians in the Southwest with the coming of warm weather. Without some military restraint on the worst troublemakers, the Comanches and Kiowas, the more peaceful inclinations of the Cheyennes and Arapahos might be harder to sustain.

William talked to the Cheyennes, especially Yellow Wolf, about the idea of the Indians farming. "It was no revolutionary idea. Tribal lore still told of the pre-horse days when the Cheyennes had raised corn and squash along the Missouri River and in the Black Hills."[107] The tribe still had some memory of when they were farmers before they got the horse, but giving up their roving horse culture held no appeal for many. Yet Yellow Wolf proposed the government should build strongholds where the farmer Indians could be safe against Indians who continued raiding.

William doubted that the government would build strongholds for Indians perceived as enemies, but all winter the Indians discussed the possibility of changing their lives. When no action took place, when equipment and annuities didn't arrive, and when the spring buffalo herds returned, the idea died. William believed that a true chance to change the future course of settling the West had been overlooked by the complacent and self-serving government.

The Indians were growing more and more dissatisfied, and they underwent internal changes as well.

> A new morality had taken hold as the old clan system broke down. Now cousins married cousins, and the old rules of courtship, marriage, and social interaction no longer applied. The people were hungry and impoverished. . . . Once the most chaste of people, the Cheyennes struggled to survive in this frightening new world.[108]

Hunger was another problem. Gifts intended for them were distributed instead to tribes in New Mexico that had been raiding. Out of his own pocket, William provided the Indians with coffee and bread—delicacies they enjoyed—to pacify them. Both William and Agent

Fitzpatrick were anxious that the spring would bring an outbreak of resentment and retribution. William continued to hope the military would arrive to control the Comanches and Kiowas.

In November Lieutenant Colonel William Gilpin arrived at the fort with the Indian Battalion's two companies of dragoons. Gilpin tried to requisition supplies, mainly beef, from William, but Ceran St. Vrain, remembering past difficulties in getting payment from the government, said no. Gilpin moved near to what is now Pueblo, Colorado, and set up a winter camp. His mission was to pacify the Cheyennes and Arapahos, though Agent Fitzpatrick and William had not been without a great deal of influence in that direction. The Kiowas, Apaches, and Comanches had been trying to recruit the Cheyennes and Arapahos to join them in the fight against the white men, but the presence of Gilpin and his troops kept them from the alliance. Gilpin's continued presence helped keep peace along the Santa Fe Trail into 1848.

However, as feared, that spring, in March of 1848, the Utes and the Apaches were on the warpath. The Indians had learned to wait until military forces had moved out of an area to continue raids. Even the Bent, St. Vrain & Company caravan was attacked by Comanches. Travel on the Southwestern trails became so difficult that premier frontiersman Kit Carson, carrying military dispatches east, avoided those trails and detoured north to the Platte River trail.

The Rise of Emigration

In these dark days Bent, St. Vrain & Company ceased to exist. The original arrangement of William running the fort and the far-flung trading locations, while Ceran ran the Taos and Santa Fe operations, and Charles had oversight of the transporting phase of the business had worked very well as long as Charles was alive. The division of labor had worked well with Charles as the common denominator that held the partnership together. However, the combination of Charles's death and the military's use of the fort during the Mexican War had been hard on William's business. He also struggled with losses from Comanche depredations when he attempted to trade in their camps.

Probably about February 1849, when Ceran rode through on his way east, Ceran and William decided to go their separate ways. Ceran and William were not particularly compatible, and their businesses were easily separated. St. Vrain believed in New Mexico as an opportunity, and he urged William to move to town. But William had become a plains man whose life was invested with the Indians. William retained his interest in the St. Vrain-Vigil land grant, where his ranch was located.

William now was forty years old, and so much had been accomplished. We don't know how introspective he might have been, but it seems like it would have been an emotional moment when the partners split. David Lavender allows us to use our imaginations to see William as Ceran rode away for the last time:

> A last julep, a handshake, and Ceran rode on down the trail. William turned back through the iron-studded gate. Conceived largely as a result of his first venture among the Cheyennes, the sprawling castle was now entirely his. But ghosts walked with him across the placita, up the stairway to the big

apartment. Three brothers, his wife. . . . It was all his now. And he was alone.[109]

As sole owner of the "mud castle," as it was called, there were too many losses and sad memories. Since the opening of the fort, William's life had been one of hard work, managing the trading business, and keeping peace among the whites and the Indians. From the outset he had realized that trade and business could only thrive with peace.

Yet periods of change just kept coming in William's life. The end of the Mexican War brought a flood of traders dealing directly with the Indians, further eroding William's business model and relations with the Cheyennes and Comanches. Freighting across the Santa Fe Trail did, however, create a business opportunity of which William would also take advantage. In *Soldiers on the Santa Fe Trail*, Leo Oliva enumerates this growing business. In 1846, about $1,000,000 worth of merchandise and military supplies traveled over the trail, more than twice as much as in 1843, topping the pre-war maximum. The trade was worth around $5,000,000 in 1855, and in 1860 16,500,000 pounds traveled the trail in over three thousand wagons. By the end of the Civil War, the volume of trade compared to 1860 had almost doubled. The Santa Fe trade had become big business.[110]

Of course, for the Indians of the plains, white opportunities translated as threats to their culture. Emigration to California and Oregon began about 1842, and even as early as 1845 the Indians grew concerned about this heavy traffic through the heart of their hunting grounds. Then the great California Gold Rush of 1849 started. Grass, wood, and game were so destroyed along the Oregon Trail on the Platte River that large trains began to use the Arkansas River route. The Cheyennes and

Arapahos lived and hunted in the country between those two rivers. The buffalo began to decrease with alarming rapidity. The tribes foresaw even hungrier years to come. "George Bent . . . mentions emigrant trains several miles long, the huge freight wagons with white canvas tops resembling ships at sea," relates Evan S. Connell in *Son of the Morning Star*.[111]

The gold rush of 1849 drove many men to high risk, low return adventures in the West. William was not impressed. He had probably been aware of rumors of gold in the area of the Rockies for some years, but he didn't feel inclined to go dig for gold.

In the summer of 1849 the gold rush brought a new horror—cholera. Cholera is an acute diarrheal infection caused by ingestion of food or water contaminated with the bacterium. Untreated, it can kill in hours. The Gold Rush carried the disease from St. Louis to Independence and Westport and from there it traveled west with the wagon trains. A plague was loose on the plains. Evan Connell characterized a broader epidemic:

> By 1848 California was in American hands, which meant that the intermediate Great Plains dividing the states no longer could be ignored, and with the '49 gold rush came not only more palefaces than an Indian could imagine but alcohol, guns, cholera, smallpox, venereal disease, and the ineradicable debris characteristic of industrial nations. The tribes grew increasingly restive. Even the monstrous buffalo herds tried to avoid this white plague.[112]

Cholera was a devastating enemy. How frightening it must have been to see people dying suddenly from something totally unknown, unexplainable, and unseen. In St. Louis at the height of the epidemic, sixty to eighty corpses were carted away daily. It felled white and Indian alike, whether Native, settler, or immigrant.

Departing from Fort Leavenworth in 1852, young Santa Fe Trail traveler Marian Sloan Russell, in her memoir *Land of Enchantment*, described the streets of the fort ravaged by cholera. "Tar barrels were burning in the streets of Fort Leavenworth to ward off the cholera, and clouds of black smoke drifted over us as we pulled out."[113] Though this preventive tactic was ineffective, many whites used it. As they rolled away from populous areas, people usually felt the air was cleaner and safer. However, cholera travelled west with the caravans on the plains and spread like wild fire to the Indians.

Some of a band of Cheyennes, after visiting a camp of emigrants, were seized by what they called "cramps," they fell from their horses, and died. Survivors had no idea what was killing their fellows, and they fled across the Arkansas River.

The disease struck along the rivers that were the roads to the West, especially the Arkansas and the Platte. On the Platte River, whole Indian camps were deserted with dead men, women, and children still in the tipis. "The Sioux and Cheyennes, closest to the emigrant road, suffered most, but the epidemic spread northward to the Blackfeet, southward into Kiowa and Comanche territory. [George] Bent visited empty villages where he saw teepees full of bodies."[114]

> A Cheyenne war party, nearly two hundred strong including women, had raided the Pawnees and were returning to their village on the Smoky Hill [now eastern Colorado and west central Kansas] when they struck an immigrant train circled. . . . The warriors investigated, for there was no movement or sound,

everything deathly quiet. . . . [T]hey discovered
to their horror dead and dying white men . . .
dying of the deadly "cramps." In panic they
wheeled their horses, running from the invis-
ible enemy. . . . But before they had gone far,
half their number fell to the disease.[115]

No one was safe. In April 1849 William took his son
Robert, eight, with him to St. Louis to sell a twenty-
wagon caravan of buffalo robes that would bring a good
price. He thought it was time for Robert to start learning the business. Left behind with Island and Yellow
Woman were Mary, George, and baby Charley.[116] A
great celebration of the Sundance was being held on
Bluff Creek, and Island and Yellow Woman took their
mother and the children. Many Cheyennes joined the
celebration of a new peace arrangement between the
Osages and Kiowas. Kiowas, Cheyennes, Arapahos,
Comanches, Prairie Apaches, and Osages were in attendance to celebrate this new agreement between two
tribes. As the dancing began, a Kiowa warrior keeled
over, writhing. He soon died. Then another onlooker
collapsed. "The Big Cramps!" reverberated through the
crowd. Everyone panicked and ran.[117]

In terror, Island and Yellow Woman gathered the
children. Eleven-year-old Mary could ride, and the
women loaded their mother and younger children on
a travois. With a limited supply of water and food, they
ran as fast as they could go. The tribes scattered and the
Cheyennes headed southwest. They traveled all night
and by the next noon had reached the Cimarron River.

> [T]he sisters carried their mother, Tail Woman
> . . . to the shade of a large cottonwood tree.
> George saw people fall down, clutching their
> stomachs, unable to stand. And he watched his
> grandmother die in the shade of the tree. The

boy helped his mother build a scaffold high in the cottonwood and saw her gently place Tail Woman on it. There was no time for ceremony.[118]

It is hard to imagine the anguish and fear of these simple people as they dealt with this ghostly enemy. The panic was all consuming. Those within a group became afraid of each other. They were afraid of the dry wind. They had no idea what caused this horror and therefore what to avoid. They split into smaller and smaller groups, thinking they might be more likely to avoid the disease that way. Island and Yellow Woman slipped away from the others and got the children back to Bent's Fort. When William got home, he found that half the Southern Cheyennes had been wiped out. Now, on top of the losses of his brothers and Owl Woman, half his adopted people had died.

Young George had to add the loss of a grandmother and other relatives and friends to the list of his losses. The trauma was intensified by the sights of funeral scaffolds in trees, empty lodges, abandoned belongings littering the trail, and corpses of men, women, and children. This must have been shocking and maybe desensitizing. To watch the family dwindle could only have been frightening for a child. It must have seemed as though they would all die. How did they cope?

After the devastation of the epidemic on the Indians, the tribes wandering up and down the Arkansas that summer were very belligerent. The Comanches, Utes, Prairie Apaches, and even the Arapahos seemed to be angry and more threatening than ever before. As tensions on the plains were growing, the government built forts along the emigrant roads to protect the travelers. The garrisons were small and manned by young, inexperienced officers who treated the Indians disrespectfully, even rudely. These young officers were highhanded and often stirred up more trouble than they could solve. All these pressures—disease, disrespectful treatment, the plundering of their land—were building to a potentially explosive consequence.

The Demise of the Fort

William was safe within the walls of the fort, but to him the fort hadn't been built to fight the Indians. During the Mexican War the military had used the fort for resupply and rest, and William was not compensated— a disastrous cost. Free traders and loafers used the fort facilities. "By 1849 life at Bent's Fort had become untenable, and William had more than a hundred fort employees and dozens of Cheyenne lodges depending on him."[119] A fresh start was needed.

William took dramatic, irreversible action to change his life in 1849. On August 21, he suddenly decided he could no longer endure the ghosts that inhabited the fort. Three of his brothers had lived at the fort and were now gone. Owl Woman had died there in childbirth. There were too many haunting memories within those walls. The fort had outlived its time. Big Timbers, thirty-eight miles away, was a better location for trade with the Cheyennes, who wintered in that area. And negotiations to sell the fort to the army broke down over price.

He ordered his employees to strip every article of value from the fort and load it into twenty wagons, each pulled by twelve oxen. His men filled the wagons with personal property and goods—timbers, iron hardware, fur presses, wagons, harnesses—anything that could be used at the new site. With his family and employees in tow, William moved everyone downriver and then returned to the fort alone.

A strange, defiant pride was in him. He could have collected many thousands of dollars from the government for this adobe fortress. But the army should not have it, nor its memories, nor its ghosts. Nor would the Indians be able to move into it, hold their dances, mock his passing, fight his white nation.[120]

William placed kegs of powder in some of the rooms and lit the accumulation of debris that littered the area. As William, a lone figure without any brothers or his wife, rode away: "Behind him, the death boom of the prairie's greatest feudal empire split the evening sky."[121]

Mr. Leon Paladay, a former employee and witness to the devastation the next day, reported he had heard a distinct explosion like gunpowder or cannon shot. Then on passing the location of the fort on August 22, he saw that "the rubbish of the buildings was all that was left."[122] He realized that the sound he had heard was the explosion of Bent's magazine. The ruins were still smoldering. He had no idea of what had become of Mr. Bent and his people.

Discrepancies about this incident exist in the historical record. There were some accounts in later years that witnesses saw the fort after 1849, so partial destruction is certainly likely. Harvey Lewis Carter, in *Dear Old Kit*, disavows the story of destruction, reinforcing that at least part of the fort was still usable in later years:

> The fort was the center of a profitable Indian trade, chiefly in buffalo hides rather than beaver, down to August 1849, when William Bent abandoned it and built his new fort in the Big Timbers, thirty-eight miles downstream. There is no truth in the legend that Bent destroyed the Old Fort by exploding barrels of

gunpowder in it, since it was used by Barlow and Sanderson as a depot on their stage line in the 1850s and 1860s.[123]

The location of the old fort on the Santa Fe Trail would probably still be used for a long time, especially if partial shelter remained. But passers-by described it as in ruins. Chalfant tells of how troops passing the site in June 1857 saw broken walls of adobe, with several chimneys and a tower still standing. "Passing travelers had used the walls as a makeshift post office to leave messages for those who followed, to try out their artistic talents, or just to endow posterity with some graffiti."[124] Some things just don't change.

Hampton Sides gives an account of this time in his preface to *Blood and Thunder,* placing emphasis on Kit Carson's feelings about the disappearing wilderness:

> The beaver he [Carson] had trapped were on the verge of extinction. The Indians he had lived among had been decimated by disease. Virgin solitudes he once loved had been captured by the disenchanting tools of the topographers. The annual rendezvous of the mountain men was a thing of the past. Even the seemingly indestructible Bent's Fort was no more. One day in August 1849 . . . William decided it was time to start over. Not wanting to sell the great fort to the government, not wanting it to be vandalized and overrun by Indians, he came up with a more dramatic solution: He filled the labyrinthine chambers with kegs of powder and blew parts of his weird, splendid castle to smithereens. If there had been any doubt before, the immolation of Bent's Fort loudly proclaimed the death of an era.[125]

Edwin Sabin's report of this event also provides some history of forts to come that William would build:

> Having rendered his old post useless to the Government and the Indians, Colonel Bent himself moved down-river about thirty-five miles into Big Timbers—a place that, three years before, he had agreed with Lieutenant Colonel [William H.] Emory of the Kearny column was an admirable site for a military post. Here he followed his log cabins trading post with the substantial stone trading post of New Bent's Fort, built in the fall and winter of 1853. This, in 1859, the Government did acquire by lease.

©Camilla Kattell

This is the site where William Bent built New Bent's Fort, on the Arkansas River.

Enlarged, it became Fort Wise, Fort Lyon, and Old Fort Lyon as differentiated from the new Fort Lyon, of later date, twenty-five miles up-river or back toward the original Bent's Fort.[126]

This story of the destruction of the original "feudal citadel" symbolizes William's defiance, pride, and determination that he should not be robbed of his years of success. It is an amazing chapter in the life of this hearty pioneer and symbolic of how his life had been changed by war, migration, and disease—forces he could not control. He was discouraged with the efforts for peace between the Indians and the white men. The Bent trading empire had come to an end, but he had the courage to build a new life at, first, a stockade and then at Bent's New Fort, a stone trading post completed by 1853. From the time of this move he chose a lower-profile life and shifted his priorities more to his family and trade with the Cheyennes. He settled down to doing just what he had been doing for seventeen years—trading with the Indians. The population served at the new location would continue to be plains Indians, French and American traders, Mexican teamsters, and their families. Despite the decimation of the Cheyenne tribe, they still needed powder, balls, kettles, knives, sugar, and other essentials. To these things he would devote his time.

A New Life

At the new fort, William was able to be just one of the traders. He no longer had to take on the huge responsibilities that he had as master at the old fort. He had downsized his life so he could live in a way dictated more by his choices and less by his responsibilities. Though he would continue trading and working hard for the rest of his days, his life didn't again have the drive for taking on the whole West.

Freighting on the Santa Fe Trail remained a growing business, and William's astute business sense was helping him turn a good profit. For the government, he would haul Indian annuities from the east, for a payload of about $400 per wagon. He could haul buffalo robes on a return trip east to sell, and then he would invest in his own trade goods for the trip back west. There were times when the old ways seemed revived.

As the years passed, he naturally rose to the top when leadership was called for. He never lost his determination to fight for the well-being of his children and the Cheyenne tribe. In the spring of 1854, for example, smallpox struck the village near William's fort. A Cheyenne brought the smallpox from a Kiowa camp. As always the Indians turned to William for help, not knowing how to deal with this threat. William knew that if they scattered they would spread the disease across the plains. He stemmed the panic and persuaded them to stay where they were. He set up strict quarantine procedures and doctored the sick. When the disease had run its course, he burned any article that could be carrying the germs and only one Cheyenne died.[127] He effectively avoided a disaster like the one only five years before when cholera had wiped out half the Cheyenne population. William continued to have a valuable influence on his adopted people.

Over the next several years William and his family spent the winters at Fort St. Vrain on the Platte River, north of Denver. Trade on the Platte River Trail was busy with the movement of gold seekers. He wanted to take advantage of that market during the winter/spring hide season. They would return to the Big Timbers the rest of the year.

Traveling to and from Fort St. Vrain, George witnessed the devastation of cholera and smallpox. He saw the sobering number of deaths from the cholera by counting the funeral scaffolds. Worse still was the number of unattended bodies left to rot because there was no one alive to provide a funeral. It wasn't difficult to see the toll taken on the Cheyenne tribe.

William had lived a dangerous and simple life demonstrating both patience and flares of temper. He cultivated deep loyalties and was an individualist. He had courage and a gruff exterior that avoided sentimentality. He had a shrewd business sense and now, with no partners to limit his choices by reminding him of their investment in the fort, he took the initiative and made a bold decision to build his business anew. William was a man who had chosen his own path. He would continue doing the kind of business he wanted to do at that stage in his life.

William's business ventures in the West had been successful, but there had been a high price. He was the survivor in his family. The Mexican War and the Gold Rush had put the final transformation on his life. He still had his children and his Cheyenne relatives, but the life he had built, when any man could carve a home out of the wilderness, was gone. He had spent time in the West when he could love and live with people of another race and culture without it limiting his happiness. That time on the plains was fast disappearing.

As the Native population became an obstacle to the flood of settlement, there was growing pressure for the government to take steps to get this obstacle out of the way—by one method or another. Racial prejudice went west with the wagon trains traveling the Santa Fe Trail, the Oregon Trail, and the California Trail. The freedoms and privileges that were available to William would not be available to his Indian children.

Now education was called for to civilize his young and energetic band. William decided it was time to send the children to school in Kawsmouth (near Westport) and St. Louis, no doubt believing that it was important to prepare his children for life with the growing domination of white culture.

Endnotes

100. Dee Brown, *Bury My Heart at Wounded Knee* (New York: Henry Holt and Company, 1970). 4.

101. Lavender, *Bent's Fort*, 321.

102. Hafen, *Broken Hand*, 249.

103. Chalfant, *Cheyennes and Horse Soldiers*, 11.

104. DeVoto, *The Year of Decision 1846*, 249.

105. Lavender, *Bent's Fort*, 320 - 321.

106. Ibid, 324.

107. Ibid, 288.

108. Halaas & Masich, *Halfbreed*, 61 - 62.

109. Lavender, *Bent's Fort*, 334 - 335.

110. Oliva, *Soldiers on the Santa Fe Trail*, 22.

111. Evan S. Connell, *Son of the Morning Star, Custer and the Little Bighorn* (New York: North Point Press, 1984), 64.

112. Ibid, 81.

113. Marian Russell, *Land of Enchantment, Memoirs of Marian Russell Along the Santa Fe Trail as Dictated to Mrs. Hal Russell* (Albuquerque: University of New Mexico Press, 1954),14. Her legal name was determined to be Marion, but it appears as Marian in her book.

114. Connell, *Son of the Morning Star*, 64.

115. Halaas and Masich, *Halfbreed*, 51.

116. Some sources say Yellow Woman took the children, others that Island was along. It may be that Island was along due to her dedication to caring for the children.

117. Lavender, *Bent's Fort*, 337.

118. Halaas and Masich, *Halfbreed*, 52.

119. A. Hyde, *Empires, Nations, and Families*, 416.

120. Lavender, *Bent's Fort*, 338.

121. Ibid, 339.

122. Unknown author. "Later from the Plains-Burning of Bent's Fort Confirmed." *Notes from the Missouri Historical Society*, 3 Feb. 64, Correspondence to the Missouri Republican. Independence, Sept. 27, 1849.

123. Harvey Lewis Carter, *'Dear Old Kit,' the Historical Christopher Carson* (Norman: University of Oklahoma Press, 1968), 81, footnote 125.

124. Chalfant, *Cheyennes and Horse Soldiers*, 95.

125. Sides, *Blood and Thunder*, 309.

126. Edwin L. Sabin, *Kit Carson Days 1809 - 1869*, 296. Lavender, *Bent's Fort*, p. 447, note 3. Records indicate that the Army leased the property in 1860.

127. Lavender, *Bent's Fort*, 353.

7 ✍ EDUCATION IN THE WHITE COMMUNITY

IN THE SPRING OF 1854, when he went to Westport to pick up the annuity goods for distribution to the Indians at the new fort, William took George, Charley, and Julia to stay with Albert Gallatin Boone, grandson of Daniel Boone and friend and relative by marriage.[128] The children would be enrolled in school. That George, in particular, needed a tighter rein became immediately apparent when George was involved in killing a buffalo calf brought into the camp. The brutality of the killing offended William's sensibilities.

He was reinforced in his belief that it was time for his children to have a civilizing influence. Though they had grown up with a lot of freedom and had seen much in a mixed-race culture, where death had often come to those closest to them, they probably needed some degree of control. If Island had been their disciplinarian they likely hadn't seen much restraint, because the Cheyennes believed that discipline would break their spirits. With the freedom of the plains that system had worked for the Natives, but in their dealings with whites, it would need to be tempered.

Other than the incident with the calf, the family traveled east without any upset. The trip must have seemed run of the mill to William. Nor did he anticipate adverse social consequences in white society. He had brought his Indian wives to Westport, and his St. Louis friends knew of his marriages by "Indian custom." He was proud of his mixed-blood children and he introduced them to high society in St. Louis where the Bent name was well known. He provided them with the best that money could buy.

William brought a lodge for Island's use when traveling back and forth to Westport. She only stayed in town long enough for William to conduct his business and would have nothing to do with the frilly petticoats offered by the white women. Conversely:

> The Westport women were intrigued and came
> in great numbers to view Colonel Bent's "tipi
> wife." Although Island did not try to draw at-
> tention to herself, her horsemanship impressed
> the ladies, who even years later remembered
> the strange Cheyenne woman who rode astride
> in her split buckskin skirt, causing sparks to fly
> from the hooves of her galloping saddle mule
> as it pounded down Westport's cobblestone
> streets. She was, recalled one dazzled witness,
> a "veritable centaur. . . ." The gossip of the town
> women annoyed Boone, who morally opposed
> mixed marriages, but William seemed not to
> mind. . . . [H]e made no distinction between
> "Indian" and "white" wives.[129]

The children, initially sharing the comforts of Island's lodge, were on the brink of living according to white ways. They would have to give up their frontier clothes and wear shoes, underwear, coats, and trousers of wool and linen.[130] Nevertheless, William anticipated a smooth transition for his children.

New boomtowns, that had originally been the sites of Native villages, were growing up along the frontier and becoming trading points for a cultural mix of people. They were comfortable communities for assimilating Indians. One of these, Kawsmouth, near Westport, was the location where William first took the children for schooling. In Kawsmouth, the mixture of French Catholics, Native people, English Presbyterians, and fur trade employees would allow the children to continue living in a multi-cultural environment. Several missionary schools and churches focused on these families of mixed race in this layered community. It would be a comfortable place for the children to begin adapting to the Eastern culture.

Arriving at the pasturage just west of Westport, eleven-year-old George had never seen so many wagons and people, even at Bent's Fort. Mexicans, Americans, French, Shawnees, Delawares, and Pawnees were all busy at various tasks. When William went into Westport to arrange for shipment of his goods to St. Louis, George was able to explore and remembered even "dancing with low down women."[131] He was a curious and adventuresome child, out to learn about the world.

William collected the family and took George, Charley, and Julia to meet Albert Boone, their new guardian. Island raised no known objection to William's plan for educating the children, but her home would always be of the mountains and plains where she could see forever. It must have been hard for her to leave behind her adopted children to whom she had been so devoted. To have them so far away when it took so long to travel the distance between them probably accentuated the loneliness for her.

Albert Boone had long been associated with William in business and they were related by marriage. Albert agreed to be a guardian for the children, as he was for Mary and Robert, until they would go to more advanced school in St. Louis, where William's sister, Dorcas Bent Carr, would look after them.

Albert's store was in the heart of Westport's industrial and trade district—a hub for proslavery radicals and border ruffians. In bustling Westport there were many jobs for blacksmiths, wheelwrights, millers, masons, carpenters, boilermakers, shipbuilders, roustabouts, doctors, lawyers, teachers, clergy, merchants, and others. It was exciting for a young boy with lots of freedom to explore this town of two thousand. In time, George and his brother Charley would be influenced by the "rebel" attitudes of the area.

George liked living at the Boone house. He easily made friends with the other mixed-blood children in the community.

> George had his mother's thick black hair—now cropped short—dark eyes, and prominent cheekbones. From his father he inherited a narrow, straight nose, square jaw, and light bronze complexion. He was tall for his age and strong, his chest and shoulders already well-muscled for a boy of eleven. . . . George sometimes acted impulsively, unable to control his curiosity and youthful enthusiasm. As the second son, he seemed to get along with everyone, and laughter came easy to him.[132]

William chose the Shawnee Indian Mission school, three miles west of the town in "Indian Country," later known as Classical Academy. A coeducational school for affluent families, it was experimental and open to white and Indian students. They would receive instruction in reading, writing, arithmetic, and the classics. "Both Scarritt and Huffaker [the school masters] were progressive educators who believed Indians, whites, and mixed-bloods were intellectual equals and could be taught in the same classroom."[133]

George found education in the East very different, and it would take some adjustment. In the Indian camps, the children learned from older members of the tribe the skills they would need as adults, often while sitting around the campfires and listening to the tribe's oral traditions. This certainly gave the older members of the tribe continued worth in the clan. Boys also learned from their own active participation in fighting skills, tracking, horse management, weapon making, reading signs to navigate, etc.

Yet in the Eastern schools they were whipped or had a hand slapped for talking or not sitting still. This new world demanded conformity. George was taught that the white, Christian way was the chosen way, though he had been taught on the prairies that the Cheyennes were the chosen people. "George and all the young Bents grappled with these contradictions. Their difficulties were compounded on the docks and streets when they were sneered down as halfbreeds . . . inferior to all."[134]

In this world that would try to change and shape George's destiny, he was now introduced to racial bigotry in the broader culture. When a fellow student quoted Patrick Henry's *Give me liberty or give me death* speech in school, George may not have identified with the precepts of the American Revolution but rather the defiance of it and the need for people stand up for their freedom. He would live up to this philosophy.[135]

A year later, George was freed in the spring of 1855 when his father's caravan rolled into Westport. George greeted this chance to go back to the fort with an Indian whoop. He and his siblings would spend the summer vacation back on the Arkansas. When George left to return to school later that summer, he had no idea it would be seven years before he would see the fort again.

In 1857 George completed his studies at Mr. Huffaker's Classical Academy. William entrusted him to his friend Robert Campbell in St. Louis. George found Campbell a fine old gentleman, tolerant and accepting of mixed-bloods.[136] George was enrolled at the St. Louis Academy of the Christian Brothers. The religious indoctrination, high academic standards, and monkish discipline fell on George like an anvil. Within a year he left.

Webster College for boys worked better for him. It was not strictly religious. Bent relatives were active financial supporters of the school, indicating philosophical compatibility with its curriculum. The course of science, classics, Latin, Greek, and German suited George better, and what he learned served him well through life.[137] After 1855 George spent his summers at his father's Westport farm. He doesn't say why this was, but maybe he worked on the ranch for the summer, or maybe no caravan was traveling at the right time so he could return to school on time, or maybe he was just spending more time in the white culture.

George also spent some of his time with the Carrs, William's sister's family, because they were closer to his new school. They were part of the aristocracy of St. Louis. Staying with the Carrs would help the children transition to the living of a lifestyle with slaves, candelabras, and snowy linens in their Aunt's mansion. What impression this new lifestyle made on these young mixed-bloods from the wilds is one of the mysteries that we will never be able to know. To judge from the future choices they made, we can guess that the effect did not include becoming enamored with "civilized culture."

The Bent children were no strangers to slavery. Charlotte Green, her husband Dick, and his brother Andrew, were slaves of the Bents. It is likely that Charles inherited them from their father, Silas Jr. Charlotte was known far and wide as a cook, especially for her pies and pancakes. Lewis Garrard mentioned her in his book *Wah-to-yah*, noting that she was the belle of the dances at the fort. They were probably taken to the fort soon after the fort's construction. The children also would have encountered slaves brought along the trails by people like Susan Magoffin, who traveled with her slave, Jane.

Interestingly, William freed the Bent slaves. In 1847, William gave Dick his freedom as reward for fighting and being wounded during the Taos revolt. Charlotte and Andrew were also freed, and they all eventually returned to Missouri.[138]

Endnotes

128. Halaas & Masich, *Halfbreed*, 68. Halaas and Masich say that George went east to school in the spring of 1854. G. Hyde, *Life of George Bent*, 94. In Hyde's book, George says the date was the spring of 1853 but editor Savoie Lottinville says it was most likely the fall of 1853. It seems a spring trip to Westport would have been most likely to sell winter furs and pick up annuities.

129. Ibid, 72.

130. Ibid, 71.

131. Ibid, 70.

132. Ibid, 71.

133. Ibid, 73.

134. Ibid, 75.

135. Ibid, 74.

136. Ibid, 77.

137. Ibid, 79.

138. Leo Oliva, *African-American Women on the Santa Fe Trail.* Presentation to the Santa Fe Trail Rendezvous, Larned, Kansas, September 23, 2016, by permission of the author.

8 ~ NO PEACE BETWEEN WARS

THROUGHOUT THE DECADE OF the 1850s, the Cheyennes, Arapahos, and Comanches on the Arkansas River faced disease, drought, dwindling buffalo herds, and the increase of human and animal traffic on the Santa Fe Trail. However, so far they had not been affected by large increases of settlement as had been happening farther north. Though they could still hunt some buffalo and were subsidized with annuities, hunger remained a problem and skirmishing would continue. As the government built more and more forts along the main trails of westward movement the Indians became more and more antagonistic. William Y. Chalfant, in *Dangerous Passage*, gives a foretaste of what was coming for the Plains Indians.

> The conquest of the country of the Plains Indians would be an odd war. There were no battle lines, no Indian armies. The war against these Indians was rather a long, drawn-out struggle, typified [defensively by the Indians] by sudden hit-and-run attacks on small trains, military units, isolated settlements, lone riders,

and sleeping camps. . . . Often attacks were made as much to obtain goods and food with which to survive as to defeat the enemy. . . . The U.S. Army was ordered to bring them to bay and force them onto reservations. It was to be a grim and tragic end.[139]

This conquest of the plains would not be a war of standing armies but a war of attrition. The only kind of war that the Natives could fight was a guerilla war, taking advantage of their mobility and knowledge of the country.

In the summer of 1854 some Brulé Sioux found a footsore ox along the road and killed it for the hide. The chiefs offered a ten-dollar indemnity payment but the owner wanted twenty-five dollars. The officer in charge felt the man who took the ox should be given up, but the Indians refused to do that. A heated standoff ensued between Lieutenant John Grattan, out of Ft. Laramie—with thirty-two men and two howitzers—and young armed warriors. Though the chief, Whirling Bear, tried to talk everyone into cooling off, hostilities were aroused. Grattan had repeatedly claimed the Indians were cowards and that they would run. When the howitzer was fired and the troops fired a rifle volley, the Indians killed Grattan and many of his men. When the troops retreated, the Indians pursued and killed the remaining troops. Grattan and his men died over the ox. The warriors were not controllable and they continued raiding. This kind of incident more and more served to arouse a need for vengeance and to fuel a cycle of attacks and retribution.

In the fall of 1854 William called the Cheyennes to New Bent's Fort to receive their annuities. He was discouraged and must have wondered if the new fort was a mistake. It seemed that each depredation by Indian or white called for revenge in an endless cycle. Even though,

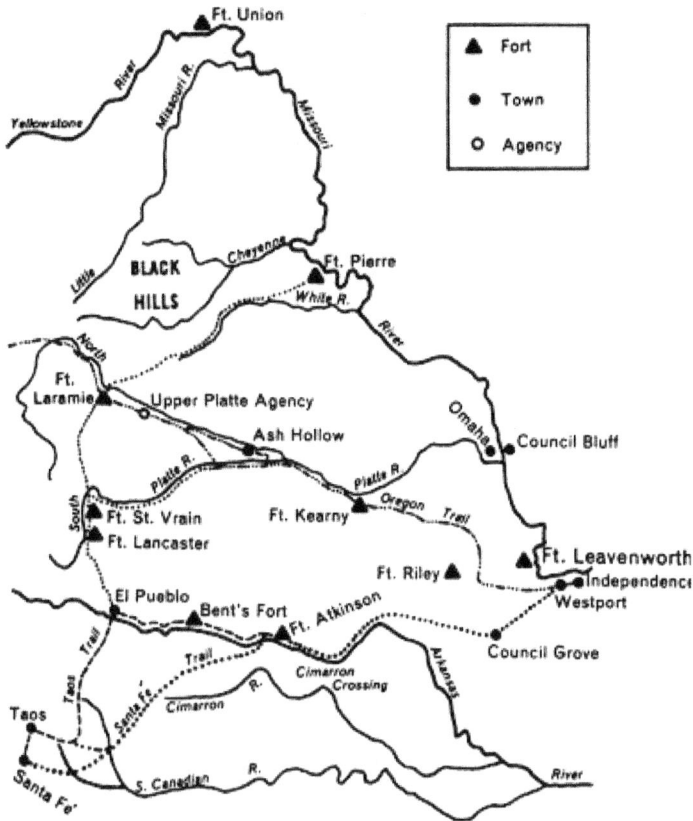

The Plains, 1850 - 60
Map originally published in The Fighting Cheyennes,
by George Bird Grinnell. Copyright ©1985 by the
University of Oklahoma Press. Reprinted by permission
of the publisher. All rights reserved.

after the Mexican War, he felt things would never be the same again, he had tried to recapture the old days of trading and hoped for peace between the races.

When the Cheyennes came together for their annuities, he spoke to them of peace, but they had lost interest. The Northern Cheyennes had been more adversely affected by the influx of settlers on the trails leading to California and Oregon. Their anger and fears were coming in more alarming proportions. The Southern Cheyennes understood the same threat and were concerned about the diminution of the buffalo herds. They decided to travel north with their brothers to winter on the Solomon River, in future western Kansas, where the chiefs could council. The disenchantment of the Indians was a concern to William.

Additional troubles were escalating in the East, with Free Soilers and slavers fighting to expand slavery in eastern Kansas and John Brown and other abolitionists causing panic and fear. Troops were being recalled from the plains to quell the unrest. Two powerful medicine men, White Bull and Dark, argued with the Cheyennes, ultimately convincing them that they should take advantage of this military withdrawal.

In the fall of 1855, near Ash Hollow on the Platte River, Colonel William S. Harney led a punitive expedition in response to the Grattan affair. He attacked and scattered a village of Brulé Sioux under Little Thunder. The camp had been forewarned, and the people were fleeing when Harney attacked. He killed eighty-six Indians, wounded five, and took seventy women and children as captives. Horses, mules, and property were appropriated. The government took revenge on an entire village, instead of just the warriors. All this was done without concern for who was guilty. Terrified, the Indians agreed to give up the man who had taken the ox that caused the Grattan affair the year before.

This fight, known as the Battle of Ash Hollow,

> . . . is a good example of the way in which Indians have often been treated by the troops, acting, of course, under orders from Washington. The individuals or groups of Indians who have

committed depredations run away, while the friendly camps, easily found, are attacked by troops and their inhabitants slaughtered.[140]

At Ash Hollow, an attack on a friendly village, the women and children suffered the brunt of the violence.

In the reports of Indians killed, the military tended to inflate the body count of warriors and overlook the innocents killed. Rarely did official military reports of clashes with the Indians report the same number killed as the Indians remembered. There were false body counts even then.

The Cheyennes were not spared, either. "What was really the first collision between the Cheyenne tribe and United States troops took place the year following General Harney's attack on the Sioux camp at Ash Hollow."[141] That spring of 1856 a white man on the Upper Platte reported to the local commanding officer that some Cheyennes had taken four horses. The Cheyennes met with the officer and agreed to return the horses. But they could only return three horses because the holder of the fourth claimed the horse had been in the camp for a long time and was not taken at the time and place claimed. The officer arrested three men who tried to escape. One was killed, one escaped, and one, Wolf Fire, was arrested, even though both the soldiers and the Indians knew that he was innocent of any offense. Wolf Fire was held in custody until he died in prison. Eventually the frightened Indians fled the area. They could get no justice.

During the summer of 1856, a party of Cheyennes was out looking for Pawnees to attack. When they saw a mail wagon coming down the road they suggested to a mixed-blood among them that he go ask for some tobacco. When he and his companion waved for the wagon to stop, the driver was frightened and he started firing at them. They shot arrows in retaliation and wounded the driver in the arm. When the rest of the party found out they had hurt the driver, they quirted the young men and drove them back to camp.

The next day a troop came looking for them in the camp. When the Indians saw the hostile intent of the troops they ran, leaving their weapons and horses. The soldiers killed six of them. A band of Indians later fell upon two different small wagon trains, killing a total of six people. This kind of cycle of attack and vengeance continued to punish the innocent.

William could only see trouble in the future. He persevered because he had an investment to protect and duties to his people, but he realized that his new stone fort could not recapture the glories of the past. He tried to sell his trading post, but the deal fell through. He continued to try to protect his investment and to serve his people, but times were fast changing. He had seen the heyday of the trappers disappear and now again the West was moving beyond his reach. The 1850s continued bringing stress and hostilities.

On October 24, 1856, Secretary of War Jefferson Davis gave his approval for a military campaign to be planned for the following year against the Cheyennes. Punishment was to be meted out for the activities of the past two years, though these activities had been previously settled and forgiven by treaty. In the spring of 1857 Secretary of War John B. Floyd gave notice that the peace concluded the previous fall with the Interior Department would be breached.

> [T]he army bore substantial responsibility by its harsh and indiscriminate treatment of Indians. It [the military plan] was the culmination of years of misunderstanding and mistrust, and was grounded on the belief that a

whole people should be responsible for the actions of a few; that Indians had no right to move freely through their own lands or hold whites accountable for wanton acts committed by them; and that the appropriate punishment for harm done to the person or property of whites was to kill Indians, any Indians, regardless of their culpability.[142]

William was caught between the needs of the Indians and the demands of the government. When new Indian Agent Robert C. Miller arrived at the fort, he refused to distribute annuities until he met with Colonel Edwin Vose Sumner, who was on the Republican River. Miller ordered William to store the goods at the fort until he was ready to distribute them. William believed that Sumner planned to provoke a fight without attempting to parlay first, and he didn't want to get involved in a fight with the Cheyennes. He negotiated with Miller to lease the fort to the government for the storage of the annuities until they were distributed. The next day, July 21, he packed up his family and belongings, and driving his cattle in front of his wagons, he once again moved away from a fort. The fort soon came back to William, but in the interim he took up residence twenty-five miles west on the Purgatoire River.[143]

On July 29, 1857, after months of planning and then campaigning on the plains, three hundred troops of the Cheyenne Expedition commanded by Colonel Sumner met a like number of Cheyenne warriors in the valley of the south fork of the Solomon River. The Cheyennes had never seen so many white soldiers and were shocked as they watched the soldiers form for a charge across the narrow valley.

Though it was intimidating to face so many powerful guns, the Cheyennes were confident because two medicine men, Ice and Dark, had convinced them that their strong medicine was going to protect them from bullets. The warriors were led by the strong chiefs of the military societies—the Kit Fox, the Crooked Lance, the Red Shield, the Bow Strings, the Dog Soldiers, and the Crazy Dogs—providing further assurance. The warriors sang their eerie war songs and death songs.

As the two lines advanced toward each other, amid the chaotic din of the war cries, one of Colonel Sumner's Indian scouts, Fall Leaf, dashed out to a mid-point and fired a shot at the advancing Indians. Colonel Sumner's orders were to try first to talk to the Indians, but now he said to First Lieutenant David Stanley, "Mr. Stanley, bear witness that an Indian fired the first shot."[144] Thus the Colonel absolved himself of any responsibility to attempt peace overtures with the Cheyennes.

The troopers expected a command to draw their carbines during the charge, fire a volley, and then continue with pistols. But to their surprise, came the order to "Draw sabres!" followed by "Charge!" The surprised Indians came to a sudden halt, not knowing how to fight the "long knives." Their mighty medicine was to protect them from bullets, and they had no idea how to fight sabers. A brave and quick-witted chief rode in front of their line and urged them to stand and do battle. When the lines were about a hundred yards apart, the Indians let loose a shower of arrows and then turned and galloped away. They broke into small groups and scattered, their will to fight was broken. The running fight went on for over five miles until "Recall" was sounded to protect the scattered troopers from the danger of being overcome by small groups of Indians. The Battle of Solomon Fork was over.

An Irish private named James Murphy, when asked how many Indians had been killed, responded by saying, "Well, really I didn't count them. But I'm dead sure of one thing, and that is that I killed as many of them as they did of me."[145]

The Southern Cheyennes migrated back to the Arkansas, hoping to avoid trouble, but they were restive and poorly fed. Some people in the village began talking about attacking the fort for supplies, but the cavalry arrived before the Cheyennes and secured the empty fort. Colonel Sumner dumped the stored annuity goods in the river, damaging the Indians more than battle could. The Cheyennes were shattered, on the run, and avoiding contact.

Gold Fever

During this period there was much speculation about whether there was gold in the Rockies, closer to the settlements than California. The Indians had talked about gold in the Rockies for years, but they had no interest in it. They seemed to know that if white men found gold they would soon take the last of the Indian lands. Some, perhaps, carried a tribal memory of the Spanish conquest in Mexico.

The effects of the 1849 California Gold Rush were exacerbated on the plains by the Pikes Peak Gold Rush in Kansas Territory and Nebraska Territory a decade later. Prospectors and people who went along to start businesses in support of the rush were the first major influx of Euro-American population in the regions. Hundreds of thousands of gold rushers traveled across Cheyenne and Arapaho lands trampling the grass, polluting the water, killing the buffalo, cutting down the trees, and even shooting Indians. "William Bent wrote to the superintendent of Indian affairs in St. Louis and begged him to establish inviolate reservations for the central Plains nations 'before they cause a great deal of trouble.'"[146] By the mid-1860s most of the hard-rock mining in the area was played out, but many cities had sprung up in Colorado. The damage to the plains and the buffalo herds, which so concerned the livelihood of the Indians, had been done.

On July 15, 1858, William arrived in Kansas City where the *Journal of Commerce* noted his arrival and commented that he had "probably transported more goods over the Great Western Plains than any one man living."[147] No one asked him about gold in July, but when he passed back through on September 15, they sent a reporter to the docks to interview him about the gold in Colorado. William was noncommittal but said the Indians had always thought there was gold there, and he had heard about it for as long as he had been trading in the area. Some gold seekers may have traveled west with his caravan, but despite gossip to the contrary, William did not set up a trading post with the idea of trading in the gold fields. Gold had no attraction for him either.

He was becoming a legend, though he never sought fame—unlike others. In 1856 frontiersman Jim Beckwourth had published a self-aggrandizing book of his Western adventures, and in 1858 army surgeon DeWitt Peters published a book about Kit Carson that helped make Kit famous.

However, William was renowned for his accomplishments in the West and was considered the man to turn to for information about the plains. He shied away from publicity. His only desire was to continue the life he had created for himself and his family on the plains. He no doubt knew that a gold rush would speed up the alteration of that life. He, like the Indians, sensed the passing of their way of life.

By November 1858 a delegation of Cheyennes and Arapahos were so desperate that they asked William to write to the white father for relief from the invasion of their homeland and hunting grounds. They were bewildered by invaders cutting down their trees and in other ways destroying their land. William knew that a new treaty was needed to define the Indians' rights and, on behalf of the chiefs, on December 1, 1858, he wrote to A. M. Robinson, Superintendent of Indian Affairs in St. Louis.

William urged prompt attention to address the continuing assault on Indian lands. He believed that Indian lands needed to be protected and a means of livelihood provided to them. William realized that helping the Indians learn farming was the only viable course for them and that they were ready. "They are anxious to get at it. If you will only give them a start they will go ahead."[148]

Though William saw an urgent problem, Congress acted slowly. Superintendent Robinson's answer to the problem was to appoint to the job of agent a man who could control the Indians until some settlement could be reached. He appointed William to the post, and President Buchanan signed the commission on April 27, 1859. Robinson gave William the news as a *fait accompli*.

William was commissioned representative to the Cheyennes, Arapahos, Kiowas, and Comanches. He was to contain the Indians until suitable lands could be apportioned. This was a nearly impossible task, but William believed that many of the Cheyennes and Arapahos would understand the need to settle down and till the soil far away from the gold rush.

He was not pleased with the additional burden of the appointment. There was nothing about this government job, plagued with red tape that William wanted. He was concerned about what would happen to the Cheyennes while he had to direct his energies to the new position. And the government compensation would not make up for the loss of time and attention to his business that the job would demand. But William accepted the appointment and decided to set up his seventeen-year-old son, Robert, with wagons and let him deliver the annuities to the South Platte. William would travel with the train and give Robert an opportunity to take more responsibility in the business. Robert was level headed and eager.

However, farming equipment was not in the government budget and never arrived for the Indians' use. William urged the Indians to remain peaceful and continued trying to get the Indian Bureau to include budgeting for farm implements so the Indians could learn to support their families. Though the young men thought farming was "squaws' work," the older men counseled that they could learn to farm and settle down to a life of peace. According to Anne Hyde:

> As father, brother, husband, son, uncle, and now agent to Cheyenne people, William Bent tried very hard to implement this plan. At his own expense be bought farm implements, seeds, lumber, and food supplies, brought them to his new stockade, and began to work from there.[149]

William was dedicated to guaranteeing the Cheyennes a future, and in time the government, the Cheyennes, and the Arapahos considered him an agent without peer. He had a well-deserved reputation—what other white man knew the Indian people the way he did? But the job would interfere with his business—he needed to oversee the freighting of goods. What would happen to the Cheyennes without him at the fort? "It was the beginning of agonizing problems that would consume most of the rest of his days."[150]

William continued to work for the Indians and reported to Superintendent Robinson that the Indians remained peaceful in his agency; however, he warned that the failure of food supplies and pressure from whites would ignite a "smoldering passion" among the Cheyennes and Arapahos. He begged for reservation land, a safe haven from the gold fields and the overland roads.

William repeatedly reported the good behavior of the Cheyennes and their willingness to learn a new way of life for peace. A report is one of few documents in William's hand that survives. In part he wrote in mid-July:

> The Chyans and Arrapahos have took my advice to them last Winter and this last Spring. I am proud to say they have behaved themselves exceedingly well. . . . Theair will be no troble settling them down and start farming. They tell me they . . . have passed theair laws amongst themselves that they will do anything I may advize. It is a pitty that the Department can't send Some farming implements and other necessarys this fall Sow as they could commence farming this Coming Spring. . . . you Must excuse my bad Spelling as I have bin so long in the Wild Waste I have almost forgotten how to Spell.[151]

This portion of William's report tells a lot about him. He certainly was fighting to do for the Cheyennes anything that he could. He had lost many of the skills of his education, but not of his mind, his good will, or his understanding of the West as it changed drastically. William further pled for the Cheyenne cause. Grinnell states:

> He said that "the Cheyenne and Arapaho tribes scrupulously maintain peaceful relations with the whites and with other Indian tribes,

notwithstanding the many causes of irritation growing out of the occupation of the gold region and the immigration to it through their hunting grounds, which are no longer reliable as a certain source of food to them."[152]

William reported a different kind of story regarding the Kiowa and Comanche tribes, who continued to be quite hostile. He recommended that military posts should be built at Pawnee Fork and Big Timbers to control them with military force. The following year his recommendations led to the establishment of Forts Larned and Wise and to a military campaign against the Kiowas and Comanches.[153]

He also informed Robinson that he could not stay with the Indians but needed to return to St. Louis to care for some unfinished business that was worth three times what they were paying him. He asked for a treaty council to be held in the next year for determining protected land for the Indians for farming. He would return to the Arkansas in the fall.

William knew that the land north of the Arkansas River, by the Treaty of 1851, belonged to the Sioux, Arapaho, and Cheyennes, but white men were settling it without concern for the treaty, and they were establishing governments following the precedents of states in the East. As a result of the influx of gold seekers, Governor Denver, of Kansas Territory, had commissioners set up the county of Arapaho to establish a system of governing similar to governing systems in the states. Neither Kansas Territory settlers nor any squatters had a legal right to claim that land. By treaty this land was Indian land.

Authorities couldn't agree about a reservation, leaving the Cheyennes no place to go. This would create huge problems for some time to come. But nothing could protect the Bents or the Indians from the turmoil of the gold rush. The next decade would determine whose country the Cheyenne lands really belonged to, and William considered the interests of the Cheyenne tribe the same as his own.

Through the summer of 1859 as the annuity distribution was delayed and as Robert waited for the Indians to return from hunting, William estimated that sixty thousand men were traveling the trails west, headed for the gold fields in Colorado. The Cheyennes continued growing restless with this invasion, and William gave priority to their needs and delayed his trip east. Even as William saw contemporaries Uncle Dick Wootton and Louis Vasquez build up trading businesses in Denver to supply this surge of population, he only wanted to continue trading with the Indians.

In October, 1859, while tending to his business in St. Louis, William wrote to Washington, pressing for a new treaty for the Indians. He said war, starvation, and extinction were inevitable without prompt action. He urged the government to build forts to keep the Indians and whites separate, even though that would have a ruinous effect on his business.

This also meant the Indians would have to cede the lands the towns were built on and the strips of territory along the main routes of travel. He knew the opponents of Indian agriculture would scoff and that many Indians would still see soil tilling as "squaw's work." He knew the young warriors would continue to desire to fight, and the temptation for plundering caravans would be strong. He believed that both the Natives and the whites would have to be protected from themselves. What more could he do?

When it looked like there was progress in Congress toward more treaty talks, William felt he could resign from the agent's job that he never wanted. However, Robinson prevailed upon him to stay because he was so pleased with William's work and he wanted him around to distribute the annuities.

In the meantime, Albert Boone reported to William that his daughter Mary was in love with a saloonkeeper, Robison M. Moore. William traveled to Westport to head off the romance of a Bent with a saloonkeeper. When he met the twenty-seven-year-old Ohioan, William found that working in a saloon was just a temporary job. Moore had put himself through Cleveland Commercial College and had a vision for his and Mary's future. William had to give him some consideration.

He could respect that Mr. Moore had arrived in St. Louis penniless and was successful with businessmen in the area. William began to cool off. He found the young people stubborn and decided that being poor wasn't something to hold against the young man. Reconciled, on April 30, 1860, William gave Mary away at a lavish wedding held at his farm. He lent his new son-in-law enough money to start a business and then he returned to the Arkansas.

On September 19, 1860, William felt his work as Indian agent was done, and he resigned. Having leased his stone fort to the government, who operated it now as Fort Wise, he went back to his holdings on the Purgatoire to work on enlarging his stockade. Once again William loaded his personal belongings and moved. He drove his cattle ahead of his wagons and abandoned what he had built at the Big Timbers. He went about twenty-five miles west of the Big Timbers and enlarged a stockade he had built three years before on the rich bottomlands of the Purgatoire River.

Close to where he and his brothers had first talked to Yellow Wolf in 1832, he claimed title to land through his interest in the St. Vrain-Vigil land grant. He spent that fall and winter on the Purgatoire.

Endnotes

139. William Y. Chalfant, *Dangerous Passage, The Santa Fe Trail and the Mexican War* (Norman: University of Oklahoma Press 1994), 275 - 276.

140. Grinnell, *The Fighting Cheyennes*, p. 109 - 110.

141. Ibid, 111

142. Chalfant, *Cheyennes and Horse Soldiers*, 61.

143. Lavender, *Bent's Fort*, 356.

144. Chalfant, *Cheyennes and Horse Soldiers*, 189.

145. Ibid, 206.

146. A. Hyde, *Empires, Nations, & Families*, 442.

147. Lavender, *Bent's Fort*, 359.

148. Ibid, 364.

149. A. Hyde, *Empires, Nations, and Families*, 442.

150. Lavender, *Bent's Fort*, 365 - 366.

151. Ibid.

152. Grinnell, *The Fighting Cheyennes*, 125.

153. Oliva, *Soldiers on the Santa Fe Trail*, 113.

9 ∞ THE BENTS AND THE CIVIL WAR

IN THE EAST THE long threatened civil war erupted in April 1861, in South Carolina, when the newly organized Confederate States Army attacked Fort Sumter. There were several reasons for the tragedy of the Civil War. The issue of states' rights versus federal power, the formation of slave or free states as the West was developed, and the fear on the part of the South of the growing strength of the industrial North—all contributed to the question of whether a state could withdraw from the Union.

The poison of slavery had come to a head, and racial issues finally required settlement. Feelings on this issue ran so strong that only violence would result in an answer—an imperfect answer. Ironically, as issues surrounding the future place for black people in the nation moved west along the trails, the debate applied to the indigenous people as well. Everyone soon chose sides.

William remained loyal to the Union, and he kept busy freighting military supplies west. When the Indians sought his advice about fighting for the army, he advised them to stay out of the white man's fight.[154]

In St. Louis, on May 10, 1861, a zealous population with diverse feelings about the war erupted into violent action. Captain Nathaniel Lyon led four volunteer regiments, mostly German immigrants, and a battalion of regular troops through the streets of St. Louis, escorting a thousand Rebel prisoners from Fort Jackson to confine them at the arsenal by the Mississippi River. Rock-throwing secessionist crowds gathered in the streets to jeer at the troops and threaten them. As the conflict veered out of control, the volunteers panicked and fired into the crowds, killing twenty-eight citizens and wounding many more. George and Charley probably witnessed this "Camp Jackson massacre."

On June 19, 1861, when school recessed, George and Charley returned to the Westport farm. They were caught up in the hysteria, and as trained warriors, couldn't wait to get in the fight. George, as an expert horseman with his own horse and saddle, hoped to serve in the cavalry. To him warfare was the mounted charge, hand-to-hand combat, and displays of personal bravery that he had learned as a youngster training to be a Cheyenne warrior. Only days before his eighteenth birthday, George enrolled in the Missouri Cavalry, a regiment of Sterling Price's newly formed army, fighting for the Confederates. Price was the same officer that William had served with during the Mexican War.

A boyish sixteen-year-old, Charley was rejected by the recruiting officer as too young, and he returned to the Arkansas River country. There, new family problems developed for William. Charley returned to his father full of anger, after having lived the white man's life in the East. He became the Bent's angry young man. It is believed that Charley was probably looked down on as a "half-breed" while living with his affluent relatives at school. He returned sullen and angry.

William begged him to stay at the ranch, while his mother wanted him to join her people, seeking a refuge with a peace faction of the Cheyennes. Though he had not been among the Indians for a half-dozen years, he had dreamed of their way of life. The excitement and freedom, relative to the degradation of being an outcast, something unbearable and new to a Bent, motivated Charley as he rode off to live with his mother's people.

On August 10, 1861, at Wilson's Creek in Missouri, Confederate and Union forces engaged in battle. Despite staggering losses on both sides, the Confederates won a stunning victory. It also was George's baptism by fire. He now learned the white man's more formal execution of important tactics and strategy, discipline, and obedience. He had to learn about horsemen riding in precise ranks and the imperatives of coordinated action and adequate military intelligence. It was not war as the Cheyennes knew it—fighting for individual honor and glory. But the knowledge of how white men fought would serve George well in years to come.

George also fought in the battles at Lexington in Missouri, Pea Ridge in Arkansas, and the siege of Corinth in Mississippi. When his cavalry regiment was converted to infantry, George chose not to fight on foot. He joined Captain John C. Landis's horse artillery.

The life of an artilleryman was often brutally short. "Casualties were appallingly high. During the Corinth campaign in the summer of 1862, Landis's battery suffered losses of more than 20 percent."[155] The Union's General Henry Halleck sent one hundred thousand men against General P. G. T. Beauregard's force of sixty-six thousand. After thirty days, Beauregard realized they could not stop this grinding war machine. He had to retreat.

George's battery was chosen to cover the retreat on May 27. These men would never forget their rearguard stand against overwhelming odds. By July, General John Pope and the Army of the Mississippi replaced the slow-moving Halleck. George and his fellow troopers covering the slow, grinding retreat were exhausted, but they fought on valiantly.

By August 26, George's unit was worn down, retreating and falling apart. They were surrounded. It isn't known whether he was captured or surrendered as the men abandoned the hopeless fight, but he was taken prisoner and detained in St. Louis. Corinth was George's last combat in the Confederate uniform.

By a strange quirk of fate, as George was marched through the streets, he was seen by an old classmate. The classmate hastened to inform Robert Bent, a loyal Union man, who was in town on business. Robert went to Robert Campbell, George's guardian since George had gone to St. Louis for school, and they were able to get George released on September 5, 1862. He had to take an oath of allegiance and swear that he would not fight again in this war.

Here again the power of William Bent and the Bent name held sway in St. Louis. That power allowed George and Robert the freedom to ride for home on the Arkansas River, much to their joy. The brothers led the Bent caravan back to their father's stone fort on the bluff overlooking the new Fort Lyon, which was situated below on the Arkansas River.

A Family Divided

George had not seen his father's new post since 1855. "The Santa Fe Trail rutted the land, but it was still a freighters' road, a trail of commerce. But now in October 1862, the trail was a deep scar on the landscape."[156] Multitudes of gold seekers had cast aside refuse and abandoned equipment. The grass had been grazed down to dry stubble. The valley of the Arkansas was now a soldier's camp—blue coats at that. A giant garrison flag flew over the frontier post that was not the flag of the Confederacy. Union troops occupied the Arkansas country less than twenty miles from William's new ranch on the Purgatoire. The soldiers were his best customers, but they were George's enemies.

William's ranch had grown into a more impressive establishment than George could remember. As before, Mexicans, mixed-bloods, mountain men, and white traders mingled, but the Cheyennes seldom came from their camps. Traders now went to them. Native life along the Purgatoire had been fairly peaceful. "The record of the years 1862 - 63 for the Indians of the central plains shows that, considering their grievances and the opportunities they had for taking matters into their own hands, the tribes were exceedingly peaceful and forbearing."[157]

The violence in the East had not yet affected things at home for William and his family, but the clash of the cultures and races was about to come home for William in ways he had not anticipated and that would create heartache. The color-blindness of the West that William had first known was changing. As immigration increased and the military was dispatched to protect the roads, new racial attitudes were brought to the West that the mountain men, early traders, and the trappers had not uniformly applied to the Indians. The crisis of being half white and half Indian had manifested itself among William's children.

Robert and Mary were living and working happily

at the stockade and ranch. They coped with their mixed blood in very different ways from George, Charley, and Julia, all products of the same environment.

Mary had married an Anglo, Robison Moore or R. M. Moore, and raised her family at the ranch. She never took her children to the Cheyenne camps and baptized them as Episcopalians and they blended into rural Colorado. Of the siblings, she seems to have come closest to living peacefully in the white culture.

After the Civil War, Robert was active in the family business and he eventually married an Arapaho woman. Julia married mixed-blood Ed Guerrier, and they lived among the Indians, as did Charley.

William tried to hold on to his son George, buying him a five-hundred-dollar horse in Denver and a good pair of field glasses. George was nineteen, and there was a place for him working with William with the caravans, trading, and farming. He was tough, intelligent, and better educated than most people he encountered. William needed and wanted his help, but George was restless.

It was more than two years since William had seen George. He had heard that George was fighting Yankees in Mississippi, but he didn't know about George's capture and release. At nineteen George was no longer a school boy but a veteran of great battles. He was now a head taller than his father, and he was lean and tough after a year of fighting.

William, on the other hand, had aged. He was in his fifties now, and his hair had turned gray. They had much to talk about. Probably George told of his campaign with Sterling Price's army and William explained the changed country along the Arkansas River and the new Treaty of 1861 that was signed while George was gone.

William's persistent advocacy helped bring about this treaty, which was signed on February 18, 1861, at

Fort Wise (formerly Bent's New Fort), by six Cheyennes and four Arapaho leaders. Cheyenne signatories were Black Kettle, White Antelope, Lean Bear (Starving Bear), Little Wolf, Tall Bear, and Left Hand. The Arapaho representatives were Little Raven, Storm, Shave-Head, and Big Mouth.

The treaty ceded most of the Indian lands that had been established in the 1851 Fort Laramie Treaty, leaving them less than one thirteenth of the land the earlier treaty had granted. The tribes opposed the treaty on the grounds that most of the people were not involved, and those chiefs could not represent them all. Most continued to live and hunt in the bison-rich lands of eastern Colorado and western Kansas. The whites, though, claimed the treaty was a solemn obligation and, therefore, those not abiding by it were hostiles. White intrusions increased along a new trail through the Smoky Hill region to new gold fields, bisecting favored hunting grounds.

William had believed the new treaty was the best way to assure some land for the Indians, but the treaty was a failure. He had done his best to assure a future for his people and his family, but, despite his efforts, a schism was opening up in the family just as this treaty was dividing the Indians. As William related to George what had been happening in his absence, George felt his father had forsaken his people by urging them to accept a worthless tract of land in southeastern Colorado.

William argued that the buffalo were gone from the Arkansas River and the Indian way of life went with them. What he had done was for the good of the Cheyennes. "[William] told the family that if the Cheyennes did not confine themselves to reservations and take up farming and the white man's ways, they were doomed.[158]"

Anxious about the future, William continued trying to convince George to stay with him to work. He felt the Cheyenne villages were dangerous, as unrest increased and the interest of the government in using the military grew stronger. William felt it was only a matter of time until wider conflict spread on the plains.

But there was also a threat to George from the men at Fort Lyon. Some thought that, as a half-breed and Confederate, he should be killed. The risk was high that some of the troops would encounter George in a vulnerable position and kill him as a wartime enemy. George decided to return to his Cheyenne family in the spring of 1863. Like Charley, who had rejoined the tribes a year before, he made the choice to go live among the Cheyennes, his mother's people, now camped in western Kansas (established as a state on January 29, 1861).

It is hard to image what it was like for William to witness this breaking up of his family along cultural lines. He loved his children and wanted to provide well for them. After all, he himself had loved the Indian way of life and spent his life married to Cheyenne women. How could he fault the choice that three of his five children made when they each had to face their own difficult options? We have no record of how the process played out. It doesn't take a lot of imagination to walk in their shoes and, except for Charley—who only saw a single choice—to feel how torn they must have been as they chose between the peoples of their parents.

1863 and 1864 were to bring grave changes for the future of the Bents and the Cheyenne Indians, as well as the other plains tribes. The rapid influx of white population into Colorado following the gold rush of 1858 placed growing pressure on the Indians. Sensational reporting in the newspapers of Indian attacks created a great deal of fear. The clash between the races was growing more heated.

Even whites were noticing the vast numbers of settlers moving west—though they typically were blind to the incursions on Indian land. Sarah Raymond Herndon in *Days on the Road Crossing the Plains in 1865*, expressed repeatedly in her diary her surprise at the amount of wagon traffic they were encountering while crossing Nebraska. She commented that one day two hundred wagons were in sight and on another day she marveled that two hundred wagons had crossed the Platte that day and they appeared to be a town of tents and wagons:

> It is wonderful, wonderful to behold how this town of tents and wagons has sprung up since yesterday morning when there was no sign of life on this north bank of the South Platte, and now there are more than one thousand men, women and children. . . . The wagons have been crossing all day, the last one has just been driven into corral at sunset.[159]

This was just the traffic observed from one perspective and one time frame. There were, no doubt, wagon trains behind and in front of her caravan. Additionally, the California Trail and the Santa Fe Trail continued to have heavy traffic, as well as several cutoffs.

The well-traveled routes of the mid-1860s gave the Indians many reasons to worry about this flood of people desecrating their homeland. "George Bent . . . mentions emigrant trains several miles long, the huge freight wagons with white canvas tops resembling ships at sea. Indians who watched these creaking trains approach every season . . . could foresee the result."[160] Stands of Cottonwood trees where they had established regular campgrounds were disappearing. Rich valleys of grazing for their herds were now barren of grass. How difficult it must have felt to watch this destruction of everything held dear and to be helpless to stem the flood.

George's Choice

George had not been in a large Cheyenne camp in seven years. Dressed as a white man, with a mustache, and leading his racehorse that William had given him, on his arrival he was not recognized. When he asked for his mother's lodge, people were amazed. They didn't recognize the man as the boy they had known. When he asked for Julia and Charley, the people understood and they told him his family was with Black Kettle on Beaver Creek. His family welcomed him with warmth and were anxious to hear the stories of his life since they had seen him.

As he gradually took on a more Cheyenne appearance, he kept his mustache, which marked him as not wholly Indian. He was a man of impressive physical stature who had been tested in eastern battles. He was a son of William Bent and grandson of the famed Arrow Keeper, White Thunder. Young warriors were immediately attracted to *Do-ha-eno* (George's Cheyenne name). These were a people who honored others for bravery and accomplishment. George entered a place of honor and respect as a very young man.

That summer the Cheyennes and Lakota held their annual Sun Dance, one of the ceremonies when the Cheyenne bands came together. It was an opportunity for the chiefs to gather in council. One of their important discussions that year concerned whether they should follow William's advice to adhere to the Fort Wise Treaty of February 1861. They had to debate the idea of giving up their hunting way of life and instead to learn farming to sustain their people. They believed it was preposterous to think there wouldn't be plenty of buffalo for a hundred years.

Black Kettle had signed the 1861 treaty. Though white men considered him the chief of all the Indians, they simply did not understand the Indian way. Each man made his own decisions. "No single chief commanded the entire nation. Most of the chiefs gathered here near Beaver Creek had never seen the treaty and had not signed it. They would continue to hunt and live on their traditional lands."[161] They felt no compunction to abide by the treaty.

Black Kettle was one of the Cheyenne signatories, but the chiefs who were not involved claimed he and others didn't understand what they were signing and were bribed with a large distribution of gifts. Black Kettle most likely did not intend to sign away their land for seeds and plows. It is hard to second guess him or know what he really understood about the concepts of the whites. Rarely, if ever, did the Indians fully understand what they were signing at treaty negotiations. They didn't have a contractual manner of thinking, and little effort was made to help them understand or have everyone present to sign. Sometimes the treaty was not even read to them and interpreted.

Because of his experience fighting with the whites, the chiefs sought George's counsel. George had fought with the Indians at Pea Ridge in Arkansas during the Civil War, where General Albert Pike's Indian allies had been decisive in that battle. Some Indians had scalped their enemies, horrifying the white people, both North and South. Somehow the whites found that mutilation more offensive than blowing a body apart with cannon fire.

When the same General Pike sent emissaries to the Cheyennes urging them to fight for the South by attacking Forts Larned and Lyon, Black Kettle wanted to know what George thought. George, with the memories of Pea Ridge, told the chiefs that the Indians did not understand the white way of warfare. It was not good for the Indians to fight in that white man's war.

Esteem grew for George as they talked and it was obvious that Black Kettle liked him. A bond grew between the two men. "[S]oon it was clear to everyone that Black Kettle not only liked this son of Bent but had taken him into his lodge to guide him as he would his own son."[162]

After George's long absence from the tribal way of life, Black Kettle could help him acclimate again to the Indian ways. When Black Kettle was selected as one of the Southern Cheyennes to be a member of the esteemed Council of Forty-Four, he had given up his membership in the Crooked Lance warrior society. Peace chiefs were peacemakers, negotiators, and counselors. But he could still teach George the ways of the Crooked Lances. Black Kettle convinced George that the Crooked Lances were the boldest of the warrior societies.

Among the Cheyennes there were now six soldier societies: Bowstrings, Crazy Dogs, Dog Soldiers, Kit Foxes, Red Shields, and Crooked Lances. These groups hunted together, fought together, sang together, prayed together, and died together as individual units. They were close-knit entities with proud identities. They had responsibilities within the band to direct hunts, oversee village moves, police the many ceremonial dances, and they led war parties. Each group was competitive for honors.

The military societies had vied for George's membership. He adjusted quickly to the excitement of the buffalo chase and the life of raiding, which were much more exciting than the white man's way. He was his mother's son again. In the late summer of 1863 George was ready to be tested for his fighting skills, not as a white soldier but as a Cheyenne warrior.

He rode out with his first Indian war party. When the war party met a small group of Delaware Indians, who were out trapping, the meeting began in a friendly manner. They agreed to meet again the next day. But the Delawares were outnumbered and feared the Cheyennes, so they slipped away in the night. This distrust angered the Cheyennes the next morning. In retribution for this perceived slight, they attacked the Delawares, actually justifying the Delaware fears. George saw his first Indian fight. The Cheyennes killed two of the Delawares and took all their horses and their packs of beaver and otter pelts. One Cheyenne, Big Head, was killed.

"George never looked favorably on this fight. There was no reason for it. The Cheyennes did not want to kill the Delawares, whom they respected as warriors. Besides, there were only a few of them and many Cheyennes."[163] Did the young warriors simply get out of hand? Was their honor truly insulted because the Delawares didn't trust them? Apparently, with hindsight, George could see how worthless the killing was. He had seen enough killing in the Civil War to be able to recognize the futility of it.

Because Big Head was killed, the Cheyennes had to throw away their scalps, negating the scalp dance celebration on the return to camp. That would be a disappointment because the scalp dance was a great celebration. George spent the winter on the Smoky Hill River, of eastern Colorado Territory and western Kansas, where the buffalo were still plentiful and no harm would come to the Cheyennes. This tranquility would not last for long.

In the winter of 1863 - 64, the Sioux had been aroused by several attacks on their tribe by the military. They sent a war pipe to the Cheyennes south of the Platt River. Smoking the pipe was a pledge to join forces in a war against the whites. But the Cheyennes and Arapahos did not smoke.

A white man living with the Arapahos told Colorado Territorial Governor John Evans that the tribes were preparing for a spring war. George related that, "I was in the Cheyenne camps at this time and know that this white man's story was a lie from beginning to end, but Governor Evans believed him."[164] Evans likewise ignored Indian Agent Samuel Colley, who had reported on September 30, 1863, that the Indians were generally friendly, though he acknowledged a lack of buffalo and other game.

Evans instead was attuned to the rumors and fear that were rampant in Colorado, with whites clamoring for protection. After the 1858 gold rush, immigration into the state had boomed. And with the growth of the territory, politicians felt pressured to solve their "Indian problem." Citizens demanded safe passage through the Indian hunting grounds.

Though the Indians had remained peaceful, by early 1864, Governor John Evans of Colorado was convinced that the Indians were preparing for war. This, despite reporting on October 14, 1863, that the Indians were quiet and that those on the Smoky Hill and Republican Rivers condemned anyone speaking of war. However, the Indian hysteria was too rampant to ignore. When General Samuel Curtis sent an order that Colorado troops were to march east to campaign against the Confederates, the Colorado cavalry made an unprovoked attack on the Cheyennes, seemingly determined to drive them to war. The military was using any excuse to attack whatever Indians they found, without any attempt to parlay and settle disputes in a peaceful manner. They created a strong motivation to need the troops in Colorado, and false accusations by whites were often the catalyst for continued white harassment.

The Cheyennes questioned: Why had the whites declared war on the Cheyennes? What was the purpose of this wave of unprovoked hostility? George later said:

> I never could understand why the soldiers made these attacks on the Cheyennes in April, 1864. There was no reason for it. One of Colonel Chivington's political enemies once hinted that there was politics back of the whole business, and that is the only possible explanation I can see.[165]

Colonel John M. Chivington, commander of the Colorado Military District, did not want to be sent east to fight in the Civil War. He had political aspirations as Colorado anticipated statehood. He was the hero of the 1862 Battle of Glorieta Pass that defeated the Confederates in New Mexico. His ambitions now were in Colorado. He wanted to gain the voters' attention in Colorado, and there was no better way than attacking the Indians to gain popularity and the hearts of voters.

It was clear that the whites didn't want to preserve the peace. Chivington made it distinctly evident that they wanted to exterminate the "Red Rebels," even after many reports that the Indians were quiet and peaceful. But the military didn't realize what a hornet's nest they were stirring up. The battles of the spring and summer of 1864 would lead to the tragedy of the Sand Creek Massacre and the violent retribution it caused.

A Shift in Policy

A new policy for policing the Indians led to these un-provoked attacks, and through the spring and summer of 1864 the Indians responded with a vengeance. A pattern of retribution and then withdrawal to a peaceful area gave the Indians a feeling of having settled matters, and an expectation of peace. They didn't understand that the policy shift would lead to continued fighting.

On April 12, 1864, about twenty bluecoats of the First Colorado Cavalry under Second Lieutenant Clark Dunn attacked a Cheyenne war party going north against the Crows, on the South Platte road at Fremont's Orchard, in Colorado Territory. The Indians had reportedly stolen a rancher's mules. Two versions of the battle that resulted were reported by the Indians and the cavalry, but likely a misunderstanding placed culpability on both sides. Whoever started the fight, the shots were the commencement of a very violent summer to come.

Mad Wolf related what had happened according to the Indian version of the battle. After a quiet winter, fifteen warriors of the Dog Soldiers had started north to join the Northern Cheyennes to raid the Crows. They found four stray mules and rounded them up, thinking they had been lost or wandered away from a wagon trail. An angry rancher showed up, claiming ownership of the mules and wanting their return. The warriors said they were willing to return the mules, but they wanted compensation for their time and trouble with the mules. They signed for the rancher to return the next day with appropriate gifts.

The next day, as they approached the South Platte River, they spotted soldiers riding in their direction. An officer advanced toward them signing for them to put down their weapons—but before they could, the soldiers starting firing at them. When a soldier charged toward Bull Telling Tales, he shot an arrow straight through the soldier and then mutilated him. The soldiers made a hasty retreat. The warriors shot a second soldier who lagged behind.

Mad Wolf reported that the warriors could have overwhelmed the soldiers, but they were not at war with the whites. The party of Dog Soldiers rode with their three wounded back to the Beaver Creek camp to report the unprovoked attack.

Again the chiefs turned to George for advice, looking to his experience with the whites. He advised them to stay away from the soldiers and avoid the roads. The soldiers were dangerous, unpredictable, and not to be trusted. The chiefs decided it would be wise to move south of the Arkansas, where there were no major roads for soldiers and emigrant traffic.

A few days later Crow Chief and his band came into the camp and reported an unprovoked attack on April 15, when seventy lodges on the Republican Fork, east of Denver, were hit. Though the people escaped, their village was destroyed. Soon thereafter, Raccoon, a Southern Cheyenne chief, reported that his small band had been attacked, and the people lost all their lodges and most of their belongings.

The Dog Soldier chiefs asked *Do-ha-eno* (George) to lead scouts to report on the soldiers' movements. George felt very proud that the Dog Soldiers, known for their fierce resistance to the white men, had selected him for a place of leadership for this scouting mission. It was a sure sign of acceptance as a warrior. Three experienced warriors were chosen to scout with George.

When George reported back, a council was held. The Dog Soldiers wanted to fight and seek revenge on the whites for all their attacks. The peace chiefs believed it was better to negotiate peace than to subject their people to a long war with the soldiers. They opted to move south and join Black Kettle's or Lean Bear's Southern Hill people as the Dog Men moved north to attack whites wherever they were found. George opted to stay with the Indians moving south to avoid conflicts with the soldiers.

Dr. Elliot Coues, a well-known scientist, came up the Arkansas in May 1864 and made the following journal entry: "At 2 P.M. we brought up at Fort Larned—mean place, built of adobe and logs, with a drunken officer in command; everybody half-drunk already; and all were whole-drunk by bed-time."[166] This was often the class of officers assigned to holding frontier posts and keeping the Indians quiet, the kind of officer William had to persuade to humane behavior.

After several unprovoked attacks by the army against the Indians, and the resulting counterattacks by the Indians, things were quiet, but the seeds for more violence were sown. However, late in May a regular army officer, Major T. I. McKenny, who made an inspection of the plains, reported to General Curtis, district commander, that if the harassment against the Indians did not end, a war on the plains would be the result. He said:

> I think that if great caution is not exercised on our part there will be a bloody war. It should be our policy to try to conciliate them, guard our mails and trains well to prevent theft, and stop these scouting parties that are roaming over the country, who do not know one tribe from another, and who will kill anything in the shape of an Indian. It will require but a few more murders on the part of our troops to unite all these warlike tribes.[167]

No prompt action was taken. False claims against the Indians continued to be the catalyst for trouble. An example of a false claim happened in April when Colonel Chivington reported to the adjutant general of the Department of Kansas that a party of Cheyennes had stolen one hundred seventy-five head of cattle from a government contractor. When an investigation was conducted a year later, there was no evidence that this had happened. Kit Carson was among those who testified that the Indians were often accused of running off cattle when the herders had just been careless and allowed animals to stray.

During the investigation, the Indians stated that some cattle had drifted to where they were hunting buffalo and some small bunches were picked up and driven into camp. When this information had been reported in Denver, Lieutenant George Eayre was sent with troops to recover the cattle. When Eayre encountered a camp of five lodges the frightened Indians wounded a soldier while trying to escape. The troops captured the camp and destroyed the lodges and dried buffalo supplies. Twenty head of cattle were recovered in the area and Eayre returned to Denver. However, Colonel Chivington reported on April, 25, that a hundred head of cattle had been recovered. And so the harassment continued.

In May as news of various attacks arrived by runners where large camps of Cheyennes and Arapahos had wintered near Fort Larned, the chiefs met in council to determine what course the tribe should take. The Dog Soldiers again argued for war and vengeance. Crow Chief and Raccoon argued for restraint, even though their people had suffered most. White Antelope and Old Little Wolf believed they should not subject their people to a long war. The wisest course would be to join Black Kettle and Lean Bear's Southern Hill people. The Dog

Soldiers headed north toward the Platte River Road. George stayed with the Hill band and headed south. So the peace Indians sought escape and the belligerent Dog Soldiers again chose to fight.

On May 16 Lean Bear and Black Kettle's two hundred and fifty lodges were camped thirty miles south of the Hill people on the Big Timber Creek near the Smoky Hill and Fort Larned. The next morning hunters rode madly into camp and reported the approach of soldiers pulling two cannons, led by Lieutenant George Eayre. Grinnell reported on what followed, quoting Wolf Chief, who was still living when Grinnell was doing his research:

> A number of us mounted our horses and followed Lean Bear . . . to meet the soldiers. . . . [We] saw the soldiers coming in four groups with cannon. . . . [W]e did not want to fight. . . . Lean Bear, the chief, told us to stay behind him while he went forward to show his papers from Washington which would tell the soldiers that we were friendly.[168]

Lean Bear wore his peace medal that Abraham Lincoln had given him the year before when he visited Washington. The soldiers, on command, fired at Lean Bear and killed him and another warrior, Star.

Chaotic battle ensued until Black Kettle arrived and intervened. Eventually the soldiers retreated. George remembered, "If Black Kettle had not stopped the fight, not one of Eayre's men would have escaped."[169] Eayre had about one hundred men and there were five to six hundred Cheyenne warriors. As a result of this murder and fight, the young warriors were so angered that the chiefs could not control them. They raided the stage road from Fort Larned to near Fort Riley, Kansas, killing white men and plundering. Lean Bear had been highly respected.

The war Indians were determined to fight for their place on the prairie. "These frequent attacks, coming all together and not at all understood by the Cheyennes, made them uneasy and angry. . . . This was the beginning of the war of 1864 - 65, which cost so many innocent lives."[170]

A few days after the fight with Eayre's troops, the main camp of Cheyennes on the Smoky Hill, seeking peace, moved south and joined the Indians that Eayre had attacked on Ash Creek. The combined camp then moved farther south to the Medicine Lodge Creek in southern Kansas. They had high hopes for moving out of the range of the troops.

Black Kettle sent a scout to find William, seeking his advice. After Lean Bear's murder, the Cheyennes dared not travel roads or approach troops, especially after the Dog Soldiers' retaliation on the Platte River. The Dog Soldiers had closed the road to Denver due to their attacks, causing general panic among the whites. Black Kettle hoped William could use his influence to stop the fighting.

The messenger from Black Kettle found William just east of Fort Lyon, riding at the head of his wagon train bound for Westport and St. Louis. William had heard of the attack on Black Kettle and Lean Bear. As always, he worried about where George and Charley were but was relieved when he heard that they had stayed on the Smoky Hill River.

Understanding how dangerous things were getting, William immediately changed his plans. Leaving Robert with the caravan, he sent a message that he would meet Black Kettle at the Arapaho camp on Coon Creek, near Fort Larned, on about June 5.[171]

In his role as diplomat between the Cheyennes and the white authorities, William arrived at the meeting point to find George was already there with the Indians. William discussed the war with Black Kettle. He felt that Lieutenant Eayre had exceeded his authority, and he urged the Indians to remain calm and give him time to ride the two hundred miles to Fort Leavenworth to confer with departmental commander Major General Samuel Curtis about Eayre's egregious behavior.

However, when William arrived back at Fort Lyon, he learned that Colonel John Chivington, commander of the Colorado Military District, would soon arrive to lead an expedition against the Cheyennes. He changed his plans again. He returned to Coon Creek to get George, and they rode to Fort Lyon to try to reason with Chivington. Father and son both understood that Chivington was dangerous to the Indians.

William knew Chivington as the hellfire preacher who had arrived in Denver in 1860 to be the presiding elder of a Methodist Church. Wearing Colt revolvers while preaching, he became a representative of what was called "muscular Christianity." With the First Colorado Volunteer Regiment, he won fame battling the Confederates at Apache Canyon, March 28, 1862. Following the Union victory in the Battle of Glorieta Pass, he succeeded to the command of the Colorado Military District. In concert with Colorado Governor John Evans, his ambitions were focused on statehood for Colorado and, for himself, a seat in the House of Representatives or the Senate. He believed he needed one more popular victory against rebels or redskins.

After five days of hard riding, William and George came within sight of the Arkansas River. George, still dressed as a Cheyenne warrior, went to William's ranch to avoid the roads and troops. William rode on to Fort Lyon to meet with Chivington.

William knew the man and his ambitions to be a

Congressman—both knew that, in Colorado, there was no better way to win an election than to take a hard line against the Indians. In the meeting William argued for peace, warning of great destruction if the forces of hate and revenge were released. Until this time, the plains tribes had never acted jointly against the white men. It was only a matter of time until they figured out that they would have greater strength in numbers against their common enemy. William later testified that he told Chivington that the Indians wanted peace. "In reply he [Chivington] said he was not authorized to make peace, and that he was then on the warpath—I think were the words he used."[172]

William argued that there was a great risk in continuing the fighting, because many government supply trains were vulnerable and there were a great many citizens, travelers, and settlers without protection.

Chivington replied that, "[T]he citizens would have to protect themselves."[173] For Chivington, the stakes were too high for withdrawal. William gave up trying to convince Chivington to consider peace. Frustrated, William returned to his stockade on the Purgatoire.[174]

William told his family that Chivington was a dangerous enemy of the Cheyennes and of the Bents. Chivington saw himself as the hand of God and that killing Indians was God's work. He especially felt that killing George would be a blow against the Indians and the Confederacy. "William warned George to stay far away from this man and his troops."[175] The warning proved prophetic.

George spent some time with his family at the ranch, recuperating from their hard ride and discussing the complications of this nearing war. Robert was in Westport with the caravan. Charley was believed to be on the Republican with his mother, Yellow Woman, and raiding with the Dog Soldiers. Yellow Woman had left William several years before, and William could not control Charley or her. Julia was with her husband in the Indian camps. Mary and Robert were with William. George was glad to see Island, but he noticed she seemed quiet when around William. The family was seriously in the thick of these unsettled times.[176]

George remained at the ranch while Black Kettle camped with the Kiowas and Comanches on Medicine Lodge Creek. They were holding sun dances and making medicine. They did not make any raids, but between the Arkansas and Platte were some large camps of Cheyennes and Sioux that remained hostile to the army. The peace chiefs could not control all the Indians, so some fought and some moved to areas where they thought they could camp in peace.

As George languished at the ranch and heard of raids where warriors were counting coups and gaining prestige, he became restless. The pull of battle was strong.

Concerned with the growing unrest among the Indians, on June 27, 1864, Governor Evans of Colorado issued a proclamation urging peaceful Indians to go to places of safety. They would be fed by the troops. His intent was to separate hostiles from peace Indians. Cheyennes and Arapahos were to come to Fort Lyon, Kiowas and Comanches to Fort Larned.

William thought this was a good idea. He tirelessly rode out in June and July, carrying some of the proclamations for delivery to the Indian camps and translating them. It was a dangerous, two-hundred-forty-mile trip. He refused a military escort because he believed that would likely draw a fight. No civilian would travel with him for fear of the palpable hostility among the Indians. So he rode out alone, knowing that he was offering a real temptation to young braves seeking glory, but he was dedicated to finding that elusive peace which would protect his children who were among the tribes. He wanted to find a peace that would allow mixed-blood offspring of the frontier to have a life in the white world or the Indian world, as they chose.

When Black Kettle's village was moving north to the Smoky Hill in July, they got word that serious raiding by the Sioux and Dog Soldiers had begun on the Platte. Several war parties decided to join the fight. The Platte Valley was an area rich in targets due to the increased building of stage lines, with stations every ten or twelve miles and daily coaches carrying mail. It was also a great emigrant and wagon-freighting route. The war parties of Cheyennes and Sioux attacked and burned ranches and stage stations, ran off stock, and forced freighters to corral their wagons and fight.

George left the quiet of the Purgatoire ranch for the excitement of joining his kinsmen on the Solomon Fork in what is now Kansas. Cheyennes, Arapahos, Sioux, and Dog Soldiers were camped there in one of the largest camps George had seen. And the camp was full of plunder, alive with celebration for the warriors' successes. Tipis overflowed with a profusion of the wealth. The raids seemed like appropriate retaliation for the unprovoked attack on the Dog Soldiers at Fremont's Orchard and Lieutenant Eayre's murder of Lean Bear. George soon heard of Dog Soldier and Lakota combined attacks on the Platte and the Little Blue Rivers. In just ten days of August, the raiders killed fifty-one whites and wounded nine. They had captured seven women and children. George realized that the conflict was no longer just about raiding for plunder and ponies. It had become "an indiscriminate war on all whites, not just the soldiers."[177] The attitudes of the tribes were changing.

He referred to the raids of July and August as terrible affairs. "[T]he Indians were wild people in those days; they had been attacked again and again by the troops without any cause, and they were retaliating in the only way they knew how."[178] That wildness called to him.

The chiefs decided to attack the Platte River Bridge, a vital crossing on the Oregon Trail. George, however, joined a party of young men who could not wait for the organized attack and for weeks they raided on the Oregon Trail, attacking ranches, stage stations, and army outposts. "His break with the white world was now complete—there could be no turning back."[179] He would fight to avenge injustices.

After several days of fighting with war parties, George and Charley rode north to join the main Cheyenne camp. George was very interested in participating in the scalp dances, for these were opportunities to meet young women. The great village was too large to remain intact for long. The main village broke up and went to hunt buffalo while the war parties renewed attacks on the white man's roads to the south.

That summer General Robert Mitchell, with a strong force of cavalry, could not catch the Indians, who kept out of the reach of troops. The Indians were great hit-and-run warriors, taking advantage of their mobility and their knowledge of the land. This summer of hardship on the plains put pressure on the government to solve the problems of violence and stress on commerce. When the road to Denver was closed, east-west communications were cut off, supplies to Denver and the area were cut off, and shortages in Colorado caused an outcry against the Indians and the military ineptitude. In Denver the price of flour per 100 pounds went from $9 to $16 then to $25. After a plague of grasshoppers ruined Colorado crops, famine in Colorado became a real threat. Not until September was the road re-opened for travel.

Major Edward Wynkoop was in charge of troops at Fort Lyon, having been appointed in May by Colonel Chivington. Wynkoop had a somewhat checkered career, beginning as a land speculator, treading a line between law and lawlessness, and finally joining the army on July 31, 1861, when he answered the call from Governor Evans for volunteers to form two companies for the Colorado Volunteers. Wynkoop entered the service as a second lieutenant but was soon promoted. He fought with Chivington at the Battle of Glorieta Pass in 1862 that destroyed the Confederate supply train, leading to a decisive defeat for the Confederates in the West.

Wynkoop reached Fort Lyon on May 8, 1864. The sandstone garrison now included Bent's New Fort that William had built in 1853 and sold to the government in 1859. The complex was named Fort Lyon in 1862. Wynkoop found the local Cheyennes were peaceful and was more focused on the threat of a new Confederate invasion of the Southwest. However, he knew that the fort was vulnerable to Indian attack. As tensions with the tribes mounted throughout 1864, he ordered that no liquor was to be sold to the Indians. He also ordered that if George Bent—known as William Bent's Cheyenne son—appeared, he was to be arrested.

To further complicate all this fighting and working for peace, William continued to be plagued by issues regarding the rights of the Indians to their land. The ownership rights of the Indians were based on the various treaties that the government had negotiated with the Indians, but no enforcement of those rights was provided as immigrants perpetually moved onto the land illegally. There seemed to be no answers in this constant strife.

William also had domestic problems that summer. Island, George's stepmother, had run off with one of William's traders, Jo Barraldo. Among the Cheyennes, if a woman was unhappy in her marriage she could simply pile a man's belongings outside the teepee, and he had to gather up his things and leave in humiliation. Since she was living at the stockade and not in a lodge, she just left; she could hardly throw out William. She joined a war party of twenty-three warriors. Often women rode along with extra horses for carrying plunder on the return trip.

This had to be a painful blow for William—Island had stood by the Bent family for many years after Owl Woman's death. In a letter to Indian Agent Samuel Colley, William wrote:

> I am not in a very good humor, as my old squaw ran off a few days ago, or rather went off with Jo. Barraldo, as she like him better than she did me. If I ever get sight of the young man, it will go hard with him.[180]

Among these mounting troubles, William knew that Samuel Colley's Indian agency was corrupt and that the annuities for the Indians were being sold by the agency. He could not blame Black Kettle for taking his people away from the agency, where they were expected to buy their own goods.

George and Charley were special worries because they were riding with the Cheyennes in the north. When the Cheyennes came south in response to William's summons, William found his sons George and Charley camped with them near Fort Larned.

Tirelessly William negotiated between the chiefs and the commander of Fort Larned, drunken Captain [first name unknown] Permeter, described by one officer as a "habitual, beastly, debased, demoralsed [sic] and brutalized drunkard."[181] The chiefs suspended negotiations, angered by the insulting Permeter.

William warned the officers at the fort to keep a special eye on Satanta, the Kiowa chief, who was touchy, surly, and aggressive. Then he sought out his sons and urged them to return to the Purgatoire. Charley refused to have anything to do with returning among white men, but George agreed.

William and George had hardly headed homeward when the incidents William feared shattered his work. Satanta's touchy behavior resulted in shooting a man in the arm. Once again William's ability to gauge the temperament of individual Indians, as he did with Satanta, was accurate.

The Kiowas arrived to camp near Fort Larned expecting sanctuary. Left Hand, a friendly Arapaho chief camped nearby with a band of Cheyennes, warned Captain Parmeter that the Kiowas intended to run off the posts' horse herd. Captain Parmeter ignored the warning and the Kiowas ran off the horses. The Cheyenne-Arapaho alliance was dismayed at this breach of faith. They were mindful of their promises to William. They had come in to Fort Larned for sanctuary and now that was threatened. The next day Left Hand rode toward the fort with a white flag, intending to offer to get the herd back. The nervous troops fired at him and the frightened Indians camped nearby scattered, no longer feeling protected.

With this disrespect of the white flag, once again the Indians had proof that the white man spoke with a "crooked tongue." Many of the Cheyennes and Arapahos gave up on negotiating. When they met Sioux runners from the Republican River, they found out that Indians there had been raiding the overland stage on the

Platte. They moved to the camps on the Republican to join those raids. Every possible motive had been given the Indians to induce them to fight and raid—and many that summer did just that.

Things were so chaotic that it was difficult for anyone to know who was fighting who and when. Cheyenne and Arapaho war parties, who had gone north, attacked ranches, stages, and wagons in a wide area on the South Platte and into Nebraska. The Lakotas and Kiowas had joined the war. Yet Black Kettle and his people stayed in the refuge of the south.

White people could be hit anywhere and at any time, a very intimidating prospect. The summer of 1864 was a very dangerous summer on the Plains. On the seventeenth of July Indians ran off stock on the South Platte, at the Bijou Ranch, the Junction Ranch, and Murray's Ranch, killing seven men in the process. On August 7, Kiowas attacked a train near Fort Lyon, and made an attack on the Cimarron, killing five men.[182]

That same day, the Kiowa leader Satanta even came to William's ranch. Though he claimed to come in peace, he said he wanted the Indian Agent Samuel Colley. William and George sensed Satanta was after blood. Much as William disliked Colley, he did not reveal the agent's whereabouts. The Kiowas rode off in anger.[183] This incident was an eye-opener for George, who for the first time had to realize that even his family was caught in a dangerous place. Many other farmers and ranchers in Colorado abandoned their properties and rode for the safety of Denver.

During the summer, an estimated two hundred travelers and settlers were killed, many isolated ranches were burned, and women were captured and abused. Terror swept Colorado towns as the Indians' pent-up anger and need for revenge was exacted against small groups. The Indian camps were nightly sustained in their thirst for revenge by scalp dances, and the daily stories of Indians with overflowing plunder sounded like a tempting way to fight the white intrusion.

Early in August 1864, Governor Evans issued another proclamation—abrogating his June announcement—in which he:

> . . . advised parties of citizens to hunt down the Indians and to kill every hostile they might meet. The result of this . . . was to put the friendly Indians at the mercy of any revengeful emigrant who had been attacked by hostiles, and any man who coveted an Indian's pony or other property could shoot him as a hostile and seize the property as his lawful prize.[184]

It was a summer of broken promises, violence, and destruction. The earlier proclamation had promised safety to Indians who came in to the forts, but now even they could be attacked. The rhetoric had changed.

It is telling that racism had reached such violent proportions in the East and in the West in 1864, despite distance and differences in the circumstances. Southern economic interests wanted to preserve slavery, while in the West manifest destiny sought the economic interests of land and minerals. Many had to pay a high price for these economic drives—especially families that were split.

George, like the other young men, thirsted for honor, status, riches, and to gain the attention of the young women. He was ready to war on Pawnees, Crows, and Utes. But warring on whites was another matter. He had lived with them, gone to school and church with them, shared their lives in Westport and St. Louis. His father was white. Was he now to kill these people? We can only imagine the pain and struggle with such divided loyalties. He loved people on both sides.

Charley resolved these conflicting loyalties by renouncing his whiteness. That Charley had been seen during the raids no doubt made life difficult for William.

> [William] and Black Kettle had always worked for peace. . . . For any Bent—to be seen riding with the raiders would undermine William's lifelong efforts to secure peace on the Arkansas River. . . . If a Bent joined the raiders, then it might be supposed that Black Kettle, too, condoned war.[185]

The dilemma had no good answer, and the choice was not as clear for George as it was for Charley. Chivington had already labeled George a renegade half-breed and Confederate agent. And among the Indians, George had risked censure when he helped Nancy Morton, a white captive, who was injured. He saw to it she was doctored and brought her to Island's lodge, where she was made as comfortable as possible. George did not want to be a part of a war on white women and children, so he risked condemnation from the Indians.

Fighting white soldiers was another matter. In mid-August a running fight between some Lakota buffalo hunters and Captain Edward B. Murphy and his troops of the Seventh Iowa Cavalry came right to the outskirts of the large Cheyenne camp on the Solomon River. George joined other Indians to chase the white troops for miles, until their ponies tired. George was glad to be part of this victory, his first against the whites as a Cheyenne warrior. Among the Indians each man fought for himself, unlike what George had seen when he fought in the Civil War. Warriors attacked again and again with war cries that panicked the troops and their horses. Traditionally the objective was not to kill as much as to demonstrate superiority. Each warrior sought personal honors, coups, horses, and scalps.

But George still had to deal with inner conflict. William and George were resolving their personal issues in ways that seemed at odds. William never quit hoping for peace, but George was drawn to his mother's people, their way of life, and the need to defend good people that he believed were being wronged.

William tried again to influence the Cheyennes toward peace. Unable to travel himself, he sent a letter to the chiefs. When the letter arrived, the chiefs asked George and Ed Guerrier to translate and then to write the response. William wanted the chiefs to come to Fort Lyon to negotiate a peace. The letter was both conciliatory and demanding. He asked that the Cheyennes exert their influence with other tribes. They would all exchange prisoners.

After hearing the letter, the chiefs held a council and decided to try to meet with the whites to attain peace. They asked George and Ed Guerrier to write two letters—one to the commandant, Major Wynkoop, at Fort Lyon and the other to Mr. Samuel G. Colley, agent for the Cheyennes and Arapahos. The letters were dated August 29, 1864, and signed, "Black Kettle and other chiefs."[186]

Their ultimatum was that peace also be made with the Kiowas, Comanches, Arapahos, Prairie Apaches, and Sioux. Only then would they be interested. They wanted peace for their whole alliance. They also offered an exchange of prisoners. After their spring and summer raids, they spoke from a position of strength.

On September 4, Lieutenant George Hawkins intercepted the return messengers, Lone Bear and Eagle Head, and brought them to Major Wynkoop. He was furious. Chivington had issued orders to fire on any Indians they saw and not to be encumbered with prisoners. Hawkins had judged that these Indians were not warlike, and Lone Bear was waving a paper that should be investigated. When Wynkoop questioned Lone Bear about his understanding that he could have been shot as he approached the fort, Lone Bear replied, "I thought I would be killed, but I knew that paper would be found upon my dead body, that you would see it, and it might give peace to my people once more."[187] Eagle Head expressed a similar devotion to their errand.

Wynkoop later wrote, "I was bewildered with an exhibition of such patriotism on the part of two savages, and felt myself in the presence of superior beings; and these were the representatives of a race that I had heretofore looked upon without exception as being cruel, treacherous, and bloodthirsty."[188] He had not expected such courage and nobility from a race he had thought to be without feelings or affection.

Wynkoop felt he should act fast to recover the white captives, and he didn't wait for orders but acted on his own authority. Troops were in the field and might attack the Cheyennes at any moment—and captives would be killed if there was an attack. He left a note for Chivington and on September 6, 1864, he rode for the Smoky Hill camps with over one hundred men, hoping to recover the captives and maybe bring peace through his efforts to meet with the Indians. This was not enough men to counter warring Indians, but Wynkoop, acting outside the chain of command, was intent on parlaying with the Indians for the return of captives.[189]

When he arrived near the camp, he encountered about seven hundred warriors. This was the largest number of plains Indians ever to confront United States troops, and they were prepared to fight if necessary.

Wynkoop thought he would be wiped out, but Lone Bear arranged a parlay. George was called on to interpret, and even Wynkoop relied on George for accuracy.

When the Indians asked why he came with troops and cannons, Wynkoop told them he was prepared to defend himself if there was treachery. The Indians accepted that, and the parlay continued with Cheyenne representatives Black Kettle, Big Wolf, White Antelope, Dog Man, and Bull Bear, as well as Arapahos Left Hand, Little Raven, Neva, and Big Mouth. Though some of the chiefs who spoke were very militant, Lone Bear and Black Kettle said they should keep their word—they had called Wynkoop to the meeting, assuring his safety. They advised Wynkoop to withdraw to a safe place while they arranged for the exchange of captives. Three days later the chiefs arrived at Wynkoop's camp with the captives they had at that location. Their behavior again was honorable—especially for "savages."

After the parlay Wynkoop felt that in Black Kettle he "had found a soul mate, someone who would join him on the precarious boundary between the races."[190]

Wynkoop suggested that the tribal leaders go with him to talk to the Great Father in Denver, where peace could be made and they could then return safely to their camps, while the rest of the Indians could remain camped on the Smoky Hill. Black Kettle, White Antelope, Bull Bear, and One-Eye represented the Cheyennes, while Neva, Bosse, Heaps-of-Buffalo, and Notanee agreed to go for the Arapahos. They hoped to meet with the governor and military authorities and secure a peace.

Wynkoop returned to Fort Lyon with his returned captives. He then loaded the chiefs in army wagons and took them to Denver. The caravan arrived on September 28 and, motivated by curiosity, all of Denver greeted it. At first Governor Evans refused to have anything to do with talking to the chiefs. Wynkoop begged, and Evans replied to his overtures saying coldly, "But what shall I do with the Third Colorado Regiment if I make peace?

They have been raised to kill Indians, and they must kill Indians."[191] This regiment was largely comprised of Coloradoans who wanted to avoid the draft for fighting in the East; battling a few poorly armed Indians was much preferred.

However, since the Indians had traveled four hundred miles to see him, Evans finally agreed to parlay. The council was held at Camp Weld, near Denver. Both Evans and Chivington gave the Indians the runaround and made no commitment to peace. Evans told the chiefs they were in the hands of the military, so he couldn't provide peace. And Colonel Chivington wouldn't tell them if they could have peace or not.

> At the Denver council Evans scolded the chiefs for not having gone into the forts in accord with his proclamation. Rightly or wrongly, the Indians—and William Bent—interpreted this as meaning that if they now reported to the forts they would be fed and protected in spite of their warfare during the summer.[192]

When they returned to Fort Lyon, Wynkoop told them to bring their people close to the fort and they would be protected. The Cheyennes and Arapahos believed that they were under the military's protection, and they were willing to comply with the directives on where they could camp.

Wynkoop was operating under the illusion that he had arranged peace, but Governor Evans and Colonel Chivington still thought it was important that the war not be ended until the volunteers had achieved a major victory against the Indians. They also accused Wynkoop of letting the Indians run Fort Lyon and of trying to negotiate peace without authority. Wynkoop was later judged by the *Rocky Mountain News*, articulating the pro-Chivington view, to have had no right to try to negotiate peace. Soon he was replaced by Major Scott Anthony, a member of the Colorado Volunteers who was not sympathetic to Black Kettle. As a result of scurvy, Anthony's eyes were red, so the Arapahos described him as an unfriendly, little red-eyed soldier chief.

George didn't go to Denver with Wynkoop and the chiefs but joined his Crooked Lance brothers in the long-awaited departure of a raiding party against the Pawnees. He rode in a party of five to the Republican River, where they expected the Pawnees to be camped. However, the Pawnees had moved; disappointed, they returned to the Cheyenne camp on the Smoky Hill.

In their absence, the camp had been attacked by Major Scott Anthony and Major General James G. Blunt. For three days the warriors had held the military off while their families moved away from the soldiers.

Black Kettle, as peace chief of his band, did not lead war parties. He recognized that the Indians didn't really have a chance to survive unless they could live with the white men, with their superior arms and numbers. With assurances from Wynkoop that they would be safe, Black Kettle once again led his people south.

All involved believed that any tribe that surrendered in good faith would be protected. For his part, William kept in contact with military authorities and civilian traders at Fort Lyon. He was convinced that peace was attainable and that his family—George, Island, Julia, and Charley—and family friends would be safe in Black Kettle's camp.

Endnotes

154. Lavender, *Bent's Fort*, 372 - 373.
155. Halaas & Masich, *Halfbreed*, 86.

156. Ibid, 93.

157. Grinnell, *The Fighting Cheyennes*, 130.

158. Halaas & Masich, *Halfbreed*, 100.

159. Sarah Herndon, *Days on the Road Crossing the Plains in 1865* (London: endeavor Press Ltd., 2016. Kindle Edition), July 2, Loc. 1188.

160. Connell, *Son of the Morning Star*, 64.

161. Halaas & Masich, *Halfbreed*, 108.

162. Ibid, 109.

163. Ibid, 112.

164. G. Hyde, *Life of George Bent*, 121.

165. Ibid, 127.

166. Ibid, 134.

167. Ibid, 136.

168. Grinnell, *The Fighting Cheyennes*, 145 - 146.

169. G. Hyde, *Life of George Bent*, 132.

170. Grinnell, *The Fighting Cheyennes*, 142.

171. Halaas & Masich, *Halfbreed*, 119. Lavender, *Bent's Fort*, 377.

172. Dee Brown, *Bury My Heart at Wounded Knee*, 73.

173. Ibid, 74.

174. Lavender, *Bent's Fort*, 377 - 378.

175. Halaas & Masich, *Halfbreed*, 122.

176. Ibid.

177. Ibid, 127.

178. G. Hyde, *Life of George Bent*, 139.

179. Halaas & Masich, *Halfbreed*, 180.

180. Ibid, 125 - 126.

181. Ibid, 125.

182. Grinnell, *The Fighting Cheyennes*, 154.

183. Halaas & Masich, *Halfbreed*, 126.

184. Grinnell, *The Fighting Cheyennes*, 154.

185. Halaas & Masich, *Halfbreed*, 128.

186. G. Hyde, *Life of George Bent*, 142.

187. Halaas & Masich, *Halfbreed*, 134. Louis Kraft, *Ned Wynkoop, and the Lonely Road From Sand Creek* (Norman: University of Oklahoma Press, 2015), 107. Attributed to an Indian named One Eye.

188. Kraft, *Ned Wynkoop*, 107.

189. Halaas & Masich, *Halfbreed*, 134.

190. Kraft, *Ned Wynkoop*, 111 - 112.

191. Dee Brown, *Bury My Heart at Wounded Knee*, 79.

192. Lavender, *Bent's Fort*, 382.

10 ∾ THE SAND CREEK MASSACRE

THE PROMISE OF PEACE was short lived. Shortly after Major Anthony assured the Indians they should return to their camp and he would notify them if he got instructions to negotiate, Colonel Chivington issued marching orders to his militia. General Curtis, commander of the district, wrote to Chivington, "I want no peace until the Indians have suffered more."[193] No effort was made to cooperate with Governor Evans's assurances of safety for those who came in to the forts, despite the Indians efforts to comply.

Six hundred fifty-two Arapahos moved near Fort Lyon as directed under Evans's June proclamation, and they surrendered their arms to Major Anthony, now in command. But after just ten days, Major Anthony gruffly told the Indians he could not provide for them. He returned their weapons and told them to go hunt buffalo. These Arapahos, under Left Hand and Little Raven, joined Black Kettle's village of about six or seven hundred Cheyennes that had moved to Sand Creek, about forty miles northeast of Fort Lyon. The women in the village numbered five hundred; that there were only two hundred men in camp suggests that most of the younger warriors were still raiding, hunting, and not ready for submission. The Dog Soldiers especially remained hostile and would never submit to military authority. Their suspicions about the true state of affairs between the tribes and the military would soon be proven.

Both Colonel Chivington and Major Anthony seemed to deliberately mask their intentions to lull the Indians into a false sense of security. George wrote to George Hyde in his letters:

> The truth probably was that he [Chivington] had already laid his plans for the attack on our camp . . . so in his talk he said nothing to alarm the chiefs or to disturb their belief that peace was soon to be concluded. He was careful . . . to make no promises.[194]

The chiefs were confused by the double talk and could not comprehend Chivington's intentions. Most of the Arapahos moved further south of the Arkansas for safety, but some stayed with Black Kettle's camp. They warned the Cheyennes at Sand Creek of Anthony's duplicity. Black Kettle and a delegation rode to Fort Lyon to reach out to Major Anthony, seeking a peaceful arrangement, as they had been led to believe was the plan.

Anthony told them he had no authority to negotiate terms. He sent them back to their camp to wait for instructions, but Anthony never asked headquarters for such instructions. Instead he gave the location of the village to district headquarters. He said he would attack if he had sufficient troops. Chivington had every intention of attacking the Sand Creek camp before his one-hundred-day volunteers fulfilled their enlistments. They were spoiling for a fight against the camp.

In the meantime, George Bent had returned to the Purgatoire ranch, but when all seemed quiet, he decided to visit Black Kettle's camp at Sand Creek. He found his brother Charley and his sister Julia there. William had no objection to George visiting the camp where everyone anticipated peace.

Chivington gathered his force of First and Third Colorado Cavalry Volunteers about November 20. These were not real soldiers. The worst class of frontier whites made up the troop—toughs, gamblers, "bad-men," miners from mining camps, and bull-whackers. They were an undisciplined mob eager to kill Indians.

As he traveled down the Arkansas, Chivington stopped all traffic and guarded every settlement so the Indians would not know of his approach. Three days after George left the ranch, on November 24, twenty dragoons rode into the stockade. They were there to threaten the Bents and to keep anyone from warning the Indians of their movements.

When Jim Beckwourth, the guide who was leading Chivington, proved incompetent to the task, Chivington didn't trust the Indian-friendly old mountain man. He ordered William's son Robert to guide him to the Cheyenne and Arapaho camps at Sand Creek or he would kill him. Chivington further coerced Robert by holding the Bents (Mary, her husband, and William) at the ranch. It must have been a horror for Robert to be leading these killers toward the camp where George, Charles, Julia, his step-mother, aunts, cousins, and friends slept, while not wanting to threaten the rest of the family by not complying.

Though William couldn't know for sure where Chivington and his troops were headed, he feared for his three children who were camped with Black Kettle—and now a fourth sibling would be in harm's way.

Chivington had been planning to attack for weeks.

> When Chivington organized this attack [Sand
> Creek], using the First and Third Cavalry,
> several junior officers protested that the
> Cheyennes had been given assurances of
> safety. Chivington . . . grew furious. He threat-
> ened these dissidents, shoved a fist at Lt.
> Joseph Cramer, and roared: "I have come to
> kill Indians, and believe it is right and honor-
> able to use any means under God's heaven to
> kill Indians!"[195]

He was also heard to say, "I long to be wading in gore!"[196]

Many of the people on the frontier felt more or less
the same. The population in general agreed that the
Indians deserved more punishment. Obviously, despite
the efforts of men like William Bent and Black Kettle to
settle a peace, there were still aggressive feelings toward
the Indians with no concern for discussion.

On November 28, Chivington surprised Major
Anthony at Fort Lyon. There was no way for Anthony
to know that Chivington was making this move. Major
Anthony objected to Chivington's revealed plan to attack the Indians because he felt Chivington was going
to cause a new outbreak of raiding and that there
weren't enough troops to handle a concerted outbreak.
Chivington, though, secured the fort to keep anyone
from warning the Indians. He prevailed and forced
Anthony and part of his garrison to join in the expedition. That evening a force of almost a thousand men
(seven hundred and fifty were Chivington's volunteers)
marched all night through deep snow and bitter cold to
reach the area of the Indian village before dawn. About
six hundred Indians were camped at Sand Creek; two-
thirds were women and children. Most of the warriors
were away hunting buffalo.

©Camilla Kattell

The site of the Sand Creek Massacre
Down below the bluff the Indians were camped along the
creek. Troops attacked from the left and the Indians that
got away scattered up the creek bed. This site is sacred to
the Indians and is protected and managed by the National
Park Service.

©Camilla Kattell

As dawn approached Chivington apparently suspected that Robert wasn't leading them to the camp. He rode beside Robert and slapped his revolver saying, "I haven't had an Indian to eat for a long time. If you fool with me and don't lead me to that camp, I'll have you for breakfast."[197]

George had arrived at Sand Creek November 26, 1864. More than one hundred Cheyenne lodges stretched for over a mile along the creek. There were also about ten lodges of Arapahos. These were the most white-friendly of all the Indians. This location was a traditional camping ground for both tribes. Women, children, and men settled into their usual peace-time pursuits, and the village took on an air of normality. Feeling assured of peace, there was no need for camp guards—just sleepy boys watching the herds.

In the early dawn light Chivington's men spotted the Indian pony herd and some moved to cut off the herd on the bluff from the lodges below. The cannons were prepared to fire.

As several women were starting their early morning chores they heard the noise of the approaching soldiers and gave the alarm. At sunrise on the 29th George awakened to the sound of rumbling hooves. He rushed outside to see what was happening and saw soldiers trotting in columns of four, heading straight for the village. George knew what this formation meant. There was total chaos and confusion on the part of the Indians as the troops rode toward the camp.

George saw Black Kettle—believing the camp was under government protection—outside his lodge with the American flag raised atop a long pole; he waved a white flag of surrender.

> At the treaty of Fort Wise in 1861 the Commissioner of Indian Affairs had presented Black

Kettle with an American flag and told him that if it flew above his lodge the village would be safe. Not unreasonably, therefore, when Chivington's militia swept toward him, he wished to make sure this flag was not overlooked. It is said to have been a large garrison flag.[198]

George recalled seeing Black Kettle waving the flag atop a long pole.

Both Black Kettle and White Antelope had traveled to Washington in 1863 and believed they were firm friends of the whites. Convinced they could not be attacked like this, Black Kettle called for the people to be calm. "Don't be afraid! There is no danger! The soldiers will not hurt you!"[199] When he belatedly realized the danger, he called for the people to run. White Antelope and Black Kettle had led the people here and the people had trusted their judgment. They had given their word that it was safe. We can only imagine their shock.

Elderly White Antelope, who had been among the first Cheyenne visitors to William's first stockade on the Arkansas thirty years before, seeing the soldiers shooting into the lodges decided to live no longer. He had been telling his people for months that the whites were good and peace was coming. He stood by his lodge and sang his death song, "Nothing lives long, Only the earth and the mountains."[200] The soldiers shot him down.

Yellow Wolf, another chief who was over eighty years old, was shot down. Chief One-Eye and Arapaho chief Left Hand were both killed. Warriors that could get to their arms fought bravely to protect the village, but the fleeing Cheyennes could offer little resistance as they awakened to chaos.

George ran west toward the high ground and joined other men who were trying to get to the horses so they could fight. When he looked back toward the village he witnessed a horrifying sight that he would never forget. He saw the soldiers galloping through the camp firing at women and children and the people too old to run. The warriors were all but helpless to fight back. Soldiers gunning down men, women, and children were committing unthinkable atrocities. Only the strongest and fastest were able to run for some cover away from the village. The screams of women, children, and constant gunfire carried the sound of the horror of the slaughter.

A bullet slammed into George's hip as he found Black Kettle still alive in the creek bed under a bluff. Together they made their way up the creek bed for about two miles, using the embankments for cover. They were besieged there by the troops throughout the day. The carnage they had witnessed left the impression that no one would survive.

As George lay in hiding he could hear the soldier's orders and conversations. How he hated them as he listened to them talk like they were hunters after cornered game. During much of his life, especially during his time in the East, George had known white arrogance and smug superiority. No doubt this was a seminal experience for George. His allegiance to white or Indian had to have taken a large shift at that moment. He would live as an Indian for the rest of his life.

As the soldiers adjusted the positioning of their two mountain howitzers, George, the former artilleryman, could judge how much danger they were effectively generating. He could tell that their shots were going wild and they were cutting their fuses too short. He believed if some of the people could survive until it got dark, they might live.

On a high bluff Colonel Chivington sat watching the bloodbath below. Robert Bent sat beside him. Black

Kettle's six-by-twelve American flag above his lodge was in plain view. Now Robert saw and watched the soldiers attack his mother's people and his brothers and sister.

> The twenty-five-year-old Bent witnessed horrors he would never forget. He saw women run out and tear their clothes off to show their sex. As they begged for mercy the soldiers shot them down. He saw a woman whose leg had been shattered by a shell fragment hold up her arm as protection from a saber-wielding soldier. The saber blow broke her arm. The woman rolled over and raised her other arm. The saber came down again, breaking that one, too. As she moaned in pain, the soldier looked down impassively, then rode off. He saw a group of women, huddled in a sandpit, send a six-year-old girl with a white flag toward the soldiers. The child had only walked a short way when the soldiers shot her. Then they turned their guns on the women and killed them all. He saw men, women, and children scalped and mutilated. He saw an unborn child cut from her mother's womb and deliberately laid beside her body. He saw infants killed in their mother's arms. . . . He saw White Antelope dead, his genitals and ears cut off. . . . And he saw Charley taken prisoner, the soldiers looking for an excuse to shoot him.[201]

Months later Robert described the atrocities that he witnessed during an investigation of the massacre. He remembered Black Kettle calling to his people to not be afraid as they were awakened at dawn with bullets whizzing through the camp and as utter chaos prevailed. His testimony was corroborated by Lieutenant James Connor: "The descriptions of brutal carnage in the pages of the congressional hearings held on the matter reflect depravity by any definition."[202] The details he provided sickened anyone reading his description of what he saw the blood-aroused volunteers do to the helpless. People who lived as witnesses of such brutality must have suffered from terrible emotional stress for the rest of their lives.

One of the few officers who challenged Chivington's methods that day was Captain Silas S. Soule. Soule retained control of his men that day and did not participate in the slaughter. He also defied Chivington in the matter of prisoners. Chivington had ordered that no prisoners would be taken. Only two had—a mixed-blood named Jack Smith, and Charley Bent. Luckily for Charley, a Mexican scout recognized him and captured him and took him to Captain Soule. Soule, having stood up to Chivington already, asked Chivington if he could take Charley back to Fort Lyon as a prisoner with the wounded. Chivington was furious with Soule's conduct on the field that day and had threatened Charley with a bullet to the head. However, deciding he wanted the rebellious Soule out of the way, Chivington eventually gave Soule his permission to take Charley to Fort Lyon. Soule had saved Charley's life. Jack Smith was not so fortunate. They executed him. Charley, however, was released to William's custody. He was a very lucky young man to be alive.

Chivington called off the slaughter of so many defenseless people in the afternoon, and as night fell the soldiers drew away. Survivors began to realize it was time to leave. Black Kettle had earlier crawled back to where he last thought his wife lay. His wife was shot and seemed dead, so he left her. After dark, Black Kettle went back again to try to find his wife's body. He found her with many wounds but still alive. He carried her on his back to where the others had grouped. When she had fallen the soldiers rode up and shot her multiple times. She too told her story to the peace commissioner's investigation in 1865.

The wounded had sought refuge by hiding all day in frigid holes they scraped out of the sandy creek bank. In the night, once they felt the soldiers weren't coming back, the wounded and underdressed survivors slowly and painfully retreated up the creek—men, women, and children. It was a bitterly cold night, and many were only half clad as they had been rousted from their sleep by the attack. Through the bitter November night, survivors had no food, water, heat, or medicines. Many who had lost loved ones went back down the ravine and looked for their people. A few still alive were found and carried along. In the night, as they escaped into the prairie, they called out to help guide any other survivors who were wandering around.

George said it was the worst night he ever knew. The wounded suffered terribly. The wind sweeping the prairie created horrible wind-chill temperatures. Some tried to burn grass to keep the children warm. They continued walking to the east to try to keep from freezing. After a time they encountered some of their men who had gone out to tend the herd before the attack and who, when they heard the soldiers' gunfire, had escaped with some horses. They loaded the worst of the wounded, including George, on the horses and all—about a hundred people—headed for camps on the Smoky Hill, fifty miles away. There was nowhere else to go for help.

A few men escaped and raced through the cold night bareback, on sweaty horses, fearing for their families, determined to seek help from those encamped on the Smoky Hill. Men from the Smoky Hill village immediately set out on the return trip, carrying blankets, robes, and food. Soon after dawn they arrived and got the survivors mounted, clothed, and fed. Late in the day they made it to the Cheyenne village, where the people saw to their every need. Everyone chipped in to provide shelter and anything else that was needed. The Indians were very communal. "All the camp was weeping. And George would never forget. Never."[203]

How the survivors struggled through that night in the bitter conditions and traveled fifty miles is a testament to the strength, endurance, and courage of these people. In the following days, George was amazed at the number of other survivors that came into the camp. It was hard to believe, with the cannon and gunfire he had heard, that any of Black Kettle's people could have gotten away. But every day stragglers on foot or horseback came in. Many Indians were able to escape because of the soldiers' lack of discipline, heavy drinking of whiskey, cowardice, and poor shooting accuracy.

The Smoky Hill camp was made up of Dog Soldiers and other Cheyennes who had refused to accept the treaty. Now their numbers increased with refugees. Within a week nearly four hundred people had arrived in the camp. We have no record of what it was like for the stragglers; some took a week to find help on that cold, wintry plain, where there was nothing to break the wind for miles. These were people who truly could survive in the most difficult of conditions.

No one knew for certain how many had died, but after talking with survivors, George estimated that 53 men and 110 women and children had been killed. Island and Charley were still missing. Many tribal leaders were killed, including eleven chiefs. Chivington claimed to have killed between four and five hundred warriors. No figures exist as to the number of the wounded. Chivington lost nine killed.

Cheyenne and Arapaho families died together on November 29, 1864. Black Kettle's people suffered the most. Only a few men survived. Yellow Wolf's band was half gone, including the eighty-five-year-old chief, White Antelope. Of about fifty Arapahos who were camped with Black Kettle, only four survived. For those who survived, hardship was their future. Their horses were gone, lodges were destroyed, clothing, camp utensils, and their entire store of food was gone. Their survival depended on the charity of the Dog Men, Lakota, and Arapaho friends.

The Sand Creek Massacre was one of the worst blows ever struck at any tribe in the whole plains region. Ironically, this blow fell upon friendly Indians, and the women and children suffered the most. The men of some bands were nearly wiped out while others that had been camped down-stream only had a few killed.

Chivington had captured all their belongings, including between six and seven hundred horses. He wanted to attack the Arapahos immediately, but his mob was too busy plundering. In Denver he and his men were welcomed as heroes with this great victory over "hostiles." At first Chivington's superiors were deceived as to the character of the Sand Creek affair.

Since the Sioux uprising in Minnesota in 1862, which took the lives of hundreds of Minnesotans, fears were raised all over the country. It was the same kind of hysteria that existed in the South before the Civil War—the fear of Negro uprisings. That revolt by the Sioux was a factor in creating an open season of violence against Native people and their mixed-blood and Anglo kin. Thus with impunity Chivington's volunteer militia gunned down a Cheyenne village as it awaited word of peace negotiations, believing in peace.

Not all in the military were of the same mind, though:

Major Anthony, no friend of the Cheyennes, wrote later, "I never saw more bravery displayed by any set of people on the face of the earth than by these Indians. They would charge on the whole company singly, determined to kill someone before being killed themselves."[204]

Anthony recognized the Cheyennes had a strong code of honor. Protecting the families and homes of the warriors was what their lives were dedicated to accomplishing. Living in an unforgiving world, their very survival depended on fighting with honor for the safety of the whole group.

For a month George stayed in the mourning camp on the Smoky Hill, but he wasn't healing well. He borrowed a horse and rode, with Ed Guerrier and another young Indian, to William's stockade on the Purgatoire. They progressed slowly because of George's wound. When they topped a hill above Fort Lyon and the ranch headquarters, soldiers dominated their view. Ed was discouraged by their numbers, and, after some discussion, he decided to give himself up. He was not treated badly, but was questioned about the location of the Indian camps. He did not give up any information of value to Major Anthony but he was out of the fight.

George made his way to the ranch, where he found Charley, alive and well. From Charley, George heard more about the atrocities of the attack that he had not seen while escaping. He and Charley were totally disillusioned with white man's civilization. They decided to return to the Cheyenne camps after George had recuperated for five days. Yellow Woman went with them, saying she would never again live with a white man.

In December George had healed enough to return to the camp, now on Cherry Creek. He took along his stepmother and two women who had been taken prisoner at Sand Creek and later put in William's custody.

Back on the Smoky Hill, the Indians were in mourning and they were angry. They decided to send a war pipe to the Sioux, Dog Soldiers, Northern Arapaho, and the Northern Cheyennes. All the tribes smoked the pipe and moved to a camp on Cherry Creek. It was very unusual to plan to fight in the winter, when the ponies were weakened by a lack of grass—and for these tribes to ally in such unity.

Black Kettle, though, was a hold out. He still felt that fighting was not the answer. As the leading proponent of peace, Black Kettle would now have his judgment questioned, so George was relieved when the council of chiefs urged the people to continue to trust in Black Kettle's leadership and wisdom. Nevertheless, the chiefs agreed that Sand Creek must be avenged. Why had this happened? Why had the soldiers attacked with such viciousness, and why had they killed and mutilated women and children?

George thought he knew why. In the East he had seen that there were rules of warfare, that war was waged among men on battlefields. Prisoners were fed and cared for. They never attacked the women and children, who were protected by law and a code of honor. George realized that men like Chivington did not see the Cheyennes as people but as vermin to be exterminated. He did not discuss this with the chiefs who didn't know white men like he did—they wouldn't understand—but he could at least talk to Black Kettle and tell him that the coming war would be for the survival of the Cheyennes and their way of life. The conflict with the whites had changed. Now the whites were destroying the land, the buffalo, and the people themselves. By the end of the 1850s:

> [T]he response of the state had changed. . . .
> [B]ureaucracies now had clear beliefs and

instructions to guide them. Certainty about the absolute good of Anglo-American political institutions and white settlement as shared goals of government encouraged citizens to demand the use of great force to impose these values. Such beliefs also enabled Colorado citizens to imagine they were taking up arms justly.[205]

They justified their actions based on the Indians' earlier response to harassment:

> [T]he attacking soldiers did not view their actions as heinous. Raiding Indians had butchered friends and neighbors, innocent people, hacking their bodies beyond recognition. Motivated by the horrific events of the spring and summer, the soldiers killed with a vengeance.[206]

The Cheyennes and Arapaho presence, whether peaceful or not, represented a dangerous barrier to the fulfillment of the ambitions of white settlers, and for this they should be killed. This change in policy led to the Indian Wars of the Sixties and an outcome like Sand Creek.

> Sand Creek indicates how far the culture crafted by nineteenth-century Anglo-Americans would go to impose its vision of conquest. That culture couldn't tolerate bison robes lodges on the Great Plains, or bodies left in trees, or visions of various spirits who guided life. The culture couldn't see or even record the Bent family, with its children of mixed race, its kinship across national and racial borders, and its Native names. This cultural vision demanded empty landscapes, without people or history, where entirely new histories could be enacted without the inconvenience of the past.[207]

That is how whites came to think of the West as an empty wilderness, there for the taking. Hence, this vision of where the nomads roamed was required. When government and the population realized the value of the lands west of the Mississippi and that indigenous peoples were in the way of the "progress" to take that land, a new paradigm had to be invented to justify their actions.

In 1858 and 1859, over a hundred thousand Euro-American people rushed across the central plains in a hopeful search for gold. "Few of these migrants had much personal knowledge of Native people, and none of them understood that they had poured into an ecological and cultural system already stressed beyond its limits."[208] Now, five years later, Black Kettle's camp reaped the end result of that ignorance

However, it wouldn't be long until the details of the Sand Creek massacre leaked out: that the Indians were camping under a promise of protection, that wholesale butchery of women and children was sanctioned, that the dead were mutilated—it all came out.

Sand Creek Exposed

On December 22, 1864, the Denver *Rocky Mountain News* published an article about the triumphant return of Colonel Chivington and the Third Regiment. They were met with a parade and much adulation for their Sand Creek "victory." It was noted that among the throng were members of the fair sex who expressed much admiration for the gallant boys who volunteered for the purpose of "protecting the women of the country, by ridding it of red-skins."[209]

A subsequent article was a copy of the order from the Headquarters, District of Colorado, signed by J. M. Chivington, Col. 1st Cavalry of Colorado, declaring that the savages for the past year had been:

> . . . committing depredations upon the property of our citizens; who have attacked and destroyed the trains conveying our supplies, who have robbed and murdered our peaceable citizens, and by their determined hostility, most seriously retarded the growth and prospority [sic] of our Territory, have been surprised, routed, and almost annihilated.[210]

He claimed that his force surprised and attacked a thousand hostile Indians, slaying more than half the forces of the savage foe, and he expressed his thanks to his gallant troops.

When the true details of the Sand Creek Massacre came out, Chivington was no longer seen as a hero. Indian Agent Samuel Colley had sent a letter to the Missouri *Intelligencer* on January 6, 1865, revealing what happened and denouncing Chivington. "Colley explained the temper of the Indians and the good prospects that there had been for peaceful outcome 'when Colonel Chivington marched from Denver, surprised the fort, killed half of them, all women and children, and then returned to Denver.'"[211] Some of Colley's facts seem a little emotional, but his letter got the attention of the army, the public, and the government.

> Under a joint resolution introduced in the Senate on Jan. 29, 1865, and adopted on March 3, the appointment of a committee was provided "to investigate the condition of the Indian tribes and their treatment by civil and military authorities."[212]

General Halleck, now chief of staff of the army, at once ordered Chivington's conduct investigated. General Curtis attempted to have him court-martialed, but unfortunately Chivington's term of service had expired and he was no longer subject to the military.

The committee began its work at Fort Leavenworth May 17, 1865. From the joint committee of the Senate and House, Senator James R. Doolittle, Vice President L. F. Foster, and Congressman Lewis W. Ross were designated as a sub-committee to investigate in Colorado and New Mexico. They began hearings in Santa Fe on July 4, 1865.

In *Kit Carson*, David Remley related, "In the words of one staff member, the committee took enough testimony . . . to convince them that Chivington . . . was 'a monster that should be loathed and shunned by every Christian man and woman.'"[213] And Senator Doolittle wrote of "the treacherous, brutal, and cowardly butchery of the Cheyennes . . . in which the blame is on our side."[214]

Major Wynkoop, who had been replaced at Fort Lyon before the slaughter occurred, received a letter from his friend and former second in command that said among other things, "I tell you Ned it was hard to see little children on their knees have their brains beat out by men professing to be civilized."[215]

The massacre was considered an outrage in its own time, though many Coloradoans still saw Chivington as a hero. A year later, Chivington's friends were trying to show that the camp at Sand Creek had been hostile, but they had no evidence. Grinnell reports:

> One of Chivington's most trusted officers said: "When we came upon the camp on Sand Creek we did not care whether these particular Indians were friendly or not." It was

well known to everybody in Denver that the Colonel's orders to his troops were to kill Indians, to "kill all, little and big."[216]

Kit Carson, now a brigadier general, testified before the committee. Though Kit had not been near Sand Creek, the government saw him as an expert on the situation of the Indians, but Kit told them there was a man who knew more—William Bent. What the government wanted from these respected frontiersmen was recommendations for the future. When William testified, he was so sure of the Indians in his area that he told the commission he could guarantee with his life that in three months he could have the Indians on the Arkansas at peace. William refused to believe that everything he had worked for was to be lost in blood now. After all, he was pleading for his own family, too.

Kit upheld William's testimony. He told the commission, "His suggestions and opinions . . . coincide perfectly with my own. . . . I have much more confidence in [his] influence with the Indians than in my own. . . . I believe that if Colonel Bent and myself were authorized, we could make a solid, lasting peace."[217] William was truly seen as the source for dealing with the southern plains tribes if peace was a goal.

David Remley reports on the lengthy testimony before the commission of both Kit Carson and William Bent. "Carson said he believed that tribes should be held to reservations 'to protect' them from such 'evils' of society as the liquor traders, and 'from the reckless injustice of those outlaws of society thronging upon the border.'"[218]

Both William and Kit criticized corrupt Indian agents for their inexperience and low quality. They felt an effective agent needed to be familiar with the Indian people. Agents who understood the culture and were able to sympathize made better advocates. And they testified that they believed the army was better equipped to handle Indian affairs than was the Interior Department's Office of Indian Affairs. Both men pointed to white provocations of the Indians and both condemned Chivington's murderous actions at Sand Creek.[219] They also believed that land needed to be set aside exclusively for Indian occupation. It was essential for the Indians to be able to live without constant white depredations.

Ultimately the committee came to the conclusion that the Interior Department was in a better position to provide oversight for the Indians, but the expertise of these two witnesses had a great influence on the committee. Their final report, submitted January 26, 1867, said:

> [T]he Committee are of the opinion that in a large majority of cases Indian wars are to be traced to the aggressions of lawless white men always to be found upon the frontier or boundary lines between savage and civilized life.[220]

This does not address the reactions from the military and government after lawless white men aroused the Indians to the cycles of revenge, but it did identify scapegoats. Further, the committee's process was so drawn-out that it had no effect on the immediate clashes to come.

Endnotes

193. Lavender, *Bent's Fort*, 382.

194. G. Hyde, *Life of George Bent*, 146.

195. Connell, *Son of the Morning Star*, 176.

196. Ibid.

197. Lavender, *Bent's Fort*, 384.

198. Connell, *Son of the Morning Star*, 176.

199. Halaas & Masich, *Halfbreed*, 141.

200. G. Hyde, *Life of George Bent*, 155.

201. Halaas & Masich, *Halfbreed*, 146.

202. A. Hyde, *Empires, Nations, and Families*, 496.

203. Halaas & Masich, *Halfbreed*, 153.

204. Lavender, *Bent's Fort*, 384 - 385.

205. A. Hyde, *Empires, Nations, and Families*, 494.

206. Kraft, *Ned Wynkoop*, 134.

207. A. Hyde, *Empires, Nations, and Families*, 496.

208. Ibid, 493.

209. Staff, "Arrival of the Third Regiment—Grand March Throtown," *Rocky Mountain News*, 22 December 1864, Front page. https://www.coloradohistoricnewspapers.org, page 1.

210. J. M. Chivington, "Head Quarters, District of Colorado, Denver, D. T. Dec. 21, 1864," *Rocky Mountain News*, 22 December, 1864. Front page. https://www.coloradohistoricnewspapers.org.,Page 1.

211. Grinnell, *The Fighting Cheyennes*, 175 - 176.

212. Keleher, *Turmoil in New Mexico, 1846 - 1868*, 352.

213. Remley, *Kit Carson*, 241 - 242.

214. Ibid, 242.

215. Kraft, *Ned Wynkoop*, 136 - 137.

216. Grinnell, *The Fighting Cheyennes*, 180.

217. Lavender *Bent's Fort*, 388.

218. Remley, *Kit Carson*, 241.

219. Ibid.

220. Grinnell, *The Fighting Cheyennes*, 176.

11 ∽ RETRIBUTION

WILLIAM AND OTHERS HAD warned federal and local
Colorado officials that the Indians had to have the
food and supplies needed as a result of their dependence on the vanishing buffalo, and they needed safety
from invaders or they would attack people passing
through their lands. In the vacuum left by the government, caravans laden with food, tools, and stock were an
obvious replacement for the destroyed buffalo and warriors pillaged them regularly. To attack them seemed, to
the Indians, like logical retribution for the Sand Creek
massacre.

By 1865, not only the young braves were keen on retaliation. On January 1, 1865, the chiefs in council for the
Sioux, Northern Cheyennes, Northern Arapahos, and
the Cheyenne Dog Soldiers made an unprecedented
decision. Having smoked the war pipe, they decided
to fight together. No such alliance had ever existed before. The horror of Sand Creek had driven them to overcome any natural antipathy and to fight back against
this invasion of their homeland. They decided to attack
Julesburg, an important depot on the South Platte River
in northeastern Colorado, that offered copious plunder,
which equaled wealth, honor, and even novelty. Winter

fighting was not traditional for the Indians, due to the condition of their horses and the difficulty of travel, but revenge for Sand Creek burned in their hearts.

In 1865 Julesburg was a major facility for the stage line. There was a restaurant, a big stable, a blacksmith and repair shop, a granary and storehouses, and a sizable corral. Located nearby was a large store stocked for travelers. The Overland Telegraph Company had an office located at this crossing of the South Platte. The town was populated by station hands, stock tenders, drivers, and telegraph operators. Also a small post was established in the summer of 1864 for a military contingent. Camp Rankin was garrisoned by a company of Seventh Iowa Cavalry.

After the tribes had completed all the preparations for battle, an unusually disciplined force of a thousand warriors rode toward Julesburg. Charley and George were among them. George was well mounted and armed with one of his father's fine carbines. Few of the Indians had guns, though the Cheyennes were acclaimed horsemen, as good as any cavalry there was.

Some women accompanied them with extra horses to carry home the plunder they expected to gather. Never before had they gone to war on such a grand scale. The tragedy of Sand Creek united these tribes; all understood that no one tribe could defeat the invaders.

At Julesburg the soldiers, after first being drawn from their fort, soon saw the number of Indians attacking and retreated behind the walls, not to be drawn out again. Their first several sorties had led to fifteen deaths, and they could see they were substantially outnumbered. A few civilians were killed, but no Indians died.

During the initial fight, George saw Big Crow count coup, and he could not understand why Big Crow hadn't killed his victim. For the Indians, counting coup was a time-honored way of fighting, and many didn't understand this was a fight to the death and for survival. But George knew the Indians had to learn to fight the white way, with no mercy for the enemy.

George was quite detailed about all the goods that the Indians explored, destroyed, enjoyed, and confiscated. At the stage station George found a Yankee officer's uniform with brass buttons. It fit him perfectly, and he wore it as a symbol of the power he would wield against his enemy. As a former Rebel, he wore the coat with pride and defiance to humiliate the hated bluecoats.

War parties ransacked the warehouse and stage depot, returning to camp with heavily laden ponies that could not carry everything they could have taken. They rode away from Julesburg late on January 7. The ponies were so heavily loaded that it took three days to reach the Cherry Creek camp again.

George remembered it as a very exciting time at the camp, with the tribes camping together and fires burning at night with celebratory dances going on every night, despite many people being in mourning. The raids had been very successful with few men wounded. The plunder included foods like bacon, ham, flour, sugar, rice, cornmeal, shelled corn, molasses, and canned meat and fruits. Other more exotic items showed up in their camps to perplex and entertain. There was hardware, silk, dress goods, clothing, boots, shoes, bolts of cloth, and many household items and personal effects that were sometimes puzzling. They threw away paper money, not knowing that it could have any value.

The first blow for revenge since Sand Creek had been struck, and great celebrations went on for days in the Indian camps. George's party continued up the Platte River destroying everything that was put there by whites.

Captured herds of horses, mules and cattle were driven away. At one site he left a note saying, "Go to Hell," telling all that the Bent boys were among the Sand Creek avengers. George reminded the chiefs that they must pull down the telegraph lines and poles, because whites could send messages with them for long distances.

On January 15, the chiefs withdrew farther to the north, for the protection of the villages, but they intended to continue hitting the whites. The chiefs met in council and made their plans. The Cheyennes would strike between Julesburg and Denver, the Arapahos would raid the Julesburg area, and the Lakotas would hit wagons, stations, and ranches along the Platte River road, east of Julesburg. The Indians demonstrated a sense of military organization for the first time.

George decided to stay with the war chiefs. He went around to the various lodges to say goodbye. By the spring of 1865 there were more than eight thousand Cheyennes, Arapaho, and Sioux camped near the Tongue River. They maintained their tribal individuality, but they began to think in their actions as one people, confident of their strength and rights to live as they pleased.

The peace Indians, however, withdrew their villages to regroup. They scattered to various camps to try to continue their seasonal life style. Still the principle leader of the peace Indians, Black Kettle opposed further fighting, believing that revenge had been exacted. He again led his seventy or eighty lodges south to join the Kiowas, Comanches, and Southern Arapahos who were wintering on the Cimarron. As they departed, things were bleak. Many were on foot. Their personal property had been destroyed at Sand Creek, and few had lodges or clothing. Once on the Cimarron, they were welcomed with friendliness and sympathy and given many presents: horses and bridles; lodges furnished with beds, kettles, and utensils; and any other needs. There was a resilient spirit of sharing. Sand Creek erased tribal boundaries, as all the plains Indians now felt a real bitterness and hatred for the whites. They knew Sand Creek could have happened to any of them.

The warriors continued to strike back in a campaign of horror all along the Platte. George and Charley were in the thick of it. The Platte River was a main thoroughfare for travel across the West by this time, rich in targets. There were no troops in the area and vengeance went unfettered. A small post like Fort Rankin had no chance against a thousand Indians. Ranchers had pioneered near the river. The government had large warehouses in Julesburg, a major depot. Stage lines and stations had been established along with telegraph lines.

The telegraph wires, when not cut by the Indians, were hot with panic, and the Overland Stage Company demanded military protection. Ten days after Julesburg, Brigadier General Robert Mitchell, commander on the Platte, set out with six hundred fifty cavalry and a hundred supply wagons to punish the Indians. Indian scouts brought word to the camps that this large force of soldiers had found the former camp on Cherry Creek, but had ridden east. Mitchell was never able to locate the fast moving Indians. The Indians were smart enough to use a hit-and-run tactic that avoided going against superior numbers and weaponry. George couldn't believe that General Mitchell was so incompetent that within a day's march of the huge village he totally missed them.

The military campaign was an attempt to keep the peace and protect settlers moving west, but they could not quell the Indians' guerilla campaign. From the

Native perspective, all this trouble was the result of Chivington's attack at Sand Creek. From the white perspective, the Indians were to blame. Fear in Denver grew to a fevered pitch. On February 6, 1865, martial law was instituted by Samuel H. Elbert, Secretary of Colorado Territory and reported in the *Rocky Mountain News* on February 7, 1865. Due to the threatening attitude of the plains Indians, three hundred and sixty mounted men were called up for ninety days of service. It was declared that "all labor and business is suspended until the number of men called for be organized and placed under my command. . . . Each man should come provided with a horse, at least two blankets, and if possible a revolver."[221] Other equipment would be issued by the government.

George said that he did not see a tenth of the things that happened along the South Platte that year, yet he saw a lot. In camp every night there was feasting and dancing in celebration of the success of this guerrilla warfare that the Indians excelled at and that flummoxed the military, which traveled too conspicuously.

In the spring of 1865, the Indians had the roads tied up again. On July 25, 1865, the Cheyennes led the allied warriors to the Platte River Bridge crossing, but after several days of fighting the results were inconclusive. As the Indians withdrew, George joined the Cheyennes and Lakotas to participate in the celebrations of a battle well fought. By summer the Indians still had the road to Denver closed. For six weeks the Indians held the road and stopped all commerce. Delayed travel to Salt Lake City, Denver, and other points caused major economic difficulties as shortages drove prices up.

The people of Denver depended on imported food from Missouri because, as yet, little was produced farther west. When the road finally was opened in the fall, it was too late for the slow-moving ox trains to get across the plains before winter set in. When they tried to rush horse or mule trains across the plains to assuage the panic of famine in Denver, the Indians hit them again, either capturing them or forcing them to wait farther east for better conditions. Food panic was exacerbated by the fact that no stages were running with mail, and the telegraph was down much of the time, cutting off communication to Denver and the West Coast.[222]

The scarcity of food affected the Indians, as well, and after a year of fighting the tribal alliances were weakened by food shortages, intertribal tensions, and the Southern Cheyennes yearning to be home on the Arkansas. George, now a battle-hardened warrior having fought in every engagement from Julesburg to the Powder River, saw the futility of this war. They had done great damage to the Colorado economy, but this fighting could not go on indefinitely. The warriors rode exhausted horses. Year-round fighting prevented villages from storing enough food for winter. Women and children could not be protected during the hard months. Indian traditions of warfare could not withstand the more technological methods of the industrial East. The whites could carry the fight to the villages anytime, because they carried provisions for the men and horses and could fight in the winter.

Savoie Lottinville, editor of *Life of George Bent*, said that George Bent's character was often misunderstood.

> He was both white and Indian, but after he was wounded at the Sand Creek Massacre in 1864, when he was in the Cheyenne camp with his mother's people, he became increasingly Indian and often hostile in his actions, outlooks, and interpretations. His clear identification of himself with "my people," the Cheyennes,

from that point becomes abundantly clear in his narrative.[223]

Sand Creek changed George forever, but he remained a shrewd observer of both white and Indian cultures. He saw that this fighting could not last.

The ease with which the Indians carried out their raids during the winter 1864 - 65 caused an outcry in the West against the generals. People thought they were being too easy on the Indians. General Patrick E. Connor was sent for in California, where he was regarded as a hero for slaughtering the Paiute Indians. He was to take command of all the troops in the plains.

First General Connor sent troops to protect the Overland Stage line. With the Civil War ending, troops were freed up in the East to come west to fight the Indians. However, the Indians in late July were off the warpath, due to their usual summer medicine ceremonies. This gave the General breathing room, and it wasn't until early August 1865 that he actually got organized to try to keep peace on the plains by quelling hostilities.

Family Cataclysm

General Connor's skilled Pawnee and Omaha scouts, sent out in August to watch the trails the Indians used to travel south to the Platte, spotted a small raiding party of Cheyennes. After successful raiding on the Upper Platte, the war party was traveling north, returning to the Powder River camps. Island was among this party, leading packhorses laden with plunder. (George Hyde and David Lavender identify Yellow Woman in this incident, while David Fridtjof Halaas and Andrew Masich report it was Island.)

On August 16, Major Frank North's Pawnee scouts, with a detachment of Seventh Iowa Cavalry, overtook the Cheyenne war party. When Island saw the approaching Pawnees she thought they were Cheyenne or Lakota Sioux warriors. The strangers waved a blanket, signaling that it was safe to approach. However, the Pawnee war cry caused Island to give warning, but it was too late. Island and her four companions were overrun, cut down, and scalped.

News of this murder did not reach Charley or George for several days. They had joined a party of Dog Soldiers, Lakotas, and Northern Cheyennes who intercepted a party of military and civilian personnel in the Powder River country. When the Indians agreed to parlay with the whites, the chiefs asked George to interpret and speak for them.

The whites said they did not come to fight. They were working to open a road into the Montana gold fields. Their leader, Colonel James A. Sawyers, asked George directly what it would take to get permission to cross Indian land. George's answer: "You can hang Colonel Chivington!"[224] George made it clear that hostilities were the result of Chivington's slaughter of women and children at Sand Creek.

Colonel Sawyers was unnerved by the vehemence of this reply, and he noticed that George used American slang with a Southern drawl, using phrases like *damn Yankees*.

George's appearance also marked him as a man apart—not entirely Indian and not quite white. This observation makes an interesting complement to an anecdote related by George, who had found the Northern Cheyennes very strange when he first went north to fight. George described how the Cheyennes in the north had grown to be much like the Sioux; they still wore buffalo clothes and spoke an unfamiliar language. The southerners wore cloth clothes and other manufactured items. To George, these northern relatives looked wild.

Similarly, George looked wild to many whites. "Even in the company of chiefs, this halfbreed [sic] Bent was an intimidating presence, a man to be reckoned with in both Indian and white worlds."[225] He had a daunting poise, dark skin and hair, and piercing black eyes. His dress was a fancy combination of white and Indian. His height, his bull neck, his square jaw, his broad shoulders, and massive chest all set him apart.[226]

Colonel Sawyers offered to pay for the right of passage, and a deal was struck by the chiefs. The Indians would allow the passage in exchange for a wagonload of supplies. George gave his word that the soldiers would be safe during the exchange. He was appalled when the Lakotas in the group swarmed in on the wagons, and during the exchange shots were fired. The chaos led to a belief among the whites that George had deceived them.

George was angered by the Lakotas breach of faith and he left the fight. This was not his idea of honorable behavior. The battle was over for George, but Charley gladly stayed to fight until long-range shooting against bows and arrows caused the Indians to lose interest, and they withdrew. Some rode back to camp, but Charley continued fighting other whites in the area.

When he finally returned to the camp, George had to tell Charley about Island's (possibly Yellow Woman's) death. This murder could only have increased Charley's rage and hatred of the whites. His sole Cheyenne blood member was Yellow Woman, and Island had been an important figure in his growing up years. The incident would put further pressure on family cohesion.

Less than a month after William made his statement before the Congressional Committee, his son Charley began a career of terror that would make him one of the worst desperados the plains had known. His pain with the way his chosen people had been treated—betrayed over and over—turned to hatred against his white blood. William's attempts to foster peace on the plains were shattered anew—this time by his own family. Eventually Charley had a price on his head and William disowned him.

A split between Charley and George also was approaching. Though George continued to feel that a fair fight was honorable, the atrocities that Charley began perpetrating were another matter.

Split Alliances

George now knew the real fight was with the whites, but he still wanted to prove himself as an Indian warrior. He joined a traditional war party against the Crow Indians, a longstanding enemy. This time he went armed with a bow, arrows, and a bull-hide shield. He missed the fine rifle his father had given him back on the Arkansas, but without ammunition it was useless.

When the war party encountered a large number of magnificent Crow warriors riding as one, with red painted faces and spiked hair in front, flowing long in back, George saw that these formidable men would soon overtake his war party. He signaled the others to ride on, and he stopped and fired at the Crows. They let loose a hail of arrows. George was riding his powerful thoroughbred that had outrun every horse he ever raced against. He knew he could escape the Crow ponies.

When he saw that his party was a safe distance away, he whirled his charger and, hugging its neck to avoid the arrows flying around him, he raced away. When he joined his compatriots they cheered him. They had seen what he had done to draw the enemy away so they could escape. George had won the approval of these Dog Soldiers, the most feared Cheyenne warriors. They would always recount his bravery while saving them from the Crow party.

As the raids and warring continued every day, camp criers reported fights. The Pawnee and Omaha Indian scouts who fought with the military were armed by the whites with the latest in firearms. The allied tribes were mostly equipped with bows and lances. When they did capture guns, it was nearly impossible to get ammunition. But they held their own against the better-equipped enemy.

Meanwhile, General Patrick E. Connor was besting Chivington in the quest for scalps, glory, and a brigadier's star. In January 1863 he had surprised a camp of Paiutes on Bear River in Utah, killing two hundred and seventy-eight Indians, including many women and children. This slaughter was very similar to the attack at Sand Creek a year later. More recently in an Arapaho village on the Tongue River, he had burned the village out. Now he was put in command of the troops in the new District of the Plains, headquartered in Denver. Because of the outcry against the generals in the West during the 1864 - 65 Indian raids, he was charged with ending the Indian wars.

A front-page article published June 9, 1865, by the *Daily Mining Journal* in Black Hawk, Colorado, complained of the failings of the military against the Indians:

> We have seen the fruitlessness of the Curtis-Mitchell-Blunt expedition: Tyler's rangers saw the smoking ruins of ranches, but not the

Indians who fired them; Dodge failed to protect the route: [T]he Third Regiment, whatever the ethics of Sand Creek, only made matters worse.[227]

Connor's army was the largest force ever to take the field against the western tribes. George's fear that the end of the Civil War would provide fresh troops to fight the Indians had come true. Connor organized a three-pronged army that would go after the allied Northern Cheyennes, Arapaho, and Lakota camps in the Powder River country. On July 4, 1865, as the Commission investigating the Sand Creek Massacre was meeting in Santa Fe, Connor issued standing orders to all commanders: "You will not receive overtures of peace or submission from Indians, but will attack and kill every male Indian over twelve years of age."[228] The evolved government policy to clear the plains of the impediment of Indians would be executed, if he had anything to say about it.

However, his campaign did not go well. Troops from the Civil War wanted to go home. Their grain-fed horses did not hold up well on the plains. They also couldn't find the Indians. By early September, when the weather turned, four hundred fourteen horses froze on the picket line in one night. Lakota warriors rode to the Cheyenne camp and told them of the soldiers' vulnerability on the Powder River. George, Charley, and other Cheyenne warriors responded quickly and arrived at the soldiers' camp on September 5, 1865.

Famous warrior Roman Nose, like George a member of the Crooked Lance Society, arrived to provide leadership. The warriors, desperately short of supplies, failed to destroy Connor's army, but they did demonstrate their superiority and forced the bluecoats into defensive positions. If the Indians had been better armed, George believed they would have broken the bluecoats, and he took satisfaction from knowing that Connor's campaign had failed.

In late September, almost a year after Sand Creek and much fighting, the Bent brothers were ready to head home to the camps in the south. They had been fighting from Julesburg to the Powder River, and the alliance was weakening. Relations with the Lakotas, in particular, were getting tense. George and Charley joined the Southern Cheyennes, led by their father's old friend Little Wolf, and rode south. In October when they reached the Platte, some Indians participated in more raids, but the Bents stayed with the homesick Cheyennes and continued on south.

When news of the negotiations of the Treaty of the Little Arkansas was reported, there was controversy in the papers about William and his role. The Leavenworth *Bulletin* reported that there was a proposal to put mountaineers Colonel Bent, of Colorado, and Colonel Kit Carson, 1st New Mexico Cavalry, in charge of the management of the Indians. "We have no confidence in Carson or Bent, so far as their management of the Indians is concerned. They are both men who have spent the greater part of their lives with the Indians. They lead a nomadic life, and their habits and customs are closely allied to those of the Indians."[229]

The New Mexico Press, published in Albuquerque, took issue with this characterization of these men, saying the *Bulletin* was deceived. The paper encapsulated both men's credentials and debunked the comment that the men lived as Indians by saying that they resided in adobe houses, not well adapted to the "nomadic life." The newspaper assured the *Bulletin* that "in their habits and customs, Colonel Bent and Colonel Carson are no more allied to the Indians than are other frontier settlers; and that they are pioneers of civilization."[230]

George knew his father was negotiating for peace, but news of The Treaty of the Little Arkansas, signed on October 14, 1865, had not reached him. On their way south, George and his party approached the Smoky Hill, where a year before there had been no stage station. Now there was a herd of cattle, a stage station, and about eight or nine men. Both parties were taken by surprise. George decided to try to parlay with the whites and called out, asking if a treaty had been signed. After an answer in the affirmative, a man named Perrin inquired who among the Indians could speak such good English. George cautiously moved into the open. "I'm the son of Bill Bent."[231]

Hearing that a treaty had been signed, the Indians laid down their arms, shook hands, and talked. George told them it was good that there was peace.

Suddenly a shot rang out, and Charley and the Dog Men, without warning, renewed the fight. George was appalled and rode away in disgust. Charley inflicted a horrible torture on a captured white man by staking him down, mutilating him in view of the holed-up whites, and building a fire on his belly. By nightfall Charley gave up on luring the whites out to fight and left.

George was shocked and disgusted by Charley's treachery. The brothers argued that night back at the village. George had given his word for the truce and Charley had endangered all the Cheyennes. The brothers, once so close, decided finally, after other separations, to pursue their chosen paths in different directions. While Charley would fight to the death, never submitting to any white domination, George had come to believe that Black Kettle's understanding of the future for the Indians was accurate. He now understood that Cheyenne survival depended on adjustment to a new world. This was a major turning point in his understanding of the future and the value of fighting.

George felt his duty now lay by the side of Black Kettle to translate for him and protect the interests of the Cheyennes. Because of his education he could bring skills to negotiations that the Indians lacked. The Indians were intelligent and able to represent themselves, but George understood the white men. "Know your enemy" applied.

Endnotes

221. Samuel H. Elbert, "Headquarters Dis't of Colorado, Denver, February 6th, 1865, General Order, No. 10," *Rocky Mountain News*, 7 February 1965, Front Page. https://www.coloradohistoricnewspapers.org

222. G. Hyde, *Life of George Bent*, 180.

223. Ibid, xv.

224. Halaas & Masich, *Halfbreed*, 189.

225. Ibid, 190.

226. Ibid.

227. No byline, "The Indians," *Daily Mining Journal*, 9 June 1865, Front page. Colorado Historic Newspapers Collection, https//www.coloradohistoricnewspapers.org/

228. Halaas & Masich, *Halfbreed*, 195.

229. Staff, "Summary of Current Items," *The New Mexico Press*, 31 October 1865, page 2. America's Historical Newspapers, Library of Congress. http://docs.newsbank.com/s/HistArchive/ahnpdoc/EANX/15226EFA1E941060/0D52805756D8EA80

230. Ibid.

231. Halaas & Masich, *Halfbreed*, 200.

12 ∾ PEACE EFFORTS

IN THE SPRING OF 1865, at the same time vengeance for Sand Creek was being exacted in the north, William and others were working for peace, hoping to avoid the war spreading in the south along the Arkansas River. Not only were the tribes themselves debating war, but Confederate authorities were trying to arrange a council with the Kiowas and Comanches to encourage them to make attacks on the Kansas border.

Colonel Jesse H. Leavenworth, named agent to these tribes and the Apaches in 1864, sent runners south to engage the Kiowas and Comanches before the Confederates had a chance. He succeeded in negotiating with the Indians, who agreed to meet on Bluff Creek in October to make another peace treaty. The agreement also included the Southern Cheyennes and Arapahos, thanks to efforts by William and Thomas Murphy, agent to the Cheyennes and Arapahos.

Colonel Leavenworth also prevented a Union attack on the tribes. Colonel James H. Ford, commander of the troops on the Arkansas River, had a strong force at Fort Larned ready to move against the camps on the Cimarron. Leavenworth declared these tribes friendly, and he succeeded in stopping the march of Ford's troops.

In October 1865, William brought Black Kettle and the Southern Cheyennes to meet the United States peace commissioners on the Little Arkansas River, near present day Wichita. The commission included Major General William S. Harney, Major General John B. Sanborn, Colonel Jesse H. Leavenworth, Judge James Steele, William Bent, Superintendent of Indian Affairs Thomas Murphy, and Kit Carson. The government wanted all Indian land claims voided so that settlers pouring into Colorado could establish clear land ownership.

Black Kettle was suspicious after what had happened at Sand Creek, but he and the other chiefs trusted William and agreed to talk. William also had the confidence of the government. "[S]ecretary of the Interior James Harlan and Major General John Pope insisted that Kit Carson and William Bent be included. Their experience and knowledge would be essential to the success of the negotiations."[232]

General Sanborn opened the council by apologizing to the Cheyennes for the massacre at Sand Creek. He also gave them assurances, in the wake of the death of Abraham Lincoln, that the new "father" (President Andrew Johnson) knew that great wrongs had been committed. He acknowledged that it was known that they had been attacked while at peace and that the nation was disgraced and shamed.

Black Kettle said, "I have always been friendly to the whites, but since the killing of my people at Sand Creek I find it hard to trust a white man."[233] It must have been a difficult conclusion for Black Kettle, who had been so determined to adapt and survive. Then he had his wife brought in and showed her nine wounds to commission members Major General John Sanborn and Major General William Harney. General Harney was so impressed with Black Kettle that he later gave him a fine horse.

Black Kettle and other chiefs registered their objection to the treaty because so few of their people were present at the negotiations. Yet they remained, and Black Kettle deferred to William to speak for the Cheyennes. William mentioned the deception of whites in former treaties but asked that all white men not be judged by that past. He said that Governor Evans and Colonel Chivington had lied to him and used him to lure the Indians into the death trap of Sand Creek.[234]

At the conclusion of negotiations, the resulting treaty declared perpetual peace with the Cheyennes and Arapahos of the upper Arkansas River. The US commissioners proposed that the Cheyenne and Arapaho reservation be located north of the Platte or south of the Arkansas, away from central overland routes that were so vital to the goldfields. Black Kettle and Little Raven agreed to the treaty if the government would make arrangements with the Comanches and Lakotas, who also had claims in the designated territory.

The Southern Cheyennes ceded all their lands between the Arkansas and Platte Rivers. The Indians' land holdings, as outlined by the treaty, were significantly reduced again. They had ceded the eastern half of Colorado, a large part of western Kansas, and parts of Nebraska and Wyoming. This victory for the government was the true outcome of Sand Creek.

The Indians did reserve hunting rights for the land between the rivers, but the commission knew that buffalo would soon be very scarce in that range anyway, and the government was anxious to get those lands for the building of the Union Pacific Railroad. The Indians agreed not to go within ten miles of any main road, post, or station without permission. They were to live on a reserve south of the Arkansas. The commission set aside special allotments of land to each chief and to each woman and child who lost a parent at Sand Creek.

It was easy to get some chiefs to sign a treaty, even if they didn't like it. This consent to relinquish so much of the traditional lands would lead to push back by those who did not participate or signed out of ignorance of the meaning.

The Treaty of the Little Arkansas was signed on October 14, 1865. Most of the Southern Cheyennes were on the Powder River at the time, but when they moved south in December 1865 the majority of them accepted the treaty. However, the government never set up the designated reservations. Two years later the treaty had to be re-negotiated, and the Indians lost more land.

The treaty indirectly impacted the Bent family. The gradual changes occurring in their lives over the previous decade had accelerated during the 1864 - 65 wars. By the end of the 1860s the Indian trade was gone for William and he made his living freighting government supplies to Santa Fe and Fort Union (present-day New Mexico). With the Indians losing their land by treaty in the south, settlers started moving into the rich Purgatoire valley. William's old lifestyle was gone, and he had to adjust to the loss of power in his part of the West. The trade empire he, his brother Charles, and Ceran St. Vrain had built had served them well, but now Bent's Old Fort eroded into the mud. Yellow Woman and Island were gone from William's life, and many Bents had died, some by violent death, levying great cost on their family.

The future would embrace a new way of life that did not include the plains Indians' influence on the Bent style of life that had defined them. William had tried to serve the Indians. But the people of the plains, as William had known them, were gone. It was a watershed in the history of the plains, where for hundreds of years these people had roamed free, following the buffalo. Now their lands and freedom were vastly diminished.

The white world had changed, too, with new attitudes and beliefs—especially racism—that were vastly different from what William had known and lived. Anne F. Hyde provides a splendid summary of the shifting concepts of race in the West during this period and the effects of the tools of conquest—railroads, armies, surveyors, reservations, censuses, and law:

> Ideas about race and how it described people and circumscribed behavior remained very shifty but soon had the power of the state to give them shape. . . . Does it mean anything to be labeled a "half-breed" or a Mexican when you used to be a Bent or a Californio? Can you talk or buy your way out of racial labeling?[235]

It is almost certain that in this atmosphere of racial prejudice, William's children easily could have been disenfranchised. They walked a dangerous path between two worlds and were particularly vulnerable to abuse from both Indians and whites. William had always worked hard to represent the interests of mixed-blood children, and in the Treaty of the Little Arkansas he saw an opportunity to guarantee, by treaty, stability for his children. "The new treaty presented the unique opportunity to guarantee his children an inheritance that he himself could not provide."[236]

Though William himself never obtained clear title to his land along the Arkansas—a sore point in his dealings with the government—he had succeeded in obtaining grants of land as reparation to a specified class of tribe members who suffered at Sand Creek and for his children (except Robert, who had received a section of land earlier).

William had earned tremendous respect among peace-loving whites and Indians during the years when he worked so hard to convince both sides that peace was advantageous. But his antipathy toward corrupt Indian agents did not go unnoticed. I. C. Taylor, the incompetent and drunken agent for the Cheyennes and Arapahos, tried to stop William from trading with the tribes. He attempted to revoke William's trading license and asked the military to remove William from the tribal lands. The military refused, saying William had Major General Pope's personal endorsement. Pope further issued orders that commanders should defer to William's counsel in all matters regarding Indian relations.

In late 1865 when George arrived at the combined camp of the Cheyennes, Arapaho, and Prairie Apache, his father and Robert were there trading. George had not seen them since the aftermath of Sand Creek. For a year he had been fighting whites, and now here they were, all trading peacefully and without fear. What he had heard from the men on the Smoky Hill was confirmed. The Southern Cheyennes had agreed to and signed the Treaty of the Little Arkansas. George learned that his father had been instrumental in the effort to end the war. For these exhausted warriors it must have been like a dream that the war was truly over and the peace treaty signed.

Only now George learned about the hearings investigating Chivington's conduct and his father's part in giving testimony, and that the official report stated that Chivington and his men had massacred a peaceful village under the protection of military authority.

Captain Silas Soule had also testified against Chivington in those hearings, and later Soule was gunned down in the streets of Denver by a crony of Chivington. This lone officer, who had refused to take part in the Sand Creek slaughter, who had ordered his men to hold their fire against women and children, and who also had saved Charley's life was that brave man that we always look for when there is a need to stand against evil. The Bents were shocked by this murder but gratified to know that Chivington's political and military ambitions were bankrupt.

George "could scarcely believe that the army had taken such a strong stand against one of its own and that the government had pledged reparations to chiefs and families who had suffered losses."[237] The horror of the Sand Creek Massacre could not be denied.

Though reparations would never be adequate for what happened at Sand Creek, George had to take heed of them, for he had lost everything. His only solace was that he had been able to inflict revenge several times over. "In fact, the allied tribes had beaten the army, closed the emigrant roads, and forced the U.S. government to take responsibility for the crime of Sand Creek."[238]

For once the Indians had won the battle, if not the war. That was big medicine.

Endnotes

232. Halaas & Masich, *Halfbreed*, 204.

233. G. Hyde, *Life of George Bent*, 248.

234. Halaas & Masich, *Halfbreed*, 204 - 205. G. Hyde, *Life of George Bent*, 247 - 248.

235. A. Hyde, *Empires, Nations, and Families*, 497.

236. Halaas & Masich, *Halfbreed*, 206.

237. Ibid, 207.

238. Ibid.

13 ⁀ ELUSIVE PEACE

IN FEBRUARY 1866, FOUR companies of cavalry escorting
Major Edward W. Wynkoop and bringing a train of annuities rode into the Bluff Creek camp of the Cheyennes,
Arapahos, and Prairie Apaches. The Indians trusted
Wynkoop, based on past dealings with him, and George
acted as an interpreter when Wynkoop traveled among
the Indians urging those that hadn't signed the Little
Arkansas Treaty to sign. His efforts also had the back-
ing of Black Kettle and Little Raven, who joined him in
urging the war factions to accept the treaty—especially
the Dog Soldiers.[239]

The Dog Soldiers continued to live and hunt in eastern Colorado and western Kansas, where there was still
sufficient buffalo. They disavowed the Little Arkansas
Treaty and felt no compunction to abide by its con-
straints. They were becoming increasingly belligerent
over the tide of white immigration flooding their lands,
particularly in the Smoky Hill River country of Kansas,
along which whites had opened a new trail to the gold
fields. Their reluctance to give in was interpreted by the
men in Kansas and some army officers as an indication
that the Indians planned war. This, of course, was a jus-
tification for considering more hostilities on their own

part. Preemptive offense on the part of a government has been around for some time.

George was instrumental in talking to Porcupine Bear, a member of the Dog Soldiers, who was a holdout to the treaty and who had lost relatives at Sand Creek. Sitting next to Porcupine Bear during negotiations, George addressed Porcupine Bear in a soft, private manner, urging him to be the first of the Dog Soldiers to sign the treaty. This attempt at influencing Porcupine Bear infuriated Bull Bear, who threatened Porcupine Bear not to betray the Dog Men.

Though George was successful with Porcupine Bear, the Dog Soldiers remained hostile. All they would say was that they would retain their country between the Smoky Hill and Republican where they had lived for so long, and they would not permit a railroad through. Major Wynkoop made a real effort to convince the Dog Soldiers to allow the road. When George succeeded with Porcupine Bear, he accomplished that at the price of his relationship with the Dog Men, but he had gained the respect of Wynkoop. Attaining a bridge between Indians and white men was costly for George.

Charley continued to encourage the Dog Soldier band to harass isolated settlements and trains. But following the Bluff Creek council, whites traveled with much more safety. Except for some small disturbances, things were peaceful in 1866 for the Southern Cheyennes. What the Indian did to the white man continued to be decried in every newspaper, but there was no mention of the incitements of the whites. Racial propaganda continued to be published.

George had proven himself in battle and often stood with the chiefs in councils. As the son of two prominent parents, he was in a highly respected position. He had skills both as a fighter and as a negotiator. In Black

Kettle's camp, the young ladies were noticing him. And he was noticing the chief's marriageable niece, whom Black Kettle regarded as a daughter.

> Her name was Magpie Woman. . . . She carried herself with a haughty pride befitting her family's high standing. . . . On mornings, he [George] made certain to be near the stream when she came to draw water. Here, among the willows, they would talk, away from prying eyes and chaperones. Her beauty and station had intimidated some of the young men, but not George. He possessed a confidence and worldliness that appealed to her.[240]

Black Kettle and William made arrangements for the union. In the spring of 1866 the two families hosted a marriage ceremony unequalled since William married Owl Woman more than thirty years before. Once again a powerful alliance was made consolidating the political and trading power of the Bents in the Cheyenne world. This marriage represented the union of two people, the union of two outstanding families, and the union of two cultures.

According to some sources, Magpie was the love of George's life. "These were happy days for us," George Bent said afterward.[241] The couple lived in Black Kettle's lodge for a couple of years. Black Kettle had no children of his own, but he loved Magpie and her brother, Blue Horse, as his own. For a while these were happy, contented, peaceful times—something the Indians had longed for. Black Kettle was a fine man, someone the tribe respected. He had found a friend in Edward Wynkoop, now their agent. And he depended on George for understanding of the white men and for honest interpretation between the white and Indian languages.

In the midst of this stability, however, the Little Arkansas Treaty remained unsettled. Ratification had been delayed in the Senate. In May 1866 William went to Washington. He had put his reputation on the line when he told the Indians that Washington would implement the provisions of the treaty, especially reparations and annuities. Neither the Cheyennes nor the Arapahos had received anything.

The chiefs were also anxious for the return of children captured at Sand Creek, and William wanted to make sure that mixed-blood offspring would receive the lands promised to them. Feeling the government had taken advantage of his word, William warned that if they betrayed what they had promised it would likely lead once again to a bloody war. He concluded his work in Washington as speedily as he could, for he had no desire to remain in the crowded city with formal airs and foppish men.

Apparently William had some success in Washington. In August he received word that the Bureau of Indian Affairs was sending men to settle claims and ensure compliance with the 1865 treaty. William was contracted to bring the Cheyenne and Arapaho annuities to talks set for later in the year. However, the councils of late summer and early fall 1866 were a dismal failure, marred by drunkenness and violence. The Dog Soldiers continued to raid. William went home to the Purgatoire in disgust.

In November he returned to Fort Zarah, northeast of present Great Bend, Kansas, with George and Robert for more talks, but things went badly. "George made up his mind to follow Black Kettle, but Charlie was an ardent disciple of Roman Nose."[242] Charley got drunk and threatened to kill his father. When George intervened, Charley exploded. He believed George had sold out the Indians. William pleaded with the military to arrest Charley to keep him away from whiskey, but they refused, fearing an uprising. The Dog Soldiers withdrew again. They continued to be recalcitrant.

Black Kettle and the peace chiefs accepted the goods and supplies as full reparation for the loss of pony herds at Sand Creek. William headed home, frustrated with the intransigence, red tape, and double-talk. George shared his father's view. He returned to the Bluff Creek village south of the fort. He could live peacefully with Magpie in Black Kettle's lodge. Free from taxing treaty negotiations, he could now focus on the life of a husband and warrior in the Cheyenne fashion. William must have felt the same kind of relief when he was able to go back to his ranch.

In December George joined a war party of eighty warriors against the Pawnees. He again conducted himself in a manner that won him honor as a warrior. Life was good for George at this time, but the calm would not last.

The Dog Soldiers continued raiding and killing on the Smoky Hill Road. The Sioux attacked Brevet Lieutenant Colonel William Fetterman and his command in Wyoming. And General William Tecumseh Sherman, commanding the Military District of Missouri, became convinced that the Indians "must be exterminated, for they will not settle down."[243] Once again the peaceful Indians were not recognized as different from the hostile Indians who continued fighting. As a direct result of this policy, Major General Winfield Scott Hancock, commander of the Department of Missouri and a Union hero of the battle of Gettysburg, decided early in December 1866 on a spring preemptive strike against the Cheyennes.

Rumors during the winter of 1866 - 67 that the Indians were planning to begin war in the spring were unfounded. The winter camps of all the tribes had white traders present. These traders would have known if there was such a plot, especially since they always stayed in the lodges of the prominent chiefs because the chiefs protected the traders and their goods.

One such trader was David Butterfield, formerly an operator of the Overland Dispatch stage line. He had hired George in January 1867 to sell goods to the Kiowa and Prairie Apache camps located twenty miles from the Cheyenne camp on Bluff Creek. Butterfield got wind that trouble with the government was brewing, and he instructed George to bring in all the goods, robes, and arms. The trade in arms and ammunition was booming as the sustenance of the Kiowas and Apaches, like the other plains Indians, now depended on guns. To survive they needed firearms for hunting and defense. For hundreds of years the plains tribes depended on buffalo for food, shelter, clothing, and tools. By increasing their kills with guns, they were participating in their own destruction, at least in a small way. They did not recognize the awful consequences of the guns-for-hides economy until the white buffalo hunters increased the slaughter exponentially.

Major Wynkoop, agent for the Cheyennes and Arapahos, reported that he had tried to assure the army that the Indians were quietly hunting, but General Hancock wasn't listening. General Sherman also turned a deaf ear. "Congress at this time wished to negotiate, which displeased the generals. In the euphemistic language favored by military men, General Sherman advised Hancock on March 14, 1867, that Congressional sentiment 'prevents our adopting preventive measures.'"[244]

George was in Black Kettle's camp with Magpie when they got news of the large body of troops under

General Hancock marching toward Fort Larned. Fear entered the village again. There was no history of respect for treaties by the whites to give any reassurance to peaceful Indians.

One has to wonder how much General Hancock understood about Indian warfare, since he set out from Fort Riley in April with a support wagon train, pontoons, journalists—and about fourteen hundred men, including cavalry, artillery, and infantry. He obviously was not getting the idea that large armies were always watched and reported on by Indian scouts, and no braves were going to ride into their path. His ponderous, noisy expedition might have been a signal that he had planned on only attacking settled villages. Clearly his march with a large force indicated that he would not be very successful against the fast, mobile warriors.

What is known is that he stated that the result of the expedition would depend on the attitude of the Indians. If they were peaceful they would not be punished for past grievances. However, if they were hostile the government was ready and able to punish them. His tone suggests that he did not differentiate between peace Indians and hostiles.

When he reached Fort Larned, Hancock sent word to the Indian agents to bring the tribes in for a council. George recalled in his letters to George Hyde that, as the runners to the Cheyenne camp reported these large numbers of troops at Fort Larned, Black Kettle, much disturbed, called his own council. "Our bitter experience with troops in the past served to make us hunt for cover when we learned of the arrival of Hancock's force at Fort Larned," reported George.[245]

Black Kettle decided to move farther south to try to stay away from Hancock and whatever his intentions were. They would travel all the way to Comanche country in Texas to seek safety. The Kiowas and Prairie Apaches followed Black Kettle's lead. The Comanches and Apaches made a similar decision, and they all moved down to the north fork of the Canadian River.

Black Kettle and his peace followers moved to avoid troops as often as they would have seasonally done to follow the herds. Francis Parkman and others gave some fascinating reports of seeing large Indian camps on the move, painting a picture of organized commotion. Watching from a hilltop as the deconstruction of the village unfolded, Parkman bequeathed to us this thrilling vision:

> [T]he whole village came into view at once, straggling away for a mile or more over the barren plains before us. . . . Here were the heavy-laden pack-horses, some wretched old woman leading them, and two or three children clinging to their backs. Here were mules or ponies covered from head to tail with gaudy trappings, and mounted by some gay young squaw, grinning bashfulness and pleasure as the Meneaska [thought to mean white person] looked at her. Boys with miniature bows and arrows were wandering over the plains, little naked children were running along on foot, and numberless dogs were scampering among the feet of the horses. The young braves, gaudy with paint and feathers, were riding in groups among the crowd, and often galloping, two or three at once along the line, to try the speed of their horses. Here and there you might see a rank of sturdy pedestrians stalking along in their white buffalo-robes. These were the dignitaries of the village, the old men and warriors, to whose age and experience that wandering democracy yielded a silent deference. . . . The

restless scene was striking and picturesque beyond description."[246]

This scene of freedom is one that we and our children will never know or see. Later, Parkman again described the scene as these rugged people functioned as a community and re-established order with a new camp:

> The little spot was crowded with the confused and disorderly host. Some of the lodges were already completely prepared. . . . Others were as yet mere skeletons, while others . . . lay scattered in complete disorder on the ground among buffalo robes, bales of meat, domestic utensils, harness and weapons. Squaws were screaming to one another, horses rearing and plunging, dogs yelping, eager to be disburdened of their loads, while the fluttering of feathers and the gleam of barbaric ornaments added liveliness to the scene. The small children ran about amid the crowd, while many of the boys were scrambling among the overhanging rocks, and standing, with their little bows in their hands, looking down upon the restless throng. . . . [A] circle of old men and warriors sat in the midst, smoking in profound indifference and tranquility. The disorder at length subsided.[247]

And so a village of hundreds of people and more livestock soon settled into their usual village life.

Others have commented on this spectacle of the moving village, an everyday activity for the plains Indians. In 1857 troops led by James Sedgwick rounded a bend in the river and spotted three to four hundred men, women, and children strung out as far as the men could see. They made the troops nervous but the Indians had no intent to cause trouble with their families and possessions so vulnerable. The Indians too were alarmed to suddenly see so many troops, and they hurried the women and children with the packhorses up the river while the warriors gathered to defend the village. A standoff took place, and Sedgwick prepared his men for battle, but when he gave an ultimatum to the warriors to return across the river, the battle was averted.

Though many bands moved south, some remained. When Hancock heard a rumor that there was a camp of Dog Soldiers and Lakota on Pawnee Fork with five hundred lodges, he assumed they were hostile. Wynkoop received a letter from Hancock instructing him to inform the Indians that he was coming to visit. The Indians were to "abandon their habit of infesting the country travelled by our over-land routes, threatening, robbing and intimidating travelers."[248] This was not a conciliatory tone.

Wynkoop called the principle chiefs of the Dog Soldiers, and the remaining Cheyennes to Fort Larned to talk to Hancock. The chiefs rode their jaded horses for thirty-five miles through deep snow. Hancock chose to talk to these chiefs at night—another indication that he knew nothing about the Indians and wasn't competent to deal with them. The Indians did not hold councils at night, and they felt suspicious.

Hancock spoke to the chiefs about white prisoners that he wanted returned. The Indians knew nothing about these prisoners (it turned out they were taken in Texas by the Kiowas), but Hancock was willing to hold them responsible, and he told them he was going to the village. Wynkoop protested, knowing this would be threatening to the women and children. Hancock was making every possible mistake that aroused fear in these people with the memory of Sand Creek.

The chiefs riding with Hancock's column toward the village were very worried. They, too, knew how the women and children would feel when they saw a large body of troops approaching. The Indians were late to their meeting with Hancock because their village was ten miles farther than had been anticipated. Hancock decided the Indians felt guilty and were not coming. He continued his threatening march toward the camp.

After marching six miles Hancock was met by three hundred warriors. He deployed his men for battle. Again Wynkoop tried to intervene and asked to ride forward to meet the Indians to reassure them. Hancock distrusted the Indians and the agent, and he rode out with Wynkoop. The parlay between the battle lines of the two forces was fractious. Roman Nose, a well-known Cheyenne warrior who Hancock insisted was a chief, wanted to kill Hancock, but Bull Bear talked him out of it because it would endanger the women and children.

Hancock asked Roman Nose if he wanted war. Roman Nose replied sarcastically that if they did they wouldn't have ridden in the open in the face of Hancock's big guns. Bull Bear asked Hancock not to approach close to the village, but Hancock insisted that he would camp near the village, and he did.

After Hancock made camp, the chiefs informed him that the women and children had fled. Hancock asked why. Roman Nose said they were afraid and hadn't Hancock heard of Sand Creek? No amount of warning could make Hancock realize how frightened the Indians were. He regarded their flight as treachery.

That evening the chiefs decided to follow the women and children and slipped away. When Hancock heard that they were decamping, he ordered his men to surround the village, but everyone was already gone except for an injured Sioux, his wife, and a little girl.

Hancock waited for three days for the Indians to return and finally ordered Lt. Colonel George A. Custer to pursue them. Then he "moved the infantry into the abandoned camp. In a methodical manner the lodges and their contents were inventoried, and then everything was burned."[249] The inventory included 251 teepees, 962 buffalo robes, 436 saddles, hundreds of parfleches, lariats, mats, and articles for cooking, eating, and living. Everything they owned, except the clothes on their backs and the ponies they rode, was destroyed.

If he couldn't catch the Indians, Hancock determined to hit them where it hurt most. Destroying their means to live would force acceptance of government control over the Cheyennes, which reinforces the impression that Hancock set out to execute General Sherman's Civil War scorched-earth tactic.

Meanwhile, Custer was not having much success. He had ordered Ed Guerrier to guide the 7th Cavalry in their pursuit. This was a difficult task for a mixed-blood who had friends in the village. Not only was he engaged to Julia Bent, he was a survivor of Sand Creek. These mixed-blood survivors had a bond that others could never understand. Worse, Julia was among the terrorized women and children fleeing from the military. As a scout riding ahead of the troops, Guerrier was able to warn the Indians away and to convince Custer that they had scattered too much for pursuit. Custer, new to this kind of warfare, believed Guerrier and rode north, away from the fleeing Indians.

After their village was burned the Indians rode to the Smoky Hill River and attacked a stage station. Payback had started. Through the summer the warriors raided in what is now Kansas and Nebraska. Since their scouts constantly reported troop locations, it was easy for the raiding parties to avoid large detachments of troops and only fight smaller groups. Custer's summer campaign on the Republican and Smoky Hill was a failure.

Hancock returned to Fort Leavenworth in May, thus ending Hancock's War, as the press had titled the campaign. His demonstration-in-force to promote "peace" was nullified by his burning of the village on the Pawnee Fork, which only insured retaliation. The plains tribes saw the destruction of tipis with all their contents— valuable buffalo robes, stored food, and all their personal possessions—as a repeat of Sand Creek and a repudiation of the Little Arkansas Treaty. With Hancock's aggression and the determination of the Indians to fight back, the plains were again in flames through Kansas, Nebraska, and the future state of Colorado.

For four months Hancock's War raged, but his fourteen hundred men reported only two Cheyennes and two Sioux killed. Custer's pursuit of the vanished village was fruitless. By May 9, 1867, the campaign was over but the trouble Hancock stirred up was not. The Indians continued burning stations and attacking coaches along the Fort Harker (central Kansas near the Smoky Hill River) to Denver road during June through September.

General Sherman reported to Secretary of War Stanton that if fifty Indians were left between the Arkansas and the Platte, it would take three thousand soldiers to guard the stage stations, trains, and railroad work parties. He felt it made little difference whether they were coaxed into peace or killed. However, commission member John Sanborn would later tell the Secretary of the Interior, "For a mighty nation like us to be carrying on a war with a few straggling nomads, under such circumstances, is a spectacle most humiliating, an injustice unparalleled, a national crime most revolting."[250]

When Black Kettle arrived on the South Fork of the Canadian River, criers brought the news of the April 14 burning of the Dog Soldier-Lakota village.

The Cheyennes held a council, and the next morning moved farther south to the Washita River. At the head of the Washita, they were joined by the other Cheyenne bands.

They were there about three weeks. Some scattered to hunt, others sent war parties north to retaliate against what Hancock had started. George went with a party of seventy-five warriors to a known camping site at the Cimarron Crossing. There they attacked a mule train going west and ran off about fifty mules. A second attempt to run off more livestock failed because some of the warriors attacked prematurely. This was always a problem for undisciplined fighters. Young warriors often just could not wait until the time to spring a trap because they were so anxious to gain glory. Individual acts of bravery won honor for them.

The commissioner of Indian Affairs summed up the disastrous summer campaign: "We lost over 300 soldiers and citizens, several millions of dollars in expenses, and an immense amount of public and private property, and killed, it is believed, six Indians, and no more."[251] Congress appointed a commission to make peace with all the hostile Indians, if possible, and remove the causes of war. Again a new treaty would be negotiated. It was decided to hold a large council on Medicine Lodge Creek south of the Arkansas.

Endnotes

239. Halaas & Masich, *Halfbreed*, 208.
240. Ibid, 210.
241. Brown, Bury *My Heart at Wounded Knee*, 149.
242. Ibid, 150.

243. G. Hyde, *Life of George Bent*, 267, n 1.

244. Connell, *Son of the Morning Star*, 134 - 135.

245. G. Hyde, *Life of George Bent*, 269.

246. Parkman, *The Oregon Trail*, 264.

247. Ibid, 340.

248. Grinnell, *The Fighting Cheyennes*, 248.

249. Brown, *Bury My Heart at Wounded Knee*, 157.

250. Ibid, 157.

251. Halaas & Masich, *Halfbreed*, 224.

14 ∾ MEDICINE LODGE
TREATY 1867

GEORGE RECOGNIZED THE FUTILITY of fighting even as he participated in the retribution for Sand Creek. He always hoped for peace and did not fight with the kind of rage that Charley expressed. He remained close to his father, Robert, Mary and Julia. His thoughts turned more toward peace, even though the memories of Sand Creek still pained him.

Since the attack at Sand Creek, George had been living with his mother's people. The border press and the press in the East created celebrity for Charley and George. False stories about the brothers abounded. These were widely circulated and believed.

When George returned to the camp after the raids at Cimarron Crossing, Black Kettle brought a Mexican named Salvatore to him. Salvatore had brought a letter to Black Kettle from Colonel Jesse Leavenworth. For several days there had been no one in the village who could read the letter so Black Kettle had come to ask George to read it.

The letter requested that the chiefs of the Cheyennes, Arapahos, Kiowas, Comanches, and Prairie Apaches come in to talk with the Colonel Leavenworth to plan for a full council in the fall. Black Kettle agreed to go meet with Leavenworth and asked George to accompany him.

Recently, when some Wichita Indians were returning from a raiding trip with a herd of stolen Texas horses, a fight had taken place with the Cheyennes and one Wichita was killed. There was fear of traveling through the Wichita country where promised revenge threatened any Cheyennes caught there. However, the Wichitas sent assurance of safety for any Cheyennes coming in to talk peace with Leavenworth. Between the possible danger from the Wichitas and his reputation due to the eastern press, it was a doubly dangerous undertaking for George. Travel for a small party of seven non-warriors (other than George) into proximity of the Wichita camp, was a risk that only Black Kettle, George, and their small group would take. The other chiefs opted out of this trip for planning a treaty council.

When they arrived at the Arkansas and crossed the high waters, Leavenworth and others, including some Wichitas, were there to greet them. The next day they met in council. Leavenworth read a long letter from Major General William S. Harney, Commissioner of Indian affairs, stating that a commission would be sent to meet with all the Indians in council. Leavenworth asked them to pick a time and place near Fort Larned for the fall council. Black Kettle said he would talk this over with his people and returned home.

The Indians expressed their main concern that the whites should abandon the roads through their hunting grounds. Railroads would drive off the game. They said they couldn't adapt to a settled life. It is unclear whether the following quote was stated at the first or second council, but one Indian summed up the feelings of the tribes when he said, "Ever since I have been born

I have eaten wild meat. My father and grandfather ate wild meat before me; we cannot give up quickly the customs of our fathers."[252] In an unsophisticated manner this unknown man's voice can still be heard explaining the basis of the problem for the Indians. You can almost hear his pain.

After the parlay, Leavenworth asked George to stay and wait for him at the mouth of the Little Arkansas. He was gone about a month. On his return he read George a letter announcing that Thomas Murphy, the superintendent of Indian affairs for the district, was already at Fort Larned and that great quantities of goods were being shipped for distribution to the Indians.

George succeeded in getting support for the treaty council from all the chiefs among the Cheyennes, Arapahos, and even the Dog Soldiers. Getting the cooperation of the Dog Soldiers was a diplomatic coup for George. Just to have them willing to participate was an important step toward lasting peace. He continued to the Kiowa, Comanche, and Prairie Apache camps and convinced those tribes to participate. He had convinced tribal leaders to participate during the height of summer fighting. This was an achievement worthy of his father. "He had already earned his place among the warrior societies; now he had earned the right to sit with the chiefs at the council fires."[253] George's role as liaison to the tribes was fast taking on a major significance. He would also act as an interpreter at the meeting, a position requiring the trust of both whites and Indians. A new role for George was emerging.

The council opened on October 16, 1867, at Medicine Lodge Creek fifty miles south of Fort Larned, a favorite site for the Indians summer medicine-making camps and for winter camps. There were one hundred seventy Arapaho lodges, one hundred fifty Kiowa lodges, eighty-five Prairie Apache lodges, and two hundred fifty Cheyenne lodges. There were fully five thousand Indians in attendance. The great camp included a two hundred cavalry escort for the commissioners, drivers for one hundred sixty-five wagons with gifts and supplies, for a total of six hundred whites with twelve hundred animals.

The Dog Soldiers made a dramatic charging entry alarming the Arapaho and Prairie Apache guard, but there was no trouble. George related that the Dog Soldiers were the head of this peace council and their leaders signed the eventual treaty, as did many chiefs.

A new policy was evolving in the government's dealings with the Indians as more and more land was needed. "No longer would the government be satisfied to acquire Indian land; now the government had decided to alter a centuries-old pattern of life—to make the savage live in a box, wear shoes, turn a furrow, and otherwise emulate wasichu [of non-indigenous descent] farmers."[254]

Buffalo Chief spoke for the southern bands and the Dog Soldiers. He said the Cheyennes did not want to live in houses or have their movements restricted by reservations. They wanted to hunt where they had always hunted between the Arkansas and the Platte Rivers. Buffalo Chief suggested that the white men and the Indians could share the land where the Cheyennes hunted, but the white men of the council did not believe in sharing any of the country north of the Arkansas.[255] He said that once the buffalo were gone they might consider settling down in one place.

The whole point of the treaty for the government was to remove the Indians from the main travel arteries in Kansas and Colorado. A deal needed to be made.

One of the commissioners, John B. Henderson, a Missouri Senator and Chairman of the Senate Committee on Indian Affairs, took George aside for a private discussion. When they returned George took the chiefs aside and explained the deal that was offered.

The Cheyennes could hunt between the Arkansas and Platte Rivers if they would sign the treaty and agree to its provisions. The commissioners believed the buffalo would soon disappear and the Indians believed the buffalo would be plentiful for years to come. This concession to hunting was used to get the participation of the Dog Soldiers. George was able to convince the leaders to sign.

Different tribes negotiated over several days at different times with the commissioners and signed the treaty on different days. The first treaty was signed October 21, 1867, with the Kiowa and Comanche tribes. The second, with the Prairie Apaches, was signed the same day. The third treaty was signed with the Southern Cheyennes and Arapahos on October 28, 1867.

The Cheyennes agreed to promises of peace, safety for emigrant travel and railroads through the Plains, surrender of their lands in Kansas, and restriction of reservation lands to the south of the Arkansas River. However, the terms of the treaty, with reparations for the loss of their land and buffalo simply being a few presents, were not likely to be adequate recompense for their losses.

> This was, in a way, the most important treaty ever signed by the Cheyennes, and it marked the beginning of the end of the Cheyenne as a free and independent warrior and hunter, and eventually changed his old range, from Saskatchewan to Mexico, to the narrow confines of a reservation in Oklahoma.[256]

When William and Charles had gone west, the Indians roamed the plains free, following the great herds and suffered white men only on the tribes' own terms. Now the buffalo were almost gone and the Cheyennes faced utter defeat, their lands reduced to small reservations. When the treaty was fully enforced, their lives would never be the same. Their priority was to live peacefully and not have to witness any more destruction of their families.

White relief at the results of the Medicine Lodge Treaty was well expressed by Alice Kirk Grierson in *The Colonel's Lady on the Western Frontier*. She was the young wife of a Lieutenant serving in the western army in 1867.

> By the end of October, news arrived that the Southern Cheyennes and Arapahoes, the Comanches, the Kiowas, and the Kiowa-Apaches had signed the Medicine Lodge Treaties. With these tribes amply supplied with government annuities and confined to two large reservations, away from white settlement and the transcontinental railroad currently under construction, the long-term prospects for peace appeared excellent.[257]

This naïve white view of the results of the treaty did not account for the fact that the government did not "amply supply" the Indians, nor for the cost to the Indians.

George's success with handling the chiefs and convincing them to sign the treaties impressed the commissioners, press corps, and officers. Without his help and understanding of the Indians, the treaty negotiations would probably not have been successful. After the council, Agent Wynkoop asked George to meet with him about an important assignment with the new Cheyenne and Arapaho Agency.

> For more than a year Agent Edward Wynkoop had observed George's skills as a negotiator.

Young Bent's abilities as a translator impressed him, as did his growing influence with the Cheyenne and Arapaho chiefs and leading men. . . . [N]o man had played a larger role in persuading these recalcitrant chiefs to sign the treaty.[258]

The Indians trusted George and he spoke their languages. George was well educated and well connected. He was comfortable mixing with officers, traders, chiefs, and warrior society headmen. He understood politics, treaty matters, and war. Given all these assets, Wynkoop saw George as an outstanding individual with much to offer. Once George was convinced that the Indians had to adapt to survive, there was no one better qualified to try to save some quality of life for them. Wynkoop, recognizing how helpful George could be to him, proposed a position with the Cheyenne and Arapaho Agency as interpreter and government representative.

George believed that the Medicine Lodge Treaty was good for his people and that only through peace could they survive. He was his father's son in this conviction. For William the Cheyennes were the only family he knew, but he wasn't born Cheyenne. George was. William never forgot his roots as evidenced by his efforts to offer guests eastern comforts and luxuries at the fort, by sending his children east for education, by maintaining strong business relationships in the east, and by his interest in contacts with his eastern family. George believed that the whites had superior technology and military power, but he never believed that white ways were superior. With all his skills and his high regard for a people often referred to as savage, how could George not be a tremendous asset for navigating between the two cultures, both of which were a part of who he was.

By working with Wynkoop he could please his father and Black Kettle. Magpie also approved. His job would bring the family money, prestige, and trade goods. However, some in the tribe viewed this job as treachery. He would be working for the white man. Dog Soldiers would see him as a spy and certainly Charley would have disapproved had he known. George respected Wynkoop and considered him a friend. After weighing the pros and cons George accepted the position. He would never be able to please both the Dog Soldiers and the whites, but he came very close to succeeding in finding a balance. This was a major turning point in his life and it would provide direction for the rest of his new life. Few were able to make that kind of adaptation. He would no longer ride the plains as a warrior, but would use his considerable skills to help the Indians transition to a new life.

As George was considering Wynkoop's offer, Charley was with the Dog Soldiers looking for revenge against the Kaws who had run off some Cheyenne horses during the council. Retribution for the insult had to be exacted. During a powwow with a scout named Charlie Coridoro, Charley was shot in the back by Coridoro. Three weeks later , in November 1867, George reported at Fort Harker that Charley had died of his wounds.

Charley never accommodated to white culture after Sand Creek. His rage never burned out. He would never give up his freedom and live on a reservation or see his father again. He could never understand his family's support of reservations and dooming the Cheyennes to trying to scratch out a living as farmers. He spent the rest of his life fighting the unwinnable war until he was killed in 1867. The clash of cultures destroyed Charley. His principles would not allow him to give in or compromise. He had the conviction of his principles just as

Black Kettle did. His sense of betrayal fueled his hatred. He threatened both William and George. William tried to save Charley from his destructive path, but eventually he could only refer to Charley as that "durn'd scoundrel."[259] Charley's response was that he would one day scalp his father, but it was he who died first, a bullet in his back.

White settlers thought that Charley's innate white intelligence and natural Indian savagery made him the most fearsome foe on the plains. Charley had been a very successful leader and warrior against the whites. His campaign of terror was effective in spreading panic. Charley's terror infused raids left whites believing that they had seen him at every Cheyenne raid from Nebraska to Texas, whether or not he was anywhere near that location when the raid occurred. He instilled that kind of fear. It isn't hard to imagine having to walk out on a dark night to check on livestock and feeling that he was watching.

Charley brought a new meaning to the respected Bent name. William had earned the reputation of working for peace, but now the name inspired fear and dread. George, Robert, and William were often called renegades, half-breeds, and "squawmen." It was unfair criticism as each had worked to find a path through the complex labyrinth of the mixed cultures without abandoning their principles of a fair space for everyone.

It was hardly fair to judge men like William, Robert, and George by the white definition of Charley's character. With a prejudice against Indians it was easy to lump all the Bent men together. Charley was no doubt a hero to many Indians for never giving up. It must have been heartbreaking for William to lose a child he loved, though it is easy to imagine a gruff, tough exterior on his part. With so much pride he had named his children after his beloved siblings labeling them as Bents. In so doing, he gave them as much opportunity to be proud Bents as he could. He had unwittingly built a future of heartbreak for himself by not anticipating the racism they would face in their lives.

Racism against the Indians was costing William the cohesion within his family that had been possible when, at his fort, diversity had been acceptable.

Not long after the Medicine Lodge Treaties were signed it was apparent that trouble would crop up again. After the Civil War, the governor of Kansas opened an advertising campaign to induce settlers to come to Kansas. The Cheyennes and Sioux still occupied the valleys of the Saline, Solomon, Republican, and Smoky Hill Rivers. In the meantime there was still some raiding by young men who had started north against the Pawnees, but also committed outrages along the Saline River.

The Medicine Lodge Treaty had not yet been approved by Congress and so was not in effect. Though some chiefs had signed the treaties, there was not yet total commitment on either side. The Indians watched sullenly as bands of white hunters continued to slaughter the herds of buffalo, taking only the hides and leaving carcasses to rot.

The Peace Commission that Congress appointed in July, 1867, reported on January 7, 1868. They concluded that in all cases they had investigated, the difficulties with the Indians, either at the time of the commission's creation or for years previously, was traced to the behaviors of white men—either civilians or soldiers. Coming to this conclusion changed nothing, but it was telling in its time.

The Medicine Lodge Treaty with the Cheyennes was not ratified by the Senate until July 1868 and not proclaimed by the President until August 1868—the treaty with the Sioux not until February 1869. This delay prevented authorities from establishing the Indians on the lands designated for them by the treaty.

Congress appropriated $500,000 to be expended by General Sherman to carry out treaty stipulations—preparing homes, furnishing provisions, tools, and farming utensils, and providing subsistence for the tribes with which treaties had been made—but the money wasn't disbursed. How much good would have been accomplished if the money had been spent as intended?

Invasion by the white people had driven off the buffalo, and according to Wynkoop, the Indians were starving. The Sand Creek Massacre of Cheyennes and Arapahos was less than four years distant, and the attack by Hancock on the village at Pawnee Fork was less than a year old. These attacks were still fresh in the minds of the Indians. Whatever peace some Indians were finding, there still was no universal settlement. Less than a year after the Medicine Lodge Treaty was negotiated, full-scale war broke out on the plains again.

Before troops could arrest the ringleaders of the Saline and Solomon River raids, troops were poured into the field. As usual in the Indian wars, the innocent suffered more than the guilty. Black Kettle knew that, though his people had nothing to do with the raids, trouble would come. Again he moved his people to try to avoid the coming trouble.

When they all reached the Arkansas River, George, Magpie, and their baby Ada, with Ed Guerrier and Julia, left Black Kettle and turned westward on the Santa Fe Trail for William's stockade. George thought Magpie and the baby would be safer there. Black Kettle continued south headed for the Washita River and safety.

When George got to the ranch William was back at Westport, but Mary and Robert were there. It was the first time they were together since Charley's death. When they arrived at Fort Lyon they learned that the fighting had spread once again. George felt there had been plenty of provocation for the recent raids, but he blamed the Indians for the mistake of starting war again. George knew that peace Indians would be blamed for the unrestrained acts of a few. Though Robert agreed to help hunt Cheyenne stock thieves, George would not take the field against the Cheyennes. George and Magpie must have been exhausted with life without peace or respect. The War Department offered George $10 a day to scout for the military, but he refused to fight against his own people.

Endnotes

252. Grinnell, *The Fighting Cheyennes*, 269.

253. Halaas & Masich, *Halfbreed*, 227.

254. Connell, *Son of the Morning Star*, p. 144

255. Brown, *Bury My Heart at Wounded Knee*, 161.

256. G. Hyde, *Life of George Bent*, 285.

257. Leckie, Shirley Anne, edit., *The Colonel's Lady on the Western Frontier, The Correspondence of Alice Kirk Grierson*. (Lincoln: University of Nebraska Press, 1989).21.

258. Halaas & Masich, *Halfbreed*, 243.

259. Ibid, 248.

15 ∽ CUSTER ON THE WASHITA

THE FIGHTING CONTINUED THROUGH the late summer and early fall of 1868 with the Indians raiding without restraint and the troops unable to strike them a decisive blow. About mid-October General Philip Sheridan was authorized to go ahead with his proposed work of punishing the Indians, and he departed Fort Hays, Kansas, on November 6th. General Sheridan was convinced that Indian campaigns in summer were barren of results and determined on a winter campaign as the only way to find the hostiles in predictable locations.

A large number of Indians, all peaceful, were camped on the Washita River (present day Oklahoma) including Black Kettle's seventy-five lodges. Downstream were more Cheyennes, Arapahos, Kiowas and Comanches. This was after the Indians signed the Medicine Lodge Treaty, but before Congress ratified it.

On November 23, General Sheridan ordered General George A. Custer to head a campaign to look for the Indians. When rumors of troops coming reached the Indians, Black Kettle and Little Robe and two Arapahos rode almost a hundred miles to Fort Cobb, headquarters of their agency, to meet with their agent, General William Hazen, whom they perceived as friendly. Black Kettle asked permission to move his lodges near the fort for protection; permission was denied. General Hazen assured Black Kettle that if they returned to their village they would be safe, though he knew of General Sheridan's war plans. The chiefs rode back to their villages through a raw north wind and snowstorm.

A few days later the Battle of the Washita took place. It was heralded as a great victory by the whites. In the peaceful quiet of early morning, Custer attacked Black Kettle's village. One hundred and three Cheyennes were killed. Eleven were warriors. Fifty three women and children were captured. Black Kettle and his wife were killed. The attack was a tragic repeat of the Sand Creek Massacre.

Custer had not scouted the area and did not know of all the Indians camped further downstream from Black Kettle's camp. During the battle, Custer ordered Major Joel H. Elliott to take some men to fight off warriors approaching from downstream. Custer burned the village and slaughtered the horses.

When Custer realized that he had been unaware of the large number of warriors in the area, he used hostages as shields and managed to withdraw before being wiped out by superior numbers. He left Major Elliott and his men behind, and they were overwhelmed. Custer's reputation was tainted by this mockery of the officer's code of responsibility. Custer's impulsive tactics would catch up to him the next time he attacked Indians imprudently and without scouting the hornet's nest he was riding into.

Finally, the army had killed one of the most respected of the peace Indians. Black Kettle never gave up on guiding his people for survival. After many years of trusted leadership he was well regarded for his courage and dedication, even after the Sand Creek Massacre. Like other peace chiefs White Antelope and Yellow Wolf, who died at Sand Creek, he died after dedicating his life to the pursuit of a place in the world for his people. These visionary men did not do this out of love of whites, who only threatened all they held dear, but out of a desire to guide their people through the forced loss of their centuries old lifestyle.

> Black Kettle was a frank, good man, who did not hesitate to expose himself to any danger if he thought that his tribe might be benefited thereby.... Black Kettle was a striking example of a consistently friendly Indian, who, because he was friendly and so because his whereabouts was usually known, was punished for the acts of people whom it was supposed he could control.[260]

Black Kettle was a farsighted man and a determined diplomat who, though considered a savage, could understand the strength and ambitions of the white men. In history outstanding individuals rise above and stand out. He was that kind of man.

Back in the fall of 1864 Wynkoop said of Black Kettle, after their prisoner negotiations:

> [His] dignity and lofty bearing, combined with his sagacity and intelligence, had that moral effect which placed him in the position of a potentate. The whole force of his nature was concentrated in the one idea of how best to act for the good of his race; he knew the power of the white man, and was aware that thence might spring most of the evils that could befall his people.[261]

Testimonials to the character of this outstanding individual merit our respect for this man now lost in time—this man many would have labeled a savage. It is beyond sad that this much admired man who loved his wife and family, as well as his tribesman, should have repeatedly been treated so brutally and yet he maintained his equanimity. He and his wife died together. He was sixty-seven years old.

The result of the winter campaign was that in the spring of 1869 the five tribes went in and settled on their new reservations. Some of the wilder bands of the Kiowas and Comanches remained on the Staked Plains. The Dog Soldiers also still held out on their old hunting grounds on the Republican River, but the Cheyennes did not go to war again until 1874.

Endnotes

260. Grinnell, *The Fighting Cheyennes*, 309.
261. Kraft, *Ned Wynkoop*, 112.

16 ∞ THE FAMILY DEALS WITH A NEW WORLD

WHEN GEORGE AND MAGPIE had separated from Black Kettle's camp, they rode to William's ranch. They found his father living on the south side of the Arkansas at the mouth of the Purgatoire River. William spent the last years of his life at his stockade trading for buffalo robes. He also sent traders out to the Indian camps.

William had worked for peace and good trade relations, but was frustrated by the government's duplicity in its dealing with the tribes, and had retired to his ranch seeking a peaceful life. Robert worked with his father on the ranch and served occasionally as army guide and scout. George had ridden with Charley and the Dog Soldiers but now saw the futility of fighting and accepted the job offer to work as liaison with the tribes.

Thanks to his work helping to bring together the Indians and the peace commissions, George, unlike his siblings, had managed to find a place in his life that worked in both the white and the red worlds. His loyalties were with the Cheyennes but he had also gained the confidence of government officials. For the next fifty years—as interpreter, advisor, special agent, school administrator—he would serve the U.S. government. It is unknown what inner conflicts he still encountered during the coming years, but he tried to master the difficult situation of living two lives and finding peace somewhere in between.

When George stopped at the ranch he found that William, while on a trip to Westport, had married a twenty-year-old mixed-blood named Adaline Harvey. She was the daughter of a Blackfoot woman and an old acquaintance from the river trade days. William had been lonely since Island left and Yellow Woman had joined the Dog Soldiers. William's servant, Billy, told George that William was drunk the night of the ceremony.

Adaline was five years younger than George, and he felt that was strange. Adaline was also pregnant. The family suspected Adaline was after William's money. They made no effort to stop her from returning to Westport to have her baby. Later, after William's death, she claimed, as William's wife, his house in Westport, but the courts evicted her and sold it at auction and awarded her $2,214 of its $15,000 value. The family seems to have considered the marriage a foolish mistake.

Soon George assumed his new duties at the Cheyenne camp on the Cimarron, south of Fort Larned. For five dollars a day he would be well paid to live in the village and report on Cheyenne activities. Agent Wynkoop was well pleased with his work and made that known to Superintendent Thomas Murphy. George was the conduit for the lines of communication with the tribe.

George reported that the camp reeked with illegal whiskey. Sometimes the whole village lay drunk. In the spring of 1868 Agent Wynkoop made his first inspection tour of Cheyenne and Arapaho villages. He brought vital supplies that had been short, though the Cheyennes had been able to hunt some buffalo. It was a tenuous situation.

The Cheyennes continued in their old ways with regards to raiding. On their minds was the determination to avenge the loss of five young men cut down by the Kaws the previous fall. Even Black Kettle had supported the warrior societies against Indian enemies. They could not rest until their enemy had paid.[262]

George was now occupied elsewhere with making peace instead of war. Wynkoop sent George on a mission to northern New Mexico with the Moache Utes and Jicarilla Apaches, traditional enemies of the Cheyennes and Arapahos. George was able to convince the tribes to agree to meet with Wynkoop and conclude a peace. His efforts as a diplomat continued to pay off.

In April, 1868, George paid a visit to William's old friend Kit Carson. Kit was grieving the recent death of his wife, Josefa. He spent time talking about the old days and George enjoyed hearing the tales of Kit and William's early adventures. Kit offered to sell George his racehorse that he had ridden in the 1864 battle at Adobe Walls. George felt lucky riding away on the famous mountain man's favorite horse. Maybe it takes a horseman to know that having Kit's favorite horse would have been an expression of esteem for George. Four weeks later he heard that Kit, a fast family friend, had died. His death was symbolic of the end of an era as the Bents were transitioning to another way of life.

William didn't know of Kit's May 23, 1868, death until he returned to the Purgatoire with a caravan. His close friend and fellow adventurer from the early days, had left this world. The loss had to be a blow to William. Although Kit died from an aneurysm, his son also attributed his demise to grieving for Josefa. Kit followed her death in less than a month.

After his peace mission, George returned to Magpie and baby Ada at Black Kettle's camp near Fort Larned, Kansas. A few days later he reported to Wynkoop that the Cheyennes were unhappy that they had not received the firearms and ammunition promised by the Medicine Lodge Treaty. Firearms were essential for them to hunt to supplement their meager government supplies.

George had some family issues and financial problems because he was not paid for seven months. He had married Kiowa Woman after Magpie had taken her mother into their lodge. By Cheyenne custom, George could not have any contact with his mother-in-law. So he had to move out. He had met Kiowa Woman as an orphan after her parents were killed at Washita, and he was more of a protector than anything else. Now he had the responsibility of two families. The new culture they were living in led to confusion and problems of adjustment. George stayed close to Magpie and loved her, but life was sometimes overwhelming as they made huge changes in all they had known.

In 1878 Little Chief and a band of thirty families from Montana arrived to visit. Among them was a twenty-year-old maiden named Standing Out Woman. She was a real beauty and an exotic Northern Cheyenne. She and George took a shine to each other. George was providing for both Magpie's and Kiowa Woman's families. The bickering between these two families and the competition for his attention wore him down. Standing Out Woman was the adoring, supportive mate he needed. She admired him and gave him much comfort through the trials of his older years. With his three wives George had a total of six children.

George sold the land that he received as settlement

after Sand Creek. It was the land that William had tried so hard to guarantee to his children. Ranching or farming just wasn't in George's make up. Colorado would not designate any land to be used for Cheyenne or Arapaho reservations. The tracts that William had negotiated for mixed-blood tribe members were soon bought out by ranchers. Rancher John Prowers, a white settler with great business acumen, bought George's land and much of the land in southeastern Colorado from the Indians. He built a cattle empire on the land William had hoped to assure for the Cheyennes and mixed-bloods. George and Magpie had settled on Cheyenne and Arapaho land in the Indian Territory in Oklahoma when the Indians were moved to reservations.

Federal policy, enforced by the military, meant that by the end of the decade all the Bent mixed-race offspring who survived the wars had to live in Indian Territory on reservations.[263]

It didn't make any difference if they [the Indians] had white attributes like education, ownership of land, friends in high places, or knew English well.[264] Once they were labeled Indian, like those of mixed Negro blood, the Indians lost their freedom of choice and were disenfranchised. The freedoms their parents had possessed were gone for them. Mary was an interesting exception. She seems to have escaped this outcome by marrying a white man and living like a white in Colorado.

From the beginning of the 19th century, when young, ambitious, and energetic William and Charles strode into the wilderness to build their lives and fortunes, until the ends of William's children's lives, the racial ethics of the country had greatly altered the prospects of the Bent family in the West. The open, free, unregulated land had favored the strong and willing men regardless of background. The Bents had thrived in that climate.

In spite of thriving commercial prospects and Bent accomplishments, the family paid a dear price for settling in this untamed land. They were influential builders in the most volatile and difficult of circumstances. Though they are not remembered as more famous settlers, such as Kit Carson, the Bent name reminds us of many stalwart, brave pioneers who were major players in our history.

On May 19, 1869, William died of pneumonia just days before his sixtieth birthday. He had started a caravan eastward from New Mexico, but the weather was foul and he became sick. When he reached the Purgatoire ranch his daughter Mary nursed him, but a doctor, called from Fort Lyon, gave her little hope and William passed away.

Ironically, "It was at the new Fort Lyon that Kit Carson died, in 1868; and nearby there died, aged sixty, while still active upon the trail, his long-time patron William Bent."[265] These two men, dear friends and yet very different, were made of the sinew that built this country. They made their share of mistakes, but they learned and persevered. We can feel free to admire what their lives gave to us.

William's death hit George hard. No man on the southern plains was better known or more influential than William. Whites saw him as the last of the great mountain men and western traders. The Cheyennes knew him as a trusted advisor and the only white man that understood them, their lives and values.

"William W. Bent spoke five Indian languages and kept the peace between the tribes on the Arkansas, negotiated treaties, and successfully lobbied congressional leaders and U.S. presidents. But as a bookkeeper he had been an abject failure."[266] The Bent heirs received very little from William, who died broke and in debt.

Within a year after William's death George settled permanently in the Indian Territory (now western Oklahoma) with his Cheyenne family. He wanted to be with his wives and children. A new life on the reservation was the only real choice left to him. Fixed trading posts, or even working the ranch, were no longer viable options.

When Agent John D. Miles took over the Cheyenne-Arapaho agency in June 1872 his first order of business was to inform the Indians that President Grant had unilaterally abrogated the old treaty and assigned the Cheyennes and Arapahos a new reservation far from their traditional lands along the Arkansas. Thus the 1867 Treaty of Medicine Lodge was nullified. As with most treaties made by the government with the Indians, Medicine Lodge was unilaterally invalidated by the government. When Miles asked George to be the interpreter to break the news to the Indians, George refused.

On the reservation there was no law enforcement, and crime by interlopers was rampant. Horse thieves, unauthorized buffalo hunters, government food shortages, and illicit alcohol sales compounded the stress of adjustment to a new live.

In 1873 a delegation of Northern Cheyennes and Arapaho chiefs and headmen went to Washington because of a project to remove the Northern Cheyennes to the Southern Cheyennes Reservation in Oklahoma. They were bitterly opposed.

On November 3, they met with President Grant and Dull Knife pointed out that the Fort Laramie treaty of 1868 gave the Northern Cheyennes the option of going onto reservations in the north or south. Nothing came of this meeting, as Dull Knife was insistent that they would not move south. But the government determined that with the influx of gold miners and railroads the buffalo in the north would be destroyed. The Northern Indians were in the way and would have to move south.

In defiance of the same treaty rights, in 1874, the government sent a military expedition into the Black Hills to investigate the finding of gold. The expedition was under the leadership of General George A. Custer. With rumors of gold came a flood of miners and commercial enterprises into the area that led to the inevitable clashes with the Indians. "That the Indians had any right to hold this country, with its mineral and other lands guaranteed to them by the treaty of 1868, apparently never entered anybody's head."[267]

The slaughter of the buffalo was the main cause of the next war in the south. White hunters were killing for hides alone, leaving carcasses to rot. The Indians were filled with bitterness and indignation at the disregard for such a vital food source. There was not much law on the border and none existed for Indians. Had authorities protected the Indians on the reservations, many future problems could have been avoided.

Reservation boundaries remained porous. Drunkenness became a major problem on the reservations causing the breakdown of families. When food shortages were critical the Bureau of Indian affairs encouraged Agent Miles to withhold annuities to ensure good behavior. If the Indians wanted food they had to send their children away to white schools and they had to begin farming.

Grants "peace policy" led to war once again in 1874. Though George was able to help quell the anger and to encourage his people to go to the agency for safety, some renegades went on the war path.

On June 27, 1874, two hundred Cheyennes, Kiowas, and Comanches attacked twenty-eight buffalo hunters and teamsters at Adobe Walls in the Texas Panhandle. The white men were able to hold out with their long range rifles against the Indian bows and arrows. The Indians killed the white men's horses and killed three men. When they could do no further damage the Indians scattered to seek revenge on ranches, wagon trains, and mail carriers in Kansas and Texas. The agency now needed military protection.

On July 20, 1874, the army received permission to hunt down the raiders and drive the warring bands back to their agencies. The Red River War had begun. "At first light on the morning of September 28, 1874, Colonel Ranald Mackenzie's Fourth Cavalry surprised a combined Cheyenne, Kiowa, and Comanche village of nearly three hundred lodges in Palo Duro Canyon in the Texas Panhandle."[268] The Indians fled and only three warriors were killed, but their village was completely destroyed. The army slaughtered nearly a thousand animals.

This attack finally shattered the Cheyenne resistance. Without lodges, food, clothing, and horses survival was impossible. The destruction drove most of the Cheyennes who had escaped, back toward the safety of the reservation. The army's scorched-earth policy was effective again.

George remained with his people and did all he could to calm and reassure them. He kept Magpie and the children safe with a sanctioned hunting party during this uprising. Throughout this time Indians had been raiding north and south.

That winter of 1874 - 75 was severe. Game was scarce and the troops active. The lot of the remaining hostiles who still held out was a hard one. Annuities were slight or non-existent. Most of the Comanches and Kiowas had returned to Fort Sill and surrendered. In January

1875 White Horse and Stone Calf, Dog Soldier leaders, surrendered. On March 6, 1875, Gray Beard and the majority of the Cheyennes still out, came in and were disarmed. About eight hundred Cheyennes finally surrendered. The army and agency officials assigned George the task of identifying Cheyennes who were guilty of committing "criminal acts." The war of 1874 - 75 was now over.

Endnotes

262. Halaas & Masich, *Halfbreed*, 249.

263. A. Hyde, *Empires, Nations, and Families*, 507

264. Ibid.

265. Sabin, *Kit Carson Days 1809 - 1868*, 296.

266. Halaas & Masich, *Halfbreed*, 268.

267. G. Hyde, *Life of George Bent*, 350.

268. Halaas & Masich, *Halfbreed*, 282.

17 ∾ WHO WAS WILLIAM BENT?

Though William's life was largely undocumented, there are eye witness accounts of him that help us to know the man. His reputation is still visible to us. We must see him through the eyes of his peers and his family.

He was not a man to keep records or journals to address his thoughts or feelings. We do know that he looked up to his older brother and was willing to join forces with him. He was just twenty years old when he chose the path for his life. He had a facility for learning languages, became a good negotiator, was skilled in dealing with people, and men looked up to him as a leader. He came to his new calling in the Southwest with the capability to respect and love the people who already lived there.

"What kind of place and time would produce men like the Bent brothers and would allow them to develop deep connections to people of other cultures?"[269] The Bent brothers would venture into the southern plains, which in a white man's mind was an empty wilderness.

It was called "Indian Country." Trade with Mexico was in its infancy, but the trail to the trade was known. Permits for trade with the indigenous people were issued, but New Spain, and later Mexico, exercised little real enforcement in the area. Many traders, hunters, and trappers functioned outside any law. "They knew that the U. S., Spanish, or Mexican governments had little effect on the region. Reputation, personal behavior, and negotiating skills mattered far more."[270] The Bent brothers were well qualified to compete in that environment.

William was a strong family man who built his life around caring for his family. He was an astute businessman who, along with steadfast partners like his brother Charles and friend Ceran St. Vrain, saw opportunity in the future of the vast undeveloped lands of the West. He built a trading empire where hard work and fair dealings with all kinds of people were the keys to success.

In 1846, George Frederick Ruxton, an English adventurer and traveler, visited Bent's Fort during his western travels that started in Mexico and went north. Of William Bent he said:

> William Bent was one of those hardy sons of enterprise with whom America abounds, who, from love of dangerous adventure, forsake the quiet monotonous life of the civilized world for the excitement of a sojourn in the far west. For many years he traded with Indians on the Platte and Arkansa, [sic] winning golden opinions from the poor Indians for his honesty and fair dealing, and the greatest popularity from the hardy trappers and mountaineers for his firmness of character and personal bravery.[271]

Traveling the Santa Fe Trail in 1856 with William Bent was James Ross Larkin, who kept a journal of the thirty-day trip. William, at forty-seven, was leading an annual caravan from Westport, Missouri, to Bent's Fort. No other diarist is known to have recorded travel on the trail with William and "Mr. Bent's Lady." Larkin gives us such a rare view of some of the things he encountered while traveling with William on the fabled Santa Fe Trail that it is worth taking some time with his observations. His writings of everyday life with William give us a many faceted view of William's character.

James was a young man of means from St. Louis who had poor health. His mother and friends urged him to try travel in the West. It was thought, when doctors ran out of other ideas, that the high, dry climate of the West was beneficial to one's health. So James sought out "Mr Wm Bent, a noted Indian Trader, & he consented that I should go out in his train to his Fort . . . distant about 550 miles from Kansas City. . . ."[272] Under William's guidance and with help from various tradesmen, James hastily put together what he would need for the journey. "I felt uneasy about starting on my trip after hearing people talk as they did, but when I saw Mr Bent my fears seemed to dissipate as he appeared to apprehend no very bad trouble," James remarked about William.[273] William's competent manner and assurance provided confidence to this "green horn."

On one occasion William showed James some of his unusual trade goods. He brought out children's spinning tops and sets of jumping jacks. They had cost William about ten cents each, and he anticipated trading them for a buffalo robe apiece. Barton H. Barbour, the editor of James's diary, notes William's inventiveness in selecting trade goods and his sharp sense of how to turn a good profit.

This incident also points out William's intuitiveness about the character of the Indians with whom he was trading. Their children were very important to them, and they would pay a good price for the opportunity to see the delight of the youngsters. They weren't brutal savages as often depicted.

Another insight that Larkin provides in his diary reflects on William's family life. "We have also Mr Bents Lady [describing the company], an Indian woman—the 'old Scwaw' as he calls her, & also her pet—a little Pawnee Indian, who was a prisoner . . . & bot by Mr Bent. He is a great favorite with the old lady."[274] Indians often held children of other tribes or white women in their camps. Some of these children thrived and grew up as members of the tribe, but often their existence was one of severe hardship. Likely William had to pay for the release of this child and apparently "Mr Bents Lady" cared for him.

When the caravan learned of a nearby camp of Cheyennes, William sent word that he would like to talk to them.

> They soon came charging up to our camp on their ponies, making quite a hubbub. Down they seated themselves in a circle & had a long talk until Mr B treated them to coffee & bread, which they eat heartily. They presented quite a warlike appearance, being young Cheyenne warriors in one War Party against the Pawnees. . . . They were very sociable to us—Mr B. being a great favorite of the tribe. . . . They had a very pleasant time chatting with Mr B & the old squaw, & seemed very much pleased. To meet them with any other man than Mr Bent—might not be to [sic] agreeable—they being rather on the savage order.[275]

Often Indians are represented as stoic and unemotional. This passage shows how they loved to visit, loved a joke, and valued William's friendship.

At this first meeting with the Cheyennes, James had an interesting experience with Mr. Bent's Lady. When some of the braves leaned their guns on the carriage wheel by where James sat, he was uncomfortable with this careless handling of guns. He remarked that the old squaw noticed this danger and reprimanded the braves and had them move their guns. This woman, with her influence on the braves, was watching out for James, their young and inexperienced guest.

As William and James approached the fort, they rode ahead of the caravan because of a report that there was trouble at the fort. They found that a Frenchman who worked for William was selling liquor to the "Kioways." William fired the Frenchman, but that evening the Kiowas came to the fort to dispute the firing. William was enraged and "abused the man and his race (Kioways) prodigiously."[276] One Kiowa drew a knife on William, but William drew his pistol and would have shot the man, but the Cheyennes intervened. Violent words were exchanged and William threw the Frenchman and the Kiowas out of the fort.

The Cheyennes, allied with William, were alarmed and anticipated an attack by the Kiowas. Larkin spent an anxious night. However, the Kiowas didn't attack. They weren't going to take on the Cheyennes. William was a man who knew the violent ways of the West and supported this anti-liquor principle with his temper. He was also setting a standard of behavior that, when disregarded, would have consequences. By this time there would be no selling of liquor to the Indians. It was against the law for traders to sell whiskey to the Indians and the sale would have endangered William's trading license. However, William had also come to know how destructive alcohol was to the Indians and he did not want the kind of trouble it brought when they were around the fort.

Barbour refers to William: "[He] and other cultural expatriots [sic] in the Southwest lived quite comfortably in two, even three, 'worlds': those of the Anglo-American, the New Mexican Hispano, or the Indian."[277] He also notes that William was not a man of Christian forbearance or restraint, citing that he had no proscription against traveling on the Sabbath.

Barbour considers Larkin a proper gentleman and notes that Larkin, "never commits to his diary a disparaging word about Bent or his Indian wife, suggesting that he found no impropriety in Bent's affinity with the aboriginal people and culture of the southern plains."[278] William was accepting of these people, respectful of their culture, and protective of them—values that seem to have impressed Larkin.

The highest of praise of William came from none other than Kit Carson, a peer of William's who gave us an additional insight into William's character. Edwin Sabin records Carson as saying, "I wish I was capable to do Bent and St. Vrain justice for the kindness received at their hands. I can only say that their equals were never in the mountains."[279] Carson honored his relationship with his long-time friend and many times associate. He often worked for William as a hunter.

Chalfant described the legacy that William would have most valued: "[He] exercised considerable influence over the Indians of the region and did much to maintain a tenuous peace between the natives and the European intruders."[280]

William Bent was not a perfect man, of course, but he was a man of his times who had a sense of honor and was honest in his dealings with other people. He was admired and respected by those who knew him. His influence in the early development of the Southwest was known as far away as Washington, DC. Maybe most importantly, he earned the respect and love of the Indians. Their value system provided some different criteria for measuring a man, and he was able to win high regard in their culture.

Harvey Lewis Carter in *'Dear Old Kit'* makes an interesting comparison between William and Kit Carson. He relates that "Bill Bent" was a hard-driving business man and Kit had no business drive at all. William was the kind of frontier individualist that rebelled against government regulation, while Kit worked for the government, regulations and all, much of his life. But these two men were very close. They had both grown and matured in a country that was challenging and dangerous. One evening, Carson rode up to Bent's ranch on the Purgatoire, with some Indians. "An eyewitness recalled that, 'Bill Bent pulled Kit off his horse and they hugged and kissed like a couple of children.'"[281] Though different in some ways these two men had shared the changing of the West. They had a unique bond. As young men they had endured every kind of hardship, had intuitive decision making skills that helped them survive, and had matured having thrived on the opportunities of the frontier.

Mr. Carter added that when Kit settled on the Purgatoire a few miles from Fort Lyon he had several reasons for going there—one was: "His old friend William Bent lived in that vicinity, where he still had some influence among both settlers and Indians. He might be able to help Kit get the Colorado Indian superintendency [sic]."[282] Old friends could count on William's loyalty.

William must have felt he had all the land he needed and since his interest had never been in holding large tracts of land, he was willing to be generous. "[He] had been promised 6,000 acres on the Purgatoire (no doubt by St. Vrain) and that he gave Kit Carson and Tom Boggs half of it."[283] He had his ranch on the Purgatoire which must have been enough. William Bent was a steadfast friend, a hard driving man who had accomplished his goals; he was no longer an "empire builder." After sharing so much with his friends from the early days, William probably liked having old friends as neighbors.

William's peers saw him as a fair man, one worth trusting and respecting. He was a man they could count on, as could his family. Black Kettle and other Indians turned to him for help and advice knowing he cared about their concerns and wanted a fair break for them. Unfortunately, this was one thing he could not accomplish. There was no turning back the white tide and no good outcome for the nomadic indigenous people of the Plains.

Traveler O. A. Nixon visiting the fort in 1855 said, "It is a very good Fort and a safe refuge to the emigrants or for who-ever seeks one; nice rooms, plastered walls, & . . . remind me of HOME and it seems that I am in a Civilized Country again."[284] That was William's intention. The new fort gave him the order he needed. He wanted for himself and his children the social structure of his youth, one defined by a clear hierarchy. Nixon had an interesting reaction to seeing Mrs. Bent. He later wrote, "Went down to the Room (Office) to see Mrs. Bent, to-day. She's pretty much Indian."[285]

Endnotes

269. A. Hyde, *Empires, Nations, and Families*, 152.

270. Ibid.

271. George Frederick Ruxton, *Wild Life in the Rocky Mountains* Edited by Outing Adventure Library, (Waxkeep Publishing, 1847 - 48) Kindle Edition, 49 - 50.

272. Larkin, *Reluctant Frontiersman*, 68.

273. Ibid, 69 - 70.

274. Ibid, 73. Larkin does not designate which of William's wives was in the company.

275. Ibid, 77.

276. Ibid, 83.

277. Ibid, 55.

278. Ibid.

279. Kit Carson as Dictated to Col. and Mrs. D. C. Peters about 1856 - 57, *Kit Carson's Own Story of His Life* (Santa Barbara, California: The Narrative Press, 2001), 44.

280. Chalfant, *Cheyennes and Horse Soldiers*, 11.

281. Carter, *'Dear Old Kit'*, 214.

282. Ibid, 172.

283. Ibid, 172 - 173.

284. Halaas & Masich, *Halfbreed*, 76.

285. Ibid.

18 ‹› SURVIVAL THROUGH RESILIENCE

THE DECADE OF THE 1870s brought immense changes to the lives of the Cheyennes and the Bent family. Hunger, poverty, loss of freedom and a familiar life-style, lawlessness, and alcohol—these and other problems stressed their lives and required adjustments they were not prepared to handle.

When the government decided, in the winter of 1874 - 1875, to arrest the Indian leadership for imprisonment at Fort Marion in Florida, nine Comanches, twenty-six Kiowas, two Arapahos and thirty-three Cheyennes were chosen for incarceration.[286] This was a devastating confinement and, for an Indian, a cruel and unusual punishment. These were a people of the outdoors. The older Indians never understood the white man's system of arrest. Grown men were never made prisoners by the Plains Indians. If captured, you were promptly killed. That was the only honorable ending to battle for the loser. Only women and children were taken captive. There was no honor in the death trap at Fort Marion.

The famous Cheyennes and Lakota defeat of General George Armstrong Custer at the Little Bighorn River in Montana in 1876, increased restlessness among the Southern Cheyennes. Custer had disobeyed his orders and rode into a huge camp without scouting the enemy first, just as he had at the Washita River. His command was wiped out, causing a huge national reaction of mourning, sadness, and anger. The Cheyennes felt the northern tribesmen had something to boast about and trophies to display. They had a great victory to commemorate for years to come while the Southern Cheyennes seemed to have only the taste of defeat.

As the Indians struggled with the transition to peaceful resettlement on reservations, hunger was a major threat to the peace as much as anything. Many people sickened and died. To supplement their food supply it was decided to let some bands have sanctioned hunts for buffalo along the Washita River under the guidance of George's brother Robert. The experiment worked well in 1875.

In October, 1876, when Agent John Miles offered George the opportunity to lead the sanctioned buffalo hunt, George jumped at the chance. For a moment the Indians could enjoy a taste of the past. But there were problems that year with controlling the restless Indians and the experience for George was disappointing.

During the hunt he learned the extent of his mixed-blood as an obstacle among the Indians. George felt he had earned a rightful place of honor among the Cheyennes and was hurt by a growing racial prejudice among the Indians. He believed he had earned the respect of the people he had chosen as his own. He was a Crooked Lance warrior and veteran of twenty-seven war parties. In 1876 he was wealthy enough to support two wives and two families. He stood with the chiefs at Medicine Lodge as a treaty was negotiated. He had married into Chief Black Kettle's family. But because he was a half-breed he would never be accepted as a chief. He struggled with that for the rest of his life. The chiefs were suspicious of his white position.[287] Now the clash of cultures struck from both racial directions. William had tried through the years to make George understand the special place he held between two worlds and now those lessons would take meaning.

George continued trying to carve out a place for himself in this confused new world. He was drawn to leadership, power, prestige, and the honor of this opportunity to lead the hunt. His white father had ruled Bent's Fort and was a leader in the Santa Fe trade. His Cheyenne grandfather had been Keeper of the Arrows, a position of great honor. Leadership was in his blood, but unlike them, he was a half-breed, and therefore, limited in opportunities—judged by race and not by skill sets. He resented this restraint.

These transition years drove a wedge between George and his Indian relationships, as well as his white connections. He gradually became a man apart from both the white and the Indian worlds when he took a position with the Indian agency. Some saw him as a traitor, particularly after he was involved in land sales of Indian land to whites. He became a scapegoat to many Cheyennes.

In the winter of 1877 discouragement was mounting in George. He had his horse herd stolen by whites who thieved from the Indians without accountability. His horse herd was his measure of wealth. He had the stress of holding down two jobs and supporting two families. He was trying to please both the agent and the chiefs.

Conditions on the reservation were bad enough that on September 9, 1878, three hundred fifty-three

Cheyennes stole horses and the equipment they would need and bolted from the reservation heading for the Powder River country and freedom. Six hundred and fifty stayed on the reservation.

George understood why the renegades ran. They longed for their old way of life. He did not betray their confidence, but he did not agree with their decision. The buffalo were gone and he believed, like his father, that the Indians had to learn another way to live or they would die.

Though liquor was illegal on the reservation it was always available. By 1876, George had gotten into the habit of drinking more than he could really tolerate and the problem only got worse. The drinking was hurting his reputation among the Cheyennes, though drinking was commonly accepted. In his position a double standard applied. He was seen as having divided loyalties, and he chose to escape through the bottle. Creating a bridge between two cultures was more than he could handle at that point.

However, George was not an idle reservation drunk—another prejudiced stereotype that began in the late-nineteenth century. He continued working as an interpreter, he worked with the agency traders, he bought and sold racehorses, and he partnered with his brother Robert in a cattle ranch. Continuing the easy sociable personality of his youth, George loved going to cowboy balls, he traveled for enjoyment in Colorado and Kansas. He liked the high life and tended to spend too extravagantly. He was confident of his position on the reservation, but there was an erosion of his status taking place among the chiefs because of his drinking sprees and non-traditional life style.

The editor of the *Arkansas City Traveler* (Arkansas City, a wild Kansas cowtown) was impressed with George.

He did not see a drunken half-breed, but a Cheyenne leader of distinction. This editor wrote, "[He]probably has more influence among his people than has any other man in the tribe."[288]

George's binge drinking did not seem to interfere with business. In May 1883 he was hired by traders Hamphill and Moy as interpreter and salesman. He was paid well for influence peddling when he urged the Indians to lease land to the growing demand from cattle ranchers. His financial situation improved and he paid as much as five hundred dollars for a team of horses and spent large sums gambling and horse racing.

However his sprees did not help his tarnished reputation on the reservation. The chiefs were unhappy with him, his agent grew tired of defending him, and though Kiowa Woman was divorced from him and remarried, she thought he should be doing more to support his children. They were, after all, still Bents.

George's behavior had convinced the chiefs that he could not be trusted. Now he had reason to lose confidence in his place in the Cheyenne community, his home. In his broad brimmed white Stetson, wool suit, and leather boots he had become the model of assimilation and was resented.

By the mid-1880s leasing Indian land had come to a head as an issue for the chiefs who believed it wasn't in the best interest of the Indians. Stone Calf and Whirlwind accused George of bullying members of the tribe into accepting lease payments. The chiefs wanted George, other mixed-bloods, and the new agent, D. B. Dyer, banned from the reservation. George's training was as a plains warrior and he didn't have the business values that were William's. He had many skills he could use in the transition to reservation life but his journey was not without failures.

At a point when warfare on the reservation over land leasing issues seemed inevitable, General Philip Sheridan, newly appointed commander of the army, visited the reservation and investigated the problems. After a week of talking to chiefs, cattlemen, and agency officials he removed the insensitive agent and put the reservation under army control. Sheridan recommended to President Cleveland the abolishment of the lease system. Cattlemen were banished from the reservation. Bent was allowed to stay on as interpreter for the army. There was a real need for stability and economic security in this baffling new world.

When things hit bottom for George, he received word of the death of Magpie Woman, the love of his life. They had been apart for some years, but they had married during the old days when the Cheyennes lived free—at a time that now seemed a dream. Though living apart after she had her mother in her lodge, they were still intimate and had children to hold them together. This was a traditional way for Indians to live.

George doted on Ada and Charley, their surviving children. With Magpie went a part of him. For years Kiowa Woman had poisoned her children against George resulting in familial battles and stress. Now for George, the centerpiece of his life was gone.

In 1887 Congress passed the Dawes Act which was intended to wipe away the concept of tribal ownership of land by allotting each family its own property. The idea was to force assimilation. It was supposed the Indians would become ranchers or farmers and, once integrated, they would get citizenship. The reservation system was a failure in terms of turning Indians into whites. The Indian culture was too strong. Only a quarter of the Cheyennes had abandoned their traditional ways. Few could speak English or read. With a stroke of the pen reformers believed the Act would destroy the tribal way of life by substituting private ownership for communal living. This struck a final blow at the very core of the Indian way of life.

George believed in private ownership, but he knew the chiefs would resist. Lawyers realized that first the Medicine Lodge Treaty of 1867, that George had helped negotiate, had to be nullified. They knew Bent was the key to acceptance of the plan, as he had been with the treaties of the past. George desperately needed the money they offered him for his help. He needed it to pay off debts. The concept of learning to live within the means of money was a new concept for an Indian and George didn't handle it well.

In the midst of this legal battle George heard that his brother Robert had died suddenly on the Canadian River ranch. George suffered from depression after his brother died. They had been close. Robert had handled George's financial affairs and been his rock of stability. Robert was seen as a model Cheyenne rancher. By working with his father all his life and learning business as a white man would, Robert had learned financial skills that George lacked. The memory of Sand Creek, where he had been forced to lead the soldiers to Black Kettle's camp, haunted Robert until his death.

Robert had a side to his personality that lightened the picture of him as a model citizen. When he heard a bunch of cowboys bragging about their prowess as Indian fighters, he rode into their saloon, guns blazing and giving an Indian war whoop. An eyewitness reported, "These brave Indian killers did not wait to go through the door but jumped through the windows, taking the sash and all with them. The last we saw of them they were on their way to Texas, not waiting to say 'Goodbye.'"[289]

Recognized by the government and the tribe as the official interpreter for the Dawes Act agreement, George had the responsibility to certify tribal acceptance.

> On November 14, 1890, Bent certified that three-quarters of the adult males approved the relinquishment "of all their right, claim, and interest in and to lands in Indian Territory." This allowed Congress in March 1891 to apply the Dawes General Allotment Act to the Cheyenne and Arapaho Reservation, thus opening it for allotment and sale. Once, the Cheyennes and Arapahos freely roamed the Central Plains—now carved up into the States of Colorado, Wyoming, Montana, Kansas, and Oklahoma Territory.[290]

Three thousand three hundred and twenty nine allotments of 160 acres each were provided to the Indians along the Canadian and Washita Rivers. The Indians were to get $1.5 million in reparations for the land claim cessation. The rest of the reservation was opened for sale and white settlement. Many Cheyennes blamed George for his influence in getting the Dawes Act implemented. Many questioned whether three quarters of the adult male signatories were legitimate and whether the certification was fraudulent.

Ultimately George was overwhelmed by drink and the politics of the white world. Government commissioners dismantled the reservation. George accepted whatever work he could get, mostly as interpreter and liaison. George had played a critical role in gaining tribal support for the sale and breakup of the reservation into individual allotments. In 1934 the government ended the failed allotment system but the damage had been done.

At Colony's Seger Indian School, where George worked as a clerk and interpreter, youngsters read white man's books. This concerned George. Every year the Colony Indian cemetery held more scaffolds and fresh graves. George realized that soon there would be no one to tell the stories and the history of their former Cheyenne lifestyle to these youngsters.

A new purpose came into George's life. In 1901 George met well-known ethnographer George Bird Grinnell, when Grinnell hired Bent as an interpreter. For eleven years George shared stories of the Cheyennes with the ethnographer. He was a gold mine of information. Bent became Grinnell's eyes and ears among the Southern Cheyennes. By 1912 Grinnell completely depended on him to get interviews with chiefs and elders. The informants were Bents friends and family. He had lived with them, fought beside them, shared sorrows and hardships as the free life came to an end. George could feel a new relevance in the tribe.

George turned to odd jobs, and he quit drinking. He leased land and sold his best horses and wagons. His drinking had marginalized him from the mainstream of Cheyenne life, but he worked at regaining their trust. He sold his house and moved to his ranch on the Canadian. He came to realize that his unique understanding and memory of Cheyenne history and culture had value, but George failed to ever sell the published story and get the worth from it that it deserved. He dedicated himself to preserving his people's history simply for the task itself.

George also developed a correspondence with George Hyde, a twenty-three-year old housebound scholar in Omaha, Nebraska. Three hundred and forty letters, written by George Bent between 1905 and 1918, left us first-hand information about the Cheyenne way of life in both peace and war.

Hyde recognized the value of George's memories. He marveled at the rich detail that George could provide.

This was unpublished, original material coming straight from an Indian source. Hyde planned to edit George's letters for publication and eventually used the letters to write *Life of George Bent*.

Grinnell and Hyde collaborated. Grinnell eventually incorporated much of the information that George Bent provided into Grinnell's book *The Fighting Cheyennes* published in 1915. Grinnell led Bent on about what he was writing and Bent waited for seven years for their collaboration to bear the fruit he expected. Preserving the memory of his people had become his sole mission.

George had grown to love telling the stories of his people. At the Seger Indian School where he worked, George regaled the children with the stories of their past and the old free life of the fighting Cheyennes, instilling pride in their culture and heritage.

George loved children and gathered them like the Piped Piper. He always had a treat and a story for them. His daughter Mary had a five-year old son that hero-worshipped George and modeled himself on his grand-father—what higher compliment? In February, 1915, the boy died suddenly. George suffered a terrible grief at this loss of youthful hope for his people. It was one thing to leave the old people in the Indian cemetery on the hill, but to lose this young image of himself as a boy at the old fort, was painful. The boy had listened to all George's stories of the old life and remembered. Now who would be the memory of the Cheyenne people and the old life? He feared their oral history would be lost.

George and Standing Out Woman lived a simple, frugal life with Standing Out Woman using traditional skills to make and sell fine beaded moccasins, buckskin dresses, and a traditional skin lodge to help earn some income. Their children and grandchildren visited often and the family enjoyed taking in entertainments like time-honored dances and ceremonies. They even enjoyed the Ringling Brothers Circus.

> George kept abreast of world events, reading more than a dozen newspapers and magazines every week. The concept of aerial combat and mechanized warfare intrigued him. Telephones, skyscrapers, automobiles, safety razors, moving pictures, medical advances—the world had changed so much from the world he had known. He found it hard, sometimes, to believe he had been born in a buffalo-hide lodge.[291]

George's determined efforts to make a record of his own and his people's history left us a rich saga of life among the Cheyennes and the struggle to live in both worlds, that of the white and the Indian. Without knowing it, he had carried on the standards of a Bent to contribute to the world. So many had died and so much had been lost—a way of life destroyed—but George Bent adapted and left us priceless knowledge.

In May 1918 the global influenza epidemic struck George down. On May 19, one week after he fell ill, George Bent died. Standing Out Woman buried George in the old Indian cemetery east of town. A rough-sawn board marked his grave.

Endnotes

286. G. Hyde, *Life of George Bent*, 364 - 365.

287. Halaas & Masich, *Halfbreed*, 291.

288. Ibid, 306.

289. Ibid, 317.

290. Ibid, 326.

291. Ibid, 347.

19 ∞ CONCLUSION

FROM THE TIME IN the late 1820s when William and his
brother Charles first started venturing West, until
1918 when William's son George died, the father and
son had a tremendous influence on the settlement of
the Southwest. It would be difficult to find two family
members who accomplished and contributed more in
the nineteenth century west.

Of the four Bent brothers that went west, William
was the survivor. He lost his other brothers to violence
and disease, but he persevered in building an important business. He built a business that contributed to
supplying the settlement of the Southwest and provided for the United States Army of conquest. There
was no other supplier in the Southwest that came anywhere near the effect that the trading from Bent's Fort
had on trail-weary travelers. The sight of Bent's Fort
made the heart beat stronger with the knowledge that
a respite from the rigors and dangers of the Santa Fe
Trail were assured.

More than just a businessman, William Bent embraced the indigenous people, treating them with love,
respect, and honesty, contributing to something even
more important—human dignity. He became a vocal,

respected advocate for the Cheyenne Indian tribe. In his efforts to negotiate peace for the Indians, he spoke for any and all peace-loving Indians. By becoming one with them he understood the tragedy that would overcome them and made every effort to help and protect them.

His son George spent his life trying to merge the two cultures flowing through his veins. Ultimately he chose with pride to live as a Cheyenne, honoring his mother's blood, and fighting for justice against a policy of subjugation and even extermination. In turn, George never lost his love and respect for his father. His efforts to serve his people were expended in a losing battle, but when the battle was lost, he learned the new way of life. Though he sometimes faltered in the arduous process of adapting and suffered the censure of some of the Cheyennes, George was accepted by the elders when they turned to telling their story. He also won the love of the children in the school where he worked by giving them pride and knowledge about where they came from at a time when Indians were degraded. Some may have condemned him and labeled him a traitor, but who among them walked the thorny path with more success. Ultimately he gave what may have been the most important contribution of his family—giving life to the memory of the Indian story.

The cost to George of the incompatibility of these two cultures hitting head to head, could have been devastating and crippling. As a child he faced the deaths of so many of his family members, neighbors, and friends that it is hard to imagine living with so much destruction and insecurity. Power struggles between stronger and weaker groups of people always leave the ground littered with broken lives.

One has to respect George's resilience and how differently he handled the devaluing of his life from the way Charley reacted. Charley was filled with rage and hate at the sight of how his mother and the other Indians were treated. He could never adjust to the end of the Indian way of life. He could not forgive and responded to violence with worse violence. George always loved his parents of both races. He had a big heart and like Charley he never gave up—his answer was simply contrary to Charley's.

Artist George Catlin devoted his life to preserving, through his art, the story of many of the Indian tribes in the West. His sensitivity to these people and his foresight for what their future would hold was expressed with great emotion. He writes:

> The lucky white man will return to his comfortable home with no misfortune, save that of deep remorse and a guilty conscience. There is plenty enough to claim his pity and engage his whole soul's indignation at the wholesale and retail system of injustice which has been, from the very first landing of our forefathers, visited upon these poor, unoffending, and untrespassing [sic] people.[292]

Catlin strongly condemned the whites who had been so anxious to destroy another people for their own good:

> For the American citizens, who live, everywhere proud of their growing wealth and their luxuries, over the bones of these poor fellows, there is a lingering terror for reflecting minds: Our mortal bodies must soon take their humble places with their red brethren, under the same glebe [cultivable land communally owned]; to appear and stand, at last, with guilt's shivering conviction, amid the myriad ranks of accusing spirits at the final day of resurrection.[293]

Catlin, it must be remembered, lived in a time when religious fervor made strong judgements and foresaw dire consequences in the afterlife. However, he does express the horrendous results that have, for time immemorial, fallen on weaker populations in the face of stronger movements. The tremendous resources this continent offered to the aggressive and ambitious immigrants from Europe led to changes to the indigenous society that had little comparison. As George grasped, from buffalo hide lodges to World War I, the Indians were the victims of the amazing changes brought on this land.

We needn't feel shame for respecting men like William Bent who contributed, though unknowingly, to the destruction of the West in its natural state, for they also built an amazing country. It is good to respect and honor men like William and George who had the courage to do the best they could in a world that was full of violence, prejudice, and mean spirited people. They were resilient men who carried on the values of the long history of strength in their family. It is an empty gesture to judge how another 'walked in their moccasins' until we have been able to assure the goodness of our own strides.

William abhorred violence from the time when he first learned some of the lessons of life on the frontier where there was no law. He made the honorable choice for peace when there was nothing to force him to make that choice. And he worked for peace on the frontier for the rest of his life.

George also preferred peace and spent much time, with his father, negotiating treaties. However, after Sand Creek he also saw a time when fighting back seemed justified. Given what had happened, it is hard to find fault in that. Would any of us choose differently? George's life took many twists and turns as he tried to accommodate to a whole new world, while also trying to preserve his Indian spirit and the love of his people.

Both of these men deserve a respected and remembered place in our history.

Endnotes

292. Catlin, Letters and Notes on the North American Indian, 349 - 350.

293. Ibid, 351.

BIBLIOGRAPHY

Abert, James William. *Expedition to the Southwest, An 1845 Reconnaissance of Colorado, New Mexico, Texas, and Oklahoma*. Lincoln: University of Nebraska Press, 1999.

Brown, Dee. *Bury My Heart at Wounded Knee*. New York: Henry Holt and Company, 1970.

Carson, Kit. *Kit Carson's Own Story of His Life--As Dictated to Col. & Mrs. D. C. Peters*. Santa Barbara, California: The Narrative Press, 2001.

Carter, Harvey Lewis. *'Dear Old Kit' The Historical Christopher Carson*. Norman: University of Oklahoma Press, 1968.

Catlin, George. *George Catlin, Letters and Notes on the North American Indians*. Edited by Michael M. Mooney. New York: Gramercy Books, 1975.

Chalfant, William Y. *Cheyennes and Horse Soldiers*. Norman: University of Oklahoma Press, 1989.

Chalfant, William Y. *Dangerous Passage*. Norman: University of Oklahoma Press, 1994.

Chivington, John M. "Head Quarters, District of Colorado, Denver, D. T. Dec. 21, 1864," *Rocky Mountain News*., 22 December 1864, Front page. https://www.coloradohistoricnewspapers.org.

Connell, Evan S. *Son of the Morning Star*, Custer and the Little Bighorn. New York: North Point Press, 1984.

Crutchfield, James A. *Revolt at Taos, The New Mexican and Indian Insurrection of 1847*. Yardley, Pennsylvania:

Westholme Publishing, LLC, 2015.

DeVoto, Bernard. *Across the Wide Missouri*. Boston: Houghton Mifflin Company, 1998.

DeVoto, Bernard. *The Year of Decision, 1846*. New York: Truman Talley Books, St. Martin's Griffin, 2000.

Duffus, Robert L. *The Santa Fe Trail*. Albuquerque: University of New Mexico Press, 1972.

Edwards, Frank S. *A Campaign in New Mexico with Colonel Doniphan*. Albuquerque: University of New Mexico Press, original 1847. Forward 1996 by the University of New Mexico Press.

Elbert, Samuel H. "Headquarters Dis't of Colorado, Denver, February 6th, 1865, General Order, No. 10." *Rocky Mountain News*. 7 February 1965, Front Page. https://www.coloradohistoricnewspapers.org

Farnham, Thomas J. *An 1839 Wagon Train Journal, Travels in the Great Western Prairies, the Anahuac and Rocky Mountains and in the Oregon Territory*. New York: Greeley & McElrath, 1843. ©1983 by Northwest Interpretive Association.

Garrard, Lewis H. *Wah-to-yah and the Taos Trail*. Norman: University of Oklahoma Press, 1955.

Grinnell, George Bird. *The Fighting Cheyennes*. Norman: University of Oklahoma Press, 1985.

Hafen, LeRoy R. *Broken Hand, the Life of Thomas Fitzpatrick Mountain, Guide, and Indian Agent*. Lincoln: University of Nebraska Press, 1981.

Halaas, David Fridtjob and Masich, Andrew E. *Halfbreed, The Remarkable True Story of George Bent Caught Between the Worlds of the Indian and the White Man,* Cambridge: Da Capo Press, 2005.

Herndon, Sarah Raymond. *Days on the Road Crossing the Plains in 1865.* London: Endeavour Press Ltd., 2016. Kindle Edition.

Hoebel, E. Adamson. *The Cheyennes, Indians of the Great Plains.* New York: Hold, Rinehart and Winston, 1960.

Hyde, Anne. F. *Empires, Nations, and Families, A New History of the North American West, 1800 - 1860.* New York: Ecco, An Imprint of Harper Collins Publishers, 2012.

Hyde, George E. *Life of George Bent. Written from his Letters.* Norman: University of Oklahoma Press, 1968.

Keleher, William A. *Turmoil in New Mexico. 1846 - 1868.* Albuquerque: University of New Mexico Press, 1952.

Kraft, Louis. *Ned Wynkoop and the Lonely Road From Sand Creek.* Norman: University of Oklahoma Press, 2011.

Larkin, James Ross. *Reluctant Frontiersman, James Ross Larkin on the Santa Fe Trail, 1856 - 57.* Edited and annotated by Barton H. Barbour. Albuquerque: University of New Mexico Press, 1990.

Lavender, David. *Bent's Fort.* Lincoln: University of Nebraska Press, 1954.

Leckie, Shirley Anne, edit., *The Colonel's Lady on the Western Frontier, The Correspondence of Alice Kirk Grierson.* Lincoln: University of Nebraska Press, 1989.

Magoffin, Susan Shelby. *Down the Santa Fe Trail and into Mexico: The Diary of Susan Shelby Magoffin, 1846 - 1847.* Lincoln: University of Nebraska Press, 1982.

Oliva, Leo E., *African-American Women on the Santa Fe*

Trail. Presentation at the Santa Fe Trail Rendezvous, Larned, Sept. 23, 2016.

Oliva, Leo E., *Soldiers on the Santa Fe Trail*, Norman: University of Oklahoma Press, 1967.

Parkman, Francis Jr. *The Oregon Trail*. New York: Penguin Classics, 1985.

Philbrick, Nathaniel. *The Last Stand, Custer, Sitting Bull, and the Battle of the Little Bighorn*. New York: Penguin Books, 2010.

Remley, David. *The Life of an American Border Man*. Norman: University of Oklahoma Press, 2011.

Rinker, Buck. *The Oregon Trail, a New America Journey*. New York: Simon & Schuster Paperbacks, 2015.

Russell, Marian Sloan. *Land of Enchantment, Memoirs of Marian Russell Along the Santa Fe Trail, as dictated to Mrs. Hal Russell*. Albuquerque: University of New Mexico Press, 1954.

Ruxton, George Frederick. *Wild Life in the Rocky Mountains*. Waxkeep Publishing, Barnes & Noble Nook. Kindle page 49 of Chapter V, Mexican Gratitude.

Sabin, Edwin L. *Kit Carson Days 1809~1868*. Lincoln: University of Nebraska Press, Vol. I, 1995.

Sides, Hampton. *Blood and Thunder, The Epic Story of Kit Carson and the Conquest of the American West*. New York: Anchor Books, a Division of Random House, Inc., © 2006 by Hampton Sides.

Simmons, Marc. *Kit Carson and His Three Wives*. Albuquerque: University of New Mexico Press, 2003.

Staff. "Arrival of the Third Regiment—Grand March

Throtown," *Rocky Mountain News*. 22 December 1864, Front page. https://www.coloradohistoricnewspapers.org.

Staff, "Summary of Current Items." *The New Mexico Press*, Albuquerque, New Mexico, 31 October 1865, page 2.

Unknown author. "Later from the Plains-Burning of Bent's Fort Confirmed." Notes from the Missouri Historical Society. 3 Feb. 64. Correspondence to the *Missouri Republican* dated Independence, Sept. 27, 1849.

Unknown author. "The Indians," *Daily Mining Journal.* 9 June 1865, front page. Colorado Historic Newspapers Collection, https//www.coloradohistoricnewspapers.org/

Webb, James J. *Adventures in the Santa Fe Trade, 1844 - 47.* Edited by Ralph P. Bieber. Lincoln: University of Nebraska Press, 1995.

Wislizenus, Friedrich A. M. D. *A Journey to the Rocky Mountains in 1839.* St. Louis Missouri Historical Society, 1912. Kindle Edition, last paragraph before Postscript, 1408.

ACKNOWLEDGEMENTS

Thanks, as always, to the support I get from my family for my continued love of writing.

Thanks to Mary Neighbour, my dedicated friend and mentor. She keeps me going.

I am indebted to Melissa VanOtterloo, of the Stephen H. Hart Library and Research Center in Denver, and to Sarah C. Smith, at the University of Oklahoma Press, for their professional and dedicated assistance. The librarians, Tomas Jaehn, Patricia Hewitt, and Photo Archivist Emily Ray Brock at the Palace of the Governors and Fray Angélico Chávez History Library, New Mexico History Museum also extended willing and skilled assistance in locating materials. It was refreshing to work with these individuals who seemed to really want to be of the greatest assistance.

ABOUT THE AUTHOR

©Orlando Diaz

Camilla "Cam" Kattell has been a wife and mother, an airplane pilot, a stock broker, and horsewoman.

Now that Cam is retired, she is pursuing her dream to write and following her passion for history. Cam's pride and joy are her two grown daughters, a son-in-law, two grandsons, and her 97-year-old mother.

Cam lives in New Mexico.